# JOB
## *WHY DO THE RIGHTEOUS SUFFER?*

By

Shawn Ward

**Copyright© 2024. Shawn Ward. All Rights Reserved.**

No part of this work covered by the copyright herein may be reproduced or used in any form or by any means—graphic, electronic, or mechanical without the prior written permission of the publisher. Any request for photocopying, recording, taping, or information storage and retrieval systems of any part of this book shall be directed in writing to the author.

This publication contains the opinions and ideas of its author(s) and is designed to provide useful advice in regard to the subject matter covered.

# IN LOVING MEMORY OF C.D.

## 9/23/95-11/27/24

## UNTIL WE MEET AGAIN

## 2 SAMUEL 12:23

# DEDICATION

I'd like to dedicate this book to all the Saints who have gone through or are going through trials and tribulations. I've heard it said that a Christian is either going through a trial, coming out of a trial, or walking toward a trial.

As Christians, we will face many trials, for Jesus said, *"In the world, ye shall have tribulations: but be of good cheer; I have overcome the world"* (John 16:33).

Trials and tribulations are hard to endure, and at times we are confused as to why they have come into our lives. Yet, God works many wonderful things in our lives through them. These trials and tribulations are very hard for us to endure, but understanding that God will do a work in our lives through them causes us to understand that there is a godly purpose for them, which strengthens us to bear them.

This grants us hope, which also strengthens us to bear them. Although God may not be the one bringing these trials and tribulations into our lives, He has allowed them to come unto us and will work a work in our lives through them. He has also promised us the grace necessary for us to bear them, for God's grace is always sufficient for any trial or tribulation we face.

God has a heavenly calling upon our lives, and in many cases, He uses trials and tribulations to prepare us for it. So, continue onward dear brothers and sisters, and remain steadfast in tribulations and trials, for God has seen fit to allow them to come into your life so that He may work a greater work in you.

— *Shawn Ward*

# ACKNOWLEDGMENTS

First and foremost, I'd like to thank God the Father for sending His Son, Jesus, to bear my curse and have His righteousness imputed to me.

I want to thank my Lord and Savior, Jesus Christ, for dying on the cross, being buried in a tomb, and rising from the dead to save a wretch like me.

I want to thank the Holy Spirit for sealing me and enabling me to write this book.

I want to thank my beautiful wife and children for always supporting me in ministry. I can't explain what each one of you means to me.

God not only calls a preacher but also his family, and you all have truly embraced the call, and do so with the grace that only God can provide. You are always understanding and helpful concerning the things that must be done in ministry, and I can't tell you how much that helps and means to me. Each one of you is a unique blessing to me. So, I want to thank Stephanie Ward, Emily Ward, and Izzy Ward for being the blessing God meant for you to be to me.

I would like to thank my mother for loving me like only a mother could. Your love amazes me, for it is purer than refined gold and always active.

I'd like to thank my brother Josh. It's not what I can say about you, but what I know of you that is special to me. You're not necessarily a person of words but of actions. I know if I ever need someone by my side, you will be there.

I'd like to thank Shane, my iron-sharpening brother. The conversations we have on the Bible are a joy to my heart. I can't count how many times God has used those conversations to reveal a greater truth to me. When desiring to fall into discourse, you're always the first one I think of.

I want to thank the Sidney Missionary Baptist Church. From the moment I met you, you have been so good to me and my family. I sort of feel like Naomi when I think of you. When I left you after the first five years, I went out full, but when I returned five years later, I was empty. Yet, after returning, God has blessed me to be filled again. You have been such an unexplainable blessing to my family and I, and I can't thank you enough for that. Your fellowship brings us great joy, and your love and prayers for us have not gone unnoticed.

I would like to thank all of my brothers and sisters in Christ, who have loved me, prayed for me, been there for me, laughed with me, and cried with me. God has blessed each and every one of you to be a part of my life. I carry bits and pieces of all of you in my heart. Each and every one of you is a special blessing to me, and I love you dearly.

# TABLE OF CONTENTS

INTRODUCTION ........................................................................ 1
CHAPTER 1 SOME TRUTHS ABOUT JOB ................................ 2
CHAPTER 2 THE SONS OF GOD PRESENT THEMSELVES BEFORE THE LORD ................................................................. 5
CHAPTER 3 THE SPIRIT OF DISOBEDIENCE ....................... 11
CHAPTER 4 A CONVERSATION BETWEEN GOD AND SATAN ........................................................................................ 41
CHAPTER 5 THE CONVERSATION CONTINUES ................. 54
CHAPTER 6 GOD'S PERMISSION ........................................... 67
CHAPTER 7 SATAN TOUCHES JOB'S STUFF ....................... 95
CHAPTER 8 ANOTHER CONVERSATION BETWEEN GOD AND SATAN ............................................................................. 109
CHAPTER 9 SATAN IS PERMITTED TO TOUCH JOB ........ 115
CHAPTER 10 CONVERSATION BETWEEN JOB AND HIS FRIENDS ................................................................................... 140
CHAPTER 11 THOSE WHO WILL BE GREAT IN THEOLOGY MUST ALSO BE GREAT IN SUFFERING ............................. 158
CHAPTER 12 THE WORD OF GOD IS TRIED, AND THE WORD OF GOD TRIES US .................................................................. 207
CHAPTER 13 SIFTED LIKE WHEAT ..................................... 246
CHAPTER 14 GETHSEMANE .................................................. 309
CHAPTER 15 HAST THOU CONSIDERED MY SERVANT JOB ................................................................................................... 346
CHAPTER 16 THE LORD APPEARS TO JOB ....................... 393
CHAPTER 17 WHY DO THE RIGHTEOUS SUFFER ............. 410

# INTRODUCTION

To the reader, this book is very dear to me. It is one of my favorite subjects to preach on. Trials and tribulations are some of the hardest things for a Christian to endure, but through them, we are blessed with greater revelation and growth. Tribulation isn't fun. Yet, we rejoice in it because God works miraculous things in our lives through it.

Tribulations work so many godly things in our lives. Things which we would never possess without them. Tribulations and trials cause us to turn loose from the world and long for heaven. They cause us to lose our affection toward the world and set our desires on glory. They cause us to despise the carnal and desire the spiritual.

Often, Christians find themselves confused when they fall into tribulations and trials. They don't understand what is going on. They can't understand why these harsh trials have come into their lives. This is the purpose of this book. It is to try and encourage those who have been or are being cast down by harsh trials and tribulations. It is to show the purpose behind the sufferings Christians face. It shows that there is a purpose for trials and tribulations in a Christian's life.

— *Shawn Ward*

# CHAPTER 1
# SOME TRUTHS ABOUT JOB

I want to start this book by giving some general truths about Job, God willing. Job was an exceedingly godly man who went through some very trying times. Job is said to be the servant of God, perfect, upright, one who feared God and eschewed (avoided, shunned) evil. We are also told in the Book of James that Job was patient (James 5:11).

Job was very wealthy, influential, respected, and wise. Job lost his health, wealth, children, and almost all his servants through the calamity that came upon him, along with his influence and respect. Job's three friends thought they understood his situation, but they didn't. They thought they knew why this catastrophe came upon him, but they didn't. Job was also confused during his affliction because he didn't understand what was happening. He didn't understand why this came upon him or the purpose of it.

Now, let's look at the character of Job. Job was the servant of God, perfect, upright, patient, one who feared God and eschewed evil. Job would have nothing to do with sin. He wouldn't dwell in the tents of the wicked or allow them to pitch their tents in his domain. Job was compassionate, caring for the poor, fatherless, and widows. Job had a spiritual knowledge of God. He even understood that the wicked desires of the heart and the evil thoughts of the mind are sins.

Job loved his children. Job's children were provided for, lived on the family ranch, were prosperous, and raised in the ways of the Lord.

Job also performed the duties of a high priest for his family, as he would offer sacrifices on behalf of his children.

God said Job had integrity and spoke highly of it, saying there is none like him on Earth.

Let's look at Job's substance. Job was extremely wealthy. He had 7,000 sheep, 3,000 camels, 500 yoke of oxen, 500 she-asses, and a very great household. It seems probable that Job would have also owned a great deal of land. I don't know the financial value of Job's substance, but it is evident that it was enormous, for we are told that Job was the greatest man in the East.

Job also had influence and wisdom and was greatly respected. Job had a seat at the gate with the nobles, princes, and great men. When Job took his seat at the gate, the young men hid, the great men stood up at his presence (reverencing him as we do in an American courthouse when the judge walks in), and the nobles placed their hands over their mouths because they knew Job was wiser than they were.

The character of Job would show us how Job used his influence, wisdom, and the respect others had for him. Job's wisdom was from God, and he would have used his influence and respect to teach this godly wisdom to the great men, princes, nobles, young men, and anyone else God placed in his path.

Job's respect, influence, and wisdom granted him a seat with the great men, princes, and nobles at the gate. Job was by no means an insignificant person upon the Earth but well known and respected throughout, and in every place the foot of Job treaded, the glorious name of the Lord would have been proclaimed.

# CHAPTER 2
# THE SONS OF GOD PRESENT THEMSELVES BEFORE THE LORD

Job 1:6: *"Now, there was a day when the sons of God came to present themselves before the LORD, and Satan came also among them."*

Now that God has blessed us to speak a little about Job's character, substance, children, compassion, wisdom, influence, and respect, let's endeavor to talk about the gathering of the sons of God when they presented themselves before the Lord.

In this verse (Job 1:6), we see the sons of God gathered before the Lord, and Satan came as well. God probably summoned Satan, and Satan may have felt it to be a great honor, but he will soon see that his summons was no more one of honor than Haman's summons unto Esther's banquet was to him.

Satan comes into this meeting and boasts about his power on the Earth. He would seek to use this meeting as a pulpit to glorify himself and all the havoc he has unleashed on the Earth.

In this meeting, we will see the audacity and pride of Satan as he addresses the Almighty God. Satan desired to be at this gathering because he was going to use it as a stage to brag directly in the face of God about his earthly conquests. God willing, we will deal with this subject in more detail later.

The sons of God (angels) had an obligation to present themselves before the Lord, and it seems Satan had the same obligation. What was the purpose of this gathering? Why did the sons of God need to present themselves before the Lord? I can't say with absolute certainty, but drawing from the question God asked Satan, it seems that this is a gathering where the sons of God were instructed to give the Lord some sort of progress report, for God asked Satan, *"Whence comest thou"* (Job 1:7)?

In other words, where did you come from, where have you been, or what have you been doing? Satan replies, *"From going to and fro in the Earth, and from walking up and down in it"* (Job 1:7).

Therefore, we may also ask, was this the same question God asked the angels (*"sons of God"*) at this gathering? If so, then their answer would have been similar to Satan's, although theirs would have been accurate and their intentions godly.

This gathering of the sons of God seems to be a progress report, as the angels give an account of their stewardship to the Lord, for they are ministering spirits sent forth unto the heirs of salvation. They would have been responsible for reporting as to the state of the Earth and its inhabitants. They may have been responsible for reporting on Earth's affairs.

Remember, the Earth is a battlefield between good and evil. It is a war between godliness and wickedness. Therefore, their report may have been on the affairs of the war. How does the battle go, and how much land is being occupied by righteousness and wickedness? When we think like this, we ask why God would need a progress report, seeing He is omniscient, omnipresent, and omnipotent.

In other words, God knows all, is everywhere, and is also all-powerful, for He can destroy every soldier of wickedness simply by speaking the word. Why would God need a progress report when He knows everything? Why would God need a progress report when He is everywhere, and why would He need a progress report when He is almighty, having the ability to win the war with the snap of His fingers? I don't know the answer to these questions, but let's try to draw from other scriptures in which angels report unto God.

When God was going to destroy Sodom and Gomorrah, He said, *"I will go down now, and see whether they have done altogether according to the cry of it, which is come unto Me; and if not, I will know"* (Genesis 18:21).

Therefore, it is apparent that someone (probably an angel or angels) reported to God on the matter of Sodom and Gomorrah, and when God personally came down and saw that the wickedness was as great as reported, He then had these wicked cities destroyed.

Here, we see that the Lord received a report on Sodom and Gomorrah before He destroyed them. It is possible that the report was given to Him by angels, maybe the same ones who accompanied Him when He witnessed the wickedness of those cities. It could have been the two angels He sent to rescue Lot and his family before the cities were destroyed.

This is probably why the angels present themselves before the Lord in the Book of Job. It is evident that God doesn't need the angels to report on the affairs of the Earth because He already knows, but it is apparent that they do report unto Him concerning such matters. God considers these reports and then acts accordingly. Remember, angels are ministering spirits sent forth unto the heirs of salvation. This is their calling, purpose, and responsibility.

Jesus also teaches us that we shouldn't offend little children because their angels do behold the face of My Father (Matthew 18:10). (Though the little ones spoken of may have to do with children, it is also apparent that this speaks of God's humble Christian children.)

God doesn't need the angels to report on the affairs of little children for Him to know what is going on with them, but the fact remains that the angels do report to God concerning them. They not only report to God concerning little children but directly unto Him concerning them. These angels don't report unto God through a written statement or indirectly in any way, but they report directly unto Him, for they behold His face. This would show the importance of the matter. The Lord places great value on little children; therefore, their angels behold the face of God.

In an earthly kingdom or government, the kings, presidents, prime ministers, and leaders don't handle everything personally, nor do they deal with every matter personally, nor do they grant every person the privilege to report unto them personally, for the things that are reported unto them personally are matters of great importance. Therefore, we see that God considers the matter of little children to be of great significance.

Most people don't report directly to the kings, presidents, prime ministers, and leaders of this Earth. Everyone working for them, or part of their cabinet, doesn't have the right to behold their face and report directly to them. For the most part, they report indirectly to them. Yet, some have the privilege to behold their face and report directly to them. These people usually deal with matters of great importance; therefore, it is necessary for them to behold their faces while reporting the matter. The angels of little children report directly unto God, for God places great value on this matter. Although it is apparent that God is omniscient, it is also evident that angels report unto God, and He considers their reports.

This gathering may have also had to do with the angels giving an account of their stewardship before God, for they are set in certain offices and have specific responsibilities.

My brother (Dr. Shane Ward) suggests that God has the angels report unto Him for their benefit, that they may behold His holiness, and that they may view how God reacts to certain situations.

We know that God doesn't need a report to know what is happening, but it is apparent that the angels report unto Him. Though we may not completely understand the full significance of this gathering, it is evident that they were gathered. It is most probable (when we look at the conversation between God and Satan) that God would have asked the angels where they'd been, and they would have given their reports unto the Lord.

When looking at this gathering of the sons of God, it seems evident that they are speaking personally unto the Lord. They are in His presence when they present themselves before Him.

The phrase *"came to present themselves before the Lord"* and the personal conversation between God and Satan seems to imply this to be so. Therefore, this may show that the matter in which the angels presented themselves before the Lord was of great importance.

Again, I feel that this was some sort of progress report. This was probably a progress report concerning the affairs of the Earth, a progress report on the war between good and evil on the Earth.

What are the affairs of the Earth? The affairs of the Earth would be good and evil. How is good and evil progressing in the Earth? What areas do they occupy? How strong have they become? This would have been the very thing that was reported unto God concerning Sodom and Gomorrah.

Sin had overrun these wicked cities and had become so prominent that the Lord destroyed them, but before doing so, a report was given unto Him concerning their state. The angels presented the evidence against Sodom and Gomorrah, and God personally came to declare judgment upon them.

Therefore, in this meeting, when the sons of God presented themselves before the Lord, He may have asked the angels the same question he asked Satan: *"Whence comest thou"* (Job 1:7)? Then, they would have given their report, as Satan did.

# CHAPTER 3
# THE SPIRIT OF DISOBEDIENCE

Job 1:6–7: *"Now, there was a day when the sons of God came to present themselves before the LORD, and Satan came also among them. And the LORD said unto Satan, whence comest thou? Then, Satan answered the LORD and said, 'From going to and fro in the Earth, and from walking up and down in it."*

Before we get into the conversation between God and Satan, let's take a moment to try and understand Satan's influence on the Earth. Satan had told the Lord that he had been going to and fro in the Earth and walking up and down in it.

We know that Satan walks about as a roaring lion, seeking whom he may devour (1 Peter 5:8), but the answer he gave unto the Lord, *"From going to and fro in the earth, and from walking up and down in it,"* may go a little deeper than that. I think we can genuinely see that Satan is going about as a roaring lion, seeking whom he may devour in this answer, but he may also be saying that he has no resistance on the Earth.

In other words, Satan is saying he can go anywhere on the Earth at any time and do as he will. Satan is implying that he has conquered the Earth, and there isn't any place he can't have his will performed therein. Satan is the god of this world. Not the owner of the Earth, but the god of this world. Satan is the god of this worldly system, for Satan is the creator of the flesh.

What is the flesh? The flesh can be described in different ways. Sure, we often refer to the flesh as our skin or bodies, which is true, but the flesh goes way beyond that. When the Bible speaks of walking in the flesh, it often means Christians are trying to live for God by their own abilities instead of the power of the Holy Spirit, who works in the lives of Saints through faith in the finished work of Christ.

The sinful nature of man also abides in the flesh (Romans 7:18). Therefore, the flesh can also be described as the sinful nature of man (Galatians 5:17), which Adam and Eve received from Satan when they ate from the Tree of the Knowledge of Good and Evil.

Satan is the creator of the flesh in this sense. Satan created the sinful nature, which is sometimes referred to as original sin, and consists of the lust of the flesh, the lust of the eyes, and the pride of life.

The sinful nature didn't come from God, but from Satan, for the scriptures say, *"For all that is in the world, the lust of the flesh, and the lust of the eyes, and the pride of life, is not of the Father, but is of the world"* (1 John 2:16).

It is incredible to think of how Satan created the sinful nature. Satan was the anointed cherub that coveted (Ezekiel 28:14), meaning he was in close proximity to God and his face was to always look in the direction of God. Satan's position placed him closer to the Lord than almost all of God's heavenly host. His calling was to spread his wings over the throne of God, and his face was to always look in God's direction. So, he created this wickedness while being surrounded by righteousness, for he created this darkness amid pure light.

Satan made the sinful nature when he looked at his own beauty and brightness, for the scriptures say, *"Thine heart was lifted up because of thy beauty, thou hast corrupted thy wisdom by reason of thy brightness"* (Ezekiel 28:17).

For Satan to have become prideful (*"lifted up"*) by his beauty, and corrupted by his brightness, he had to do something else first. For Satan to look at himself, he had to first look away from God. This is doubt, and out of doubt came the sinful nature. All sin originates in doubt, for the Bible says, *"For whatsoever is not of faith is sin"* (Romans 14:23).

Out of doubt came the lust of the flesh, the lust of the eyes, and the pride of life, and all sin can be traced back to these three categories. So, Satan created the sinful nature and gave it to humanity when Adam and Eve fell in the Garden of Eden.

Genesis 3:1–6: *"Now, the serpent was more subtle than any beast of the field which the LORD God had made. And he said unto the woman, Yea, hath God said, Ye shall not eat of every tree of the garden? And the woman said unto the serpent, we may eat of the fruit of the trees of the garden: But of the fruit of the tree which is in the midst of the garden, God hath said, Ye shall not eat of it, neither shall ye touch it, lest ye die. And the serpent said unto the woman, Ye shall not surely die: For God doth know that in the day ye eat thereof, then your eyes shall be opened, and ye shall be as gods, knowing good and evil. And when the woman saw that the tree was good for food and that it was pleasant to the eyes, and a tree to be desired to make one wise, she took of the fruit thereof, and did eat, and gave also unto her husband with her, and he did eat."*

When Eve was tempted to eat from the Tree of the Knowledge of Good and Evil, she doubted the word of God, which would mean she believed the lie (word) of the serpent. When Eve doubted God's word, we see the sinful nature springing up in her before she ate of the Tree of the Knowledge of Good and Evil, for she saw that the tree was good for food (the lust of the flesh), pleasant to the eyes (the lust of the eyes), and a tree to be desired to make one wise (the pride of life).

Here, we see that the sinful nature began to influence her through doubt because she hadn't even eaten the forbidden fruit yet. When Eve doubted the word of the Lord, the sinful nature began to push her to eat from the Tree of the Knowledge of Good and Evil. Doubt was the beginning of the downfall of mankind, but after doubting, the sinful nature began to push Eve to do the unthinkable (eat from the Tree of the Knowledge of Good and Evil). Sin always works in our lives through doubt.

Now that Adam and Eve have fallen, the sinful nature is now present in their lives. They will never be able to rid themselves of it in their natural lifetime. It will remain with them all their days, and not only that, but they will pass this horrible thing down to their children through natural procreation. Therefore, every descendant of Adam will be born with this sinful nature. God blessed David to say it like this, *"Behold, I was shapen in iniquity; and in sin did my mother conceive me"* (Psalms 51:5).

This is our inheritance from Adam, for we are born in his fallen image and likeness (Genesis 5:3). The sinful nature abides in every single person that has ever been born with the exclusion of One. Christ wasn't born with a sinful nature because He was born of a woman whom God impregnated. This is why Christ is called the Son of God, not the Son of Adam.

Christ wasn't a Son of Adam because he wasn't born of natural procreation, but by God impregnating Mary. This is why the virgin birth was necessary and why the doctrine of the virgin birth is so essential unto us. If Christ weren't born of a virgin whom God impregnated, then Christ would have been shapen in iniquity and conceived in sin (Psalms 51:5), as is every other person who has ever been born.

All humanity is born with this sinful nature; we can even see it in toddlers, for they can be selfish, greedy, and fight with one another over toys & etc. I've heard Jimmy Swaggart say, If you want to see the sinful nature in children, place two two-year-olds in the same playpen and give them one toy.

Humanity is born with a sinful nature, and there is nothing we can do to rid ourselves of it during this lifetime. There is also nothing we can do to overcome it in this life because the sinful nature is stronger than we are. Our own willpower and godly desires aren't strong enough to overcome the sinful nature.

The sinful nature is more powerful than we are, dragging us toward sin. It causes us to be prisoners of war. We fight against it with everything we have, but it is stronger than we are and drags us kicking and screaming into the P.O.W. camp of sin and death (Romans 7:23; 8:2). Often, Saints find themselves there.

Saints are citizens of God's Kingdom, yet we are defeated in battle by the sinful nature and placed in the P.O.W. camp of sin and death. We try to break free but can't. We are God's soldiers, yet the sinful nature defeats us, and we languish away in the P.O.W. camp Satan has built.

We didn't want to go into this awful camp, but we were overpowered by the sinful nature and forced into bondage. Therefore, we are slaves to sin, for Jesus said, *"Whosoever commits sin is the servant of sin"* (John 8:34). Humanity has been born in this fallen condition of slavery (Romans 7:14).

A slave is someone who isn't free. A slave has a master who commands them how to order their life. A slave doesn't have the liberty to live as they desire to live, but are made to live and do all that their master commands them to do. Why do slaves remain slaves for the most part? They don't have the power to break free. Their masters are more powerful than they are. They are forced to follow their master's will because they don't have the power to resist him.

The sinful nature has enslaved humanity, and Christians who try to live for God by their own abilities (walking in the flesh) are also brought into this bondage. How? Doubt! The sinful nature works in the lives of people through doubt.

The Bible says, *"The strength of sin is the law"* (1 Corinthians 15:56). The law mentioned here is the law of Moses or the law of God. This is the law that God gave unto Moses, which he delivered to Israel. The law tells us what we should and shouldn't do, and yet, Christians can't keep the law with their hearts and hands by their own abilities. Our own abilities aren't sufficient to keep the law.

One may say, Isn't the law spiritual, holy, just, and good (Romans 7:12;14)? Yes, it is, for there is nothing wrong with the law, but there is something wrong with us.

Romans 8:3–4: *"For what the law could not do, in that it was weak through the flesh, God sending His own Son in the likeness of sinful flesh, and for sin, condemned sin in the flesh: That the righteousness of the law might be fulfilled in us, who walk not after the flesh, but after the Spirit."*

Let's notice a couple of things at the beginning of these verses. First, the law couldn't do something. Secondly, we see why the law couldn't do something. What couldn't the law do? The law couldn't sanctify us (cause us to be holy or live a holy life), for the law is the ministration of death written and engraved upon stones (2 Corinthians 3:7). The scriptures also say that the law doesn't have the ability to give life (Galatians 3:21).

Why couldn't the law give life? First, the law was never meant as a means of eternal life but was meant to show the children of promise how they should live before God. If it were possible for the law to give life, which it isn't, we wouldn't be able to obtain it through the law, because all have sinned and come short of the glory of God (Romans 3:23). The law was given to show the children of promise how to live a sanctified life before God, or what it took to live a sanctified life before God. Yet, none could live this sanctified life before God, for all have sinned and come short of the glory of God.

So, the law couldn't give us life, sanctify us, or make us righteous. Why couldn't the law do these things? The law is weak through the flesh. What flesh? How is the law flesh? The law isn't flesh, for it was written and engraved on stones and parchment. So, what does this mean when it says the law is weak through the flesh? It is speaking of our flesh.

Mankind can't keep the law through the means of the flesh (our own abilities) because of the sinful nature (original sin, the spirit of disobedience, the lust of the flesh, the lust of the eyes, and the pride of life). The sinful nature pushes us toward sin, and we have already stated that it is stronger than we are, which we will speak of later, God willing.

When we look at the law, we see good and evil. We see what we should do and what we shouldn't do. We see thou shalt, and thou shalt not. The mind of the Christian will desire to keep the law many times, most of the time, or all the time, but the sinful nature never will.

Again, the sinful nature is stronger than we are, and when we try to live for God through our own abilities, the sinful nature will overcome us. The sinful nature desires that which is forbidden, and therefore, the law is the strength of sin. God blessed Paul to say it like this,

Romans 7:7–8: *"What shall we say then? Is the law sin? God forbid. Nay, I had not known sin, but by the law: for I had not known lust, except the law had said, 'Thou shalt not covet. But sin, taking occasion by the commandment, wrought in me all manner of concupiscence. For without the law, sin was dead."*

The law is the strength of sin because it shows us what we should or shouldn't do, and the sinful nature desires that which is forbidden. When we see the knowledge of the law, the sinful nature uses that knowledge against us, as it drags us toward sin in both desire and action. Sin is born in the heart before it manifests itself in the hands. Sin must be created in the heart before the actions of these ungodly desires come to fruition.

Notice that Paul said he didn't even know what lust was until he read it in the law, and then, after he read it in the law, sin took occasion by the commandment and worked all manner of evil desires (*"concupiscence"*) in him.

In other words, Paul was never tempted by lust until he read *"Thou shalt not covet"* in the law, for he couldn't be tempted by something he didn't even know existed. Paul didn't know what lust was, but when he read *"Thou shalt not covet"* in the law, the sinful nature desired that which was forbidden and began to work *"concupiscence"* in him.

The Bible states that the law is the knowledge of sin (Romans 3:20), not that the law is sin, but the knowledge of it. The law shows us what sin is. There is nothing wrong with the law, for it is spiritual, holy, just, and good, but we aren't (Romans 7:12–14). We are born with a sinful nature, which desires the opposite of what God commands. Therefore, the law can't give us life, sanctify us, or make us righteous because we can't keep it by our own abilities.

Though the law couldn't give us life, sanctify us, or make us righteous, Jesus could. The blood of Christ cleanses us of our sins; through Christ, we are made the righteousness of God, and through Christ, we are sanctified.

The Bible says the Christian is washed, sanctified, and justified (1 Corinthians 6:11). The Saint of God has the ability to live a sanctified life because God sent His only Son: *"Who condemned sin in the flesh: That the righteousness of the law might be fulfilled in us, who walk not after the flesh, but after the Spirit."*

In other words, through His finished work, Christ caused sin to lose its power over us, and this will be manifest in our lives when we walk in the Spirit and not in the flesh.

Earlier, God blessed me to make a statement, saying that all sin comes from doubt. The question might be, How is trying to keep the law doubt? How is it doubt to try and do that which God commands?

To look unto the law for righteousness is to trust in one's own abilities to keep it. We can't keep the law because of the sinful nature, for this point has already been proven. Therefore, to trust in one's own abilities to keep the law is to doubt Christ's finished work (death, burial, and resurrection).

When Christians try to live for God by any other means than faith in the finished work of Christ, then they doubt Christ's finished work, as they trust in their own abilities and make an idol out of their own hands and willpower.

To trust in something other than Christ's finished work for eternal salvation, sanctification, and blessing is to doubt Christ's finished work for these things. When Christians place themselves under the law, they doubt Christ's finished work, for they are trusting in their own abilities for their righteousness instead of the finished work of Christ. When Saints do this, the sinful nature will become stronger in their lives, for the law is the strength of sin (1 Corinthians 15:56).

This is what the Bible speaks of when it mentions Christians walking in the flesh. Therefore, a Christian walking in the flesh is a Christian trusting in their own power to live for God, which will not grant them the ability to do so. This is why we fail so many times as Christians. We are trying to live for God through our own abilities, and the sinful nature is stronger than we are.

The Bible teaches us that the sinful nature is more powerful than we are. The Bible teaches us that the sinful nature is stronger than our own abilities. This is alluded to throughout the Bible, and God blesses Paul to mention his struggles with the sinful nature in the following verses.

Romans 7:15–25: *"For that which I do I allow not: for what I would, that do I not; but what I hate, that do I. If then I do that which I would not, I consent unto the law that it is good. Now then it is no more I that do it, but sin that dwelleth in me. For I know that in me (that is, in my flesh,) dwelleth no good thing: for to will is present with me; but how to perform that which is good I find not. For the good that I would I do not: but the evil which I would not, that I do. Now if I do that I would not, it is no more I that do it, but sin that dwelleth in me. I find then a law, that, when I would do good, evil is present with me. For I delight in the law of God after the inward man: But I see another law in my members, warring against the law of my mind, and bringing me into captivity to the law of sin which is in my members. O wretched man that I am! Who shall deliver me from the body of this death? I thank God through Jesus Christ our Lord. So then with the mind I myself serve the law of God; but with the flesh the law of sin."*

These verses show Paul struggling with sin and losing the battle. What he wants to do, he can't do, and what he doesn't want to do, he can't stop himself from doing. Have you ever been there? Wanting to do the good things of God and abstain from the evil things of this world, yet you fail repeatedly?

We get confused and frustrated to the point of giving up, as we are frequently defeated by the sinful nature. We sometimes come to the place where we think we are hypocrites because we continue to fall into the clutches of the sinful nature. We feel we should just give up on trying to be a Christian because we continue to fail in our walk before the Lord. We try so hard to do the good but end up doing the bad. This is where Paul was. He tried to do the good but ended up doing the bad.

Paul is saying, What I want to do, I don't do, but what I don't want to do, I end up doing. So, what does Paul desire to do that he can't? Paul desires to keep the law (the law of Moses, the law of God). Paul desperately wants to live a life that is pleasing unto the Lord.

Paul is a Christian, but he is failing in his walk for the Lord. So, what is keeping Paul from doing the good and forsaking the bad? The sinful nature, for Paul, is continually being defeated by it. Paul is a Christian, but he made the same mistake that most, if not all, Christians have made or make. Paul is saved by grace through faith, but now he is trying to live for God by placing himself under the law, or law in principle. Paul is a Christian, but he is trying to live for God by his own abilities instead of through faith in the finished work of Christ. The Bible refers to this as walking in the flesh, which is trying to live for God by fleshly abilities.

All Christians do this when they place themselves under the law, for they are trusting in their abilities to live for God. This is why the law can't sanctify us, for it is weak through the flesh. The sinful nature is stronger than our own fleshly abilities, and therefore, it drags us away in the direction of sin.

As we look at these verses in Romans, let's notice that Paul says the sinful nature is stronger than he is. Paul says what he doesn't want to do, he ends up doing, and what he wants to do, he doesn't do. Paul states that he possesses willpower, but it is defeated by the sinful nature, as he says, *"For to will is present with me, but how to perform that which is good I find not."*

He also says, *"For I know that in me (that is, in my flesh,) dwelleth no good thing,"* speaking of the sinful nature.

Paul goes on to describe himself as being in a battle with the no-good thing that is in him, as he says, *"But I see another law in my members, warring against the law of my mind, and bringing me into captivity to the law of sin which is in my members."*

Paul's mind desired to do what the law said, *"For I delight in the law of God after the inward man."* So, we see that Paul delighted in the law of God after the inward man (the regenerate part of Paul), but the sinful nature, which was in him, went to war against his mind (the knowledge of God which Paul desired to do) and brought Paul into captivity to the law of sin, which was in his members. It is easy to see that Paul didn't want to walk in sin but was forced to walk in it because the sinful nature overpowered him.

This brings us to another question: Was Paul responsible for walking in sin if he tried to avoid sinning, having been overpowered by the sinful nature and brought into captivity to the law of sin and death? Yes, he was. He was just as responsible as David when he committed adultery and murder. It is interesting to note that David said something very similar to Paul's statement when he asked God to forgive and restore him after he had sinned so greatly.

When David is speaking to God about his sin, he acknowledges his responsibility for it, but he also states why he did it, as he says, *"I was shapen in iniquity; and in sin did my mother conceive me"* (Psalms 51:5).

In this Psalm, David is saying he is responsible for his sinful actions, and God is righteous in His judgment against him, but he also states that it was the sinful nature he was born with that pushed him toward sin.

The question that now arises is this: If the sinful nature is stronger than we are, then why are we held responsible for being overpowered by it? If the sinful nature is more powerful than we are, why are we held accountable for the sin it drags us into? If the sinful nature is mightier than we are, why are we held responsible for sins we don't want to commit or try not to do?

In the Bible, we see that a woman is not held responsible, nor is it accounted as a sin on her behalf if she is raped. Although it is sinful for her to have sex with someone to whom she isn't married, it isn't reckoned to her as sin, for she didn't commit this sexual act willingly but was overcome by a stronger person than herself. She cried out for help, and there was none to deliver her (Deuteronomy 22:25–27).

The sinful nature is stronger than we are, yet Saints are still responsible for the sins the sinful nature forces them to commit. Why? There is help for us. Again, if the sinful nature is more powerful than we are, why are we held accountable for sins we don't desire to commit? The answer is the sinful nature is stronger than we are, but it isn't stronger than the Holy Spirit, Who dwells within every single believer.

Now, the next question that arises is: Why didn't the Holy Spirit stop the sinful nature from dragging me into sin? The answer is the Holy Spirit works in our lives in a certain way. There is a prescribed order of victory over the sinful nature for every child of God. Yet, we must understand that the Holy Spirit doesn't give us victory over the sinful nature simply because He is in us. If that were so, every child of God would live a perfect life and never fail. Yet, we know this isn't the case, for Christians often fail.

All Christians fail at some point in their Christian life. Sure, the Holy Spirit is the seal of our salvation and certifies that we are saved children of God who are on our way to glory, but He doesn't always produce victory over the sinful nature in our lives.

Why? Again, the Holy Spirit works in our lives by God's prescribed order. When we follow God's prescribed order, the Holy Spirit will give us victory over the world, the flesh, and the devil.

How does the Holy Spirit work in our lives? Through faith! Yet, it must be proper faith, not faith in our own abilities to live for God, for proper faith is to trust Christ's finished work for eternal salvation, sanctification, and blessings.

Our faith must be in the gospel, which Paul proclaimed to be Christ's death, burial, and resurrection (1 Corinthians 15:1–4). Our faith must be in the finished work of Christ if the Holy

Spirit is going to give us victory over the sinful nature. This is how the Holy Spirit works in our lives.

Romans 8:2 says, *"For the law of the Spirit of life in Christ Jesus hath made me free from the law of sin and death."*

Notice that the law of the Spirit of life is in Christ Jesus, not in willpower or any other fleshly ability.

When we trust Christ's finished work for life and godliness, the Holy Spirit will give us victory over the sinful nature. When we trust Christ's finished work for sanctification, the Holy Spirit will work it out in our lives. The power of the Holy Spirit will overpower the sinful nature and lead us into all godliness. This is what the Bible refers to as walking in the Spirit.

I won't say that the Holy Spirit doesn't benefit us when we are walking in the flesh because He does, and in many circumstances, He may help us beyond our faith, but His workings will be greatly limited in our lives when we walk in the flesh.

The finished work of Christ is His death, burial, and resurrection, which is what Paul proclaims as the gospel (1 Corinthians 15:1–4). Christ died on the cross for our sins, was buried in the tomb, and rose again for our justification. Although the cross of Christ is the centerpiece of His finished work, all three parts are essential for the gospel.

The Bible teaches us that Christ died for our offenses and was raised again for our justification (Romans 4:25). Therefore, Christ had to rise from the dead for the gospel to be complete.

The Bible also says, *"That if thou shalt confess with thy mouth the Lord Jesus, and shalt believe in thine heart that God hath raised him from the dead, thou shalt be saved. For with the heart, man believeth unto righteousness; and with the mouth, confession is made unto salvation"* (Romans 10:9–10).

So, we see that salvation comes from believing in Christ's death, burial, and resurrection. Christ died for our sins, was buried, rose from the dead, and now sets on God's right hand as our eternal High Priest, making intercession for us. Therefore, Christ's high priestly ministry keeps us in favor with God, which secures our salvation.

Our faith should always be in the cross of Christ for our forgiveness, sanctification, and righteousness, but also in the high priestly ministry of Christ for our security as believers, seeing He forever lives to make intercession for us (Romans 8:34; Hebrews 7:25).

Again, the cross is the centerpiece of Christ's finished work, and our faith should always be there, but the resurrection is essential to our salvation as well, and we should also rest in it. This is what I mean by the finished work of Christ.

Now that we have seen how the Holy Spirit works in the lives of Christians let's look at the reasons why He won't work, or why His work will be hindered in our lives. When Christians walk in the flesh (trying to live for God by their own abilities), the Holy Spirit won't give us victory over the sinful nature. Why? The Holy Spirit will not honor our pride, self-righteousness, and idolatry.

When Saints walk in the flesh, they pridefully feel that they can live for God by their own abilities; they also feel that their work has produced a certain amount of righteousness and blessings in their lives. They feel they have pleased God or are pleasing God by their own abilities, as they trust in themselves for eternal salvation, sanctification, and blessings. Therefore, when walking in the flesh, Christians are walking in pride, self-righteousness, and idolatry.

The Holy Spirit will not honor our works, but He will always honor the finished work of Christ. If the Holy Spirit honored our works, then we would pat ourselves on the back, but because He only honors faith in the finished work of Christ, he that glories must only glory in the Lord (2 Corinthians 10:17).

Satan also tempts us through the sinful nature, for the Bible says, *"But every man is tempted, when he is drawn away of his own lust, and enticed"* (James 1:14).

Here, we see that we are tempted by our own lust. It's sort of like this. A largemouth bass is lying under a log, and fishermen are all around him. While the bass lies under the log; he is safe, but the fisherman will cunningly play upon the hunger of the bass to try and cause him to come out from under the log and swallow his hook.

The fisherman runs the lure by the log repeatedly in the sight of the bass. The hunger of the bass moves him toward the lure, while the mind and instincts of the bass counsel him to stay under the log. The hunger of the bass is drawn toward the lure, never considering that there is a hook hidden within it. If the bass is moved by hunger, he will have a hook in his jaw, dragging him, kicking and screaming unto a place he doesn't want to go.

Satan does the same with us. Satan runs lures of temptation before our faces as he plays upon our lust and pride. Our lusts and pride are drawn toward it, never considering that there is a hook hidden within it. The believer's mind doesn't want to go after it, but the lust and pride of the believer are pushing him toward the temptation.

When a bass is hooked, there is very little he can do because he has a hook in his mouth. Though the bass fights with all his might, it seldom does him any good. Yet, the bass has a well-known move in which he jumps up out of the water, creating slack in the fishing line, and sometimes has the ability to spit the hook out of his mouth.

The same is true with us when we are hooked by the temptations of Satan. We should head toward higher ground. Yes, we should look up, not trusting in our own strength and abilities to deliver us. We should look up to God and trust in Him to take the hook out of our mouths. We should look unto the hills from whence cometh our help, for our help cometh from the Lord who made heaven and Earth (Psalms 121:1–2).

We should look unto Calvary, where the cross of Christ was erected. We should look unto the finished work of Christ for help. When our faith is in Christ's finished work, the Holy Spirit will overpower the sinful nature that is dragging us toward sin or has drug us into sin and will deliver us from its darkened clutches.

There may be times when Christians, who have been dominated by the sinful nature, feel like they aren't even saved, yet if we look at a couple more points in these verses, we can see proof of Paul's salvation, although he was being overcome by the sinful nature. Paul says, If I do what I don't want to do, then it is no longer me who is doing it, but sin that dwells in me.

Paul had come to a place where the sinful nature had so dominated his life that he cried out, *"O wretched man that I am! Who shall deliver me from the body of this death?"* (Romans 7:24)

Paul also shows us the only one who can deliver us from the sinful nature, as he says, *"I thank God through Jesus Christ our Lord."* (Romans 7:25)

But he also teaches us the very best a saved person walking in the flesh can do, as he says, *"So, then, with the mind, I myself serve the law of God, but with the flesh the law of sin."* (Romans 7:25)

The point I'm driving at is that Paul made a difference between himself and the sinful nature that dwelled within him. Paul made a difference between himself and the sinful nature that dominated him.

Paul made a difference between what he wanted to do and what the sinful nature compelled him to do. Paul states that his mind wanted to serve God, but the sinful nature didn't. Dear Saints, you may feel as Paul did when he cried out, *"O wretched man that I am! Who shall deliver me from the body of this death?"* (Romans 7:24)

You may be so dominated by the sinful nature that you're uncertain of your salvation. You may be so dominated by the sinful nature that you are wondering if you're even saved. You want to do the good things that are pleasing to God but don't, and now, you have found yourself in the good company of Paul. It is not good to have your life dominated by the sinful nature, but it is good to know you want to do good, as Paul did. It is good to know that your mind wants to serve God, although the sinful nature is overcoming your mind's desire. You are striving against sin, but you're being defeated by the sinful nature.

No, this isn't the place any Christian wants to be, but it is still in the good company of Paul, for the godly desire of your mind may very well be a proof of salvation in your life, even though you are being dominated by the sinful nature. Although it is a miserable place to be, take heart in knowing that your mind's desire is right; therefore, the sinful nature is not you.

The righteous desire of your mind may very well prove that you are saved. It very well may be proof of your love for God. You don't want to go in the evil direction the sinful nature is dragging you. You don't want to disappoint God. You don't want to fail in your service unto the Lord. Yes, the desire of the mind to walk in godliness may very well be proof that you love God and are saved, although you are failing in your battle against the sinful nature.

Take heart in this, dear Saints, and look unto Jesus, the Author and Finisher of your faith. Take heart, dear brothers and sisters, and place your faith in the finished work of Christ to grant you victory over the sinful nature. Then, the Holy Spirit will take up the battle you are losing and grant you victory over the spirit of the world.

The sinful nature is also called the spirit of the world or the spirit of disobedience (Ephesians 2:2). Now, before we get back to the topic of God and Satan's conversation, let's deal with the sinful nature a little more. Again, the sinful nature is referred to as the spirit of disobedience or the spirit of the world.

Ephesians 2:1–2: *"And you hath he quickened, who were dead in trespasses and sins; Wherein in time past ye walked according to the course of this world, according to the prince of the power of the air, the spirit that now worketh in the children of disobedience."*

Here, in these two verses, God shows us many things concerning the topic of the spirit of disobedience. First, we see that the saved have been quickened, made alive, or resurrected from the sinful state in which they were born and participated. All of humanity is born in a dead state of sin, and we must be resurrected if we are to be made alive.

Romans Chapter 6 likens salvation to a resurrection. We are baptized into the death of Christ and raised by the same Holy Spirit that raised Jesus from the dead so that we may walk in newness of life.

To walk in the newness of life is not to walk in the dead manner we walked in before we were saved. To walk in the newness of life would be to live as the saved and living, not as the lost and dead. To walk in the newness of life is to walk in the Spirit through faith in the finished work of Christ, not to walk according to the sinful nature. The saved have been raised from the dead state of sin into the living state of righteousness.

Now, let's notice what this spirit of disobedience is. The spirit of disobedience is in accordance with the course of this world and the prince of the power of the air. The course of this world is worldliness, and the prince of the power of the air is Satan. So, we can see in these verses that trespasses and sins are the course of this world, set by the prince of the power of the air through the spirit of disobedience.

Satan set the course of this world, and we can see that the course of the world is sinful and in one accord with the spirit that works in the children of disobedience. This worldly and disobedient spirit is the sinful nature.

The very sin nature Satan gave unto Adam and Eve when they fell in the Garden, for all humanity has been given the spirit of Satan, but the saved have also received the Spirit of God. This wicked spirit of Satan is a disobedient spirit. Not disobedient unto Satan, for it came from him, not disobedient unto the world, for it sets its course, but disobedient unto God, for it rebels against His every word.

So, how did Satan set the course of this world? Satan set the course of this world through the spirit of disobedience. Satan set the course of this world through the fall of humanity. When Adam and Eve fell, they received this disobedient spirit.

Earlier, we mentioned that one could see the sinful nature in Eve when she doubted God's word, even before she had eaten from the Tree of the Knowledge of Good and Evil, for she saw that the tree was good for food (the lust of the flesh), pleasant unto the eyes (the lust of the eyes), and a tree to be desired to make one wise (the pride of life) before she ever ate of the tree. Humanity's domain is upon the Earth, and Satan has given the entire human race the sinful nature through the fall of Adam in the Garden.

To take this a little further, let's revisit a point we made earlier. The sinful nature is stronger than mankind. I won't spend much time on this, seeing we recently mentioned it, but it is very important that we understand this. If the sinful nature is stronger than humanity, then the sinful nature can overpower us. Paul said that he was carnal (fleshly), sold under sin (Romans 7:14).

In other words, Paul is saying that he is a slave to sin, and he is a slave unto sin because he is carnal. Carnality doesn't have the power or ability to overcome the sinful nature; therefore, if that is all we have or rely on, then we will be enslaved to it.

Saints of God should never rely on their own abilities to grant them victory over the sinful nature because they are inadequate for such a task, but we should trust solely in the finished work of Christ for victory over it. Faith in the finished work of Christ is the only way to live a victorious life over the sinful nature.

Again, to revisit a previous point made earlier, slaves, for the most part, are slaves because their masters overpower them. Most slaves aren't slaves by choice but are placed in these chains of bondage by others who are more powerful than they are. Whether it is by the laws of the government or any other forces that place them into this bondage, many slaves are born as slaves simply because their parents were slaves when they were born.

Many of them spend their whole lives as enslaved people, never tasting freedom or having the sweet kiss of liberty blow upon their faces. They, for the most part, are enslaved and remain slaves because they don't have the power to break free from their bondage.

The same is true with mankind. We are born into this bondage of sin, brought forth out of the womb bound by these chains of darkness. We have been overpowered from birth, and the law of sin and death causes us to remain there. We can't break free because we don't have the power within ourselves. This is humanity's fallen condition.

Again, many are born slaves and have never experienced anything other than slavery, and there have been documented cases of freed slaves struggling or not understanding how to live as a free person.

This is also true with some people who have spent most of their lives in prison. They become institutionalized. Meaning they have been incarcerated so long that they don't know how to live when they are released from prison. Some even fear freedom because it has become unknown to them. They understand how to live an incarcerated life but don't know or have forgotten how to live free lives.

The same is true with mankind, for all we have experienced is slavery; we were born into it, and we don't understand how to act as free people when God grants us liberty through Christ. Even the children of Israel desired to return to Egypt after God had delivered them through the hand of Moses. They wanted the fleshpots of Egypt over the manna God provided for them.

Often, Saints revert back to their knowledge of slavery when trying to live for God because we know nothing other than this, yet when we learn the manner in which God has called us to live as free people, then we should forsake the ways of bondage and embrace the practices of liberty. We should no longer look to our own abilities to live for God but look to the finished work of Christ, which grants us the power and skills of the Holy Spirit.

The sinful nature is more powerful than we are and will keep us in shackles and chains all the while we try to live for God by our own abilities (law or law principles). We will pine away in the P.O.W. camp of sin and death, crying out, *"O wretched man that I am! Who shall deliver me from the body of this death?"*

Yet, there is hope, for we don't have to abide in such slavery as this, for the scriptures say, *"For sin shall not have dominion over you: for ye are not under the law, but under grace"* (Romans 6:14).

What is this verse saying? It's saying that the sinful nature will not have dominion over Saints who haven't placed themselves under the law but under grace. The sinful nature will not rule over the Saints who stop relying on their own power to live for God and start relying on the finished work of Christ to live for Him, for this will cause the power of the Holy Spirit to break us free from the P.O.W. camp of sin and death.

The sinful nature will not have power over Saints who have placed faith in Christ for eternal salvation, sanctification, and blessing. The sinful nature cannot dominate the lives of Saints who trust in the finished work of Christ because such faith causes them to walk in the Spirit, and the Holy Spirit is stronger than the sinful nature.

Now, let's see how Satan uses the sinful nature (spirit of disobedience) for his power in the Earth. If humanity is carnal (fleshly) and enslaved to sin, which we are, then we must obey our master because it is stronger than we are. Mankind is forced into this ungodly and worldly direction by the sinful nature. The sinful nature rules over us like a hard taskmaster, as we are made to plow the fields of wickedness.

We are bound with the black and darkened chains of the sinful nature, and we don't have the ability to break them. Therefore, we are forced to go in the direction the sinful nature leads us. This is the consequence of the fall of man in the Garden, for every death, every sickness, every rape, every murder, etc., came unto us through the fall of man in the Garden.

Every sin and desire to sin came unto us by the sinful nature through our first parents. The sinful nature we are born with is the spirit that now works in the children of disobedience. This disobedient spirit moves humanity in a direction opposite to God's ways.

Now that we have established mankind to be enslaved by the sinful nature let's go a little further with this bondage and what it means. Satan set the course of this world. The course of this world is sinful and is produced by the spirit of disobedience. The spirit of disobedience, sinful nature, the spirit of the world, carnality, or worldliness moves people in the direction of disobedience, which would be the ungodly direction Satan has traveled. Therefore, the sinful nature is 100% lined up with the direction and desires of Satan. It is wickedness with a capital WICKEDNESS, and humanity is in bondage to it.

Mankind is enslaved unto the sinful nature, the spirit of disobedience, the very spirit of Satan. If humanity is in slavery unto the sinful nature, then how will their direction and desires line up with Satan's agenda on Earth? The sinful nature mirrors Satan's desires and agenda for the Earth. Every place the sinful nature drags us would be the direction Satan wants us to travel. So, being slaves to the sinful nature places us in bondage to perform Satan's desires.

Mankind has dominion upon the Earth, for God said in Genesis 1:26–28: *"Let us make man in our image, after our likeness: and let them have dominion over the fish of the sea, and over the fowl of the air, and over the cattle, and over all the Earth, and over every creeping thing that creepeth upon the Earth."*

Though humanity rules over the Earth, humanity is ruled by the sinful nature and, therefore, under the lordship of Satan. Satan is the god of this world because he created the sinful nature which rules over mankind. If the sinful nature has enslaved mankind, and the sinful nature mirrors Satan's desires and agenda, then who lords over humanity?

All who are moved by the sinful nature are moved in the ways of Satan. This means Satan reigns over them. The sinful nature enslaves mankind and forces them to perform the will of Satan. Therefore, Satan is the god of this world, for Satan sets the world's course, for the spirit of disobedience rules humanity in a manner pleasing unto him.

Satan is the god of this world because he rules mankind through the sinful nature. The sinful nature is worldliness, and therefore, Satan rules over humanity through the sinful nature, for he is the god of this world.

When Adam and Eve fell, Satan became the god of this world because Adam and Eve received the sinful nature. The spirit of disobedience was placed in them and ruled over them. However, Satan doesn't own the Earth; the Lord does (Psalms 24:1–2). Yet, Satan has given the spirit of disobedience to humanity, who has dominion upon the Earth, and therefore, Satan is the god of this world.

Remember, God gave mankind dominion over the Earth. Therefore, they have authority on the Earth. Mankind has dominion over the Earth, but the sinful nature rules humanity. So, under these circumstances, how will humanity rule the Earth?

Mankind will rule the Earth in accordance with the prompting of the sinful nature. The sinful nature is the spirit of Satan. Therefore, the sinful nature moves humanity in the wicked direction of Satan, which means mankind rules the Earth in accordance with the desires of Satan.

Thus, Satan has set the course of this world through his dominion over mankind by the sinful nature. Satan has set the course of this world through humanity because he has placed the spirit of disobedience in them. Therefore, the world rebels against God, for the sinful nature always moves in an ungodly direction.

Mankind received the spirit of disobedience through the fall in the Garden, and the sinful nature moves humanity in the direction of Satan. This is the spirit of the world mankind has received, and it will move mankind in the direction of disobedience unto God.

When a person is saved, the sinful nature is still in them. It is not removed at the moment of conversion and will remain in them until our heavenly change comes. The sinful nature has the ability to rule over Christians all the while we are trusting in our own abilities to live godly, but when Saints trust in the finished work of Christ for godliness, then the Holy Spirit will overpower the sinful nature and move us in the ways of righteousness.

This is God's prescribed order of victory over the sinful nature in the lives of Christians, and there is no other way to overcome it outside of faith in the finished work of Christ.

Satan is the god of this world, and many times, he has dominion over Christians through the sinful nature, but when we trust in the finished work of Christ for sanctification, then we will be lights in this dark world. The sinful nature continually rules over the unredeemed, and from time to time, many Christians, but when the Saints of God trust in the finished work of Christ, the Holy Spirit will crucify the sinful nature and move us in the path of righteousness.

# CHAPTER 4

# A CONVERSATION BETWEEN GOD AND SATAN

Job 1:6–12: *"Now, there was a day when the sons of God came to present themselves before the LORD, and Satan came also among them. And the LORD said unto Satan, whence comest thou? Then, Satan answered the LORD, and said, 'From going to and fro in the Earth, and from walking up and down in it. And the LORD said unto Satan, Hast thou considered my servant Job, that there is none like him in the earth, a perfect and an upright man, one that feareth God, and escheweth evil?' Then Satan answered the LORD, and said, 'Doth Job fear God for nought? Hast, not thou made an hedge about him, and about his house, and about all that he hath on every side? Thou hast blessed the work of his hands, and his substance is increased in the land. But put forth thine hand now, and touch all that he hath, and he will curse thee to thy face.' And the LORD said unto Satan, 'Behold, all that he hath is in thy power; only upon himself put not forth thine hand. So, Satan went forth from the presence of the LORD."*

Let's comment somewhat on the conversation between God and Satan at this gathering.

First, let's notice that God initiated the conversation with Satan. God says unto Satan, *"Whence comest thou?"* These are the first words in this conversation between God and Satan.

Let's look at this question from a couple of different viewpoints, although they both apply. First, God is the one being reported to, and all the angels wouldn't speak at once. Although Satan shows up at this meeting, it is an orderly meeting, a meeting in which the Judge of all the Earth moderates. Therefore, it seems unlikely that the angels would speak unless called upon.

When called upon, they would have given their report. This meeting may have been ordered like this: God would call upon a certain angel by name and then ask him where he has been and what he has been doing, how goes the war between good and evil in the area I have sent you to minister unto the heirs of salvation, then the angel would answer.

Although Satan is full of pride and presumption, it doesn't seem that he disrupts the order of this meeting because he wouldn't dare do so in the presence of the Lord. Therefore, Satan doesn't speak until spoken to. This may be one of the reasons God initiates the conversation between Himself and Satan.

Secondly, God knows where this conversation will lead. God knows that Satan will brag and be exposed as a liar at this meeting. Yet, God also knows that this conversation will lead to Job being tried and increased on the Earth, which means Satan will be decreased on the Earth. God knows that this will lead to Job having more power on the Earth and Satan's power and influence decreasing on the Earth. Therefore, God initiated the conversation between Himself and Satan. So, God, in His omniscience, asks Satan a three-word question, which will set the Book of Job into motion.

God asks Satan, *"Whence comest thou?"*

Satan replies to God's question by saying, *"From going to and fro in the Earth, and from walking up and down in it."*

So, Satan is saying, I can go anywhere I want and do anything I want on the Earth. I am the strongest power on the Earth. Wickedness is stronger than righteousness, and evil triumphs over good. Yes, I'm the most influential being in the Earth.

Before we go any further concerning Satan's proclamation of being the earthly power, let's ask a couple of questions concerning the Earth. Who owns the Earth, and who has dominion over the Earth? First, God owns the Earth, for the Bible says, *"The Earth is the LORD'S, and the fulness thereof; the world, and they that dwell therein"* (Psalms 24:1).

Secondly, God has given dominion over the Earth unto mankind, for the Bible says, *"And God said, Let us make man in our image, after our likeness: and let them have dominion over the fish of the sea, and over the fowl of the air, and over the cattle, and over all the Earth, and over every creeping thing that creepeth upon the Earth"* (Genesis 1:26).

Now that this has been established, let's look a little deeper into how wickedness or righteousness prevails in the Earth. God moves people in the ways of righteousness, and Satan moves people in the ways of wickedness. We also understand that there are times that God personally does something on the Earth and Satan as well, but we also know that God and Satan both use people.

Righteousness and wickedness are mostly wrought on the Earth by people who are influenced by God or by Satan. Therefore, the more people are influenced by God, the more righteousness will increase on the Earth, and the more that Satan influences people, the more wickedness will increase on the Earth.

Let's get back to the conversation between God and Satan. God asked Satan, *"Whence comest thou?"*

Satan replies by saying, *"From going to and fro in the Earth, and from walking up and down in it."*

Again, Satan is proclaiming to have the ability to do anything he desires on Earth. He is saying there is nothing to hinder him in the Earth. He is saying I can do anything at any time I want on the Earth. Satan is proclaiming to be the dominant force in the Earth. Satan is boasting of his power in the Earth at this gathering.

The angels may have given their progress reports, but now Satan is giving his. Satan is saying that he is the most influential power in the Earth. He is saying that he can do anything he wishes. He is proclaiming that nothing can stop him. He is proclaiming that there isn't a square inch of the Earth where he isn't the dominating power.

Satan is saying that wickedness has overcome righteousness. He boasts in this meeting that he is the great power in the Earth. Yes, he is so brazen that he brags before God in the company of these angels, proclaiming himself as winning the war between good and evil on Earth. He boasts that he has conquered the Earth.

This was a very brazen move on Satan's part, for he was at a meeting in which angels were presenting themselves before God. As we have stated earlier, this meeting may have been a meeting in which the angels reported to God concerning the affairs on Earth. They were probably giving their progress reports concerning these affairs.

Each may have reported on the areas in which they were sent to minister. They may have been giving God their report on the war between good and evil. During the time of this gathering, Satan proclaims himself to be the victor on the Earth, as he states that he has been going to and fro in the Earth and walking up and down in it. Satan is saying wickedness is victorious in the Earth, making him the victor.

Think of this meeting where the angels are gathered to present themselves before the Lord, and the dark prince boasts of his victory over God in the Earth. Is Satan so bold as to make such a claim as this in the presence of the angels and the Holy God? Yes, he is.

Satan gives his progress report, which says, I'm winning, evil has conquered good, I'm the victor, and I have overcome God in the Earth, for it is evident that wickedness has triumphed over righteousness.

I'm sure Satan sought to brag on what he claimed to be victory and sought to shame the angels and the Glorious God in this meeting. Therefore, Satan says, I have been going to and fro in the Earth and walking up and down in it.

Earlier, I stated that God is omniscient and, therefore, would have known what Satan's response would be before He asked him, *"Whence comest thou?"*

God knew Satan would seek to use this stage to boast about his conquests on the Earth, to claim wickedness to have overcome righteousness, and to claim himself the victor. This didn't catch God off guard. God didn't think, Well, I wish I hadn't called upon Satan to speak and give his report.

God didn't feel like Satan had embarrassed Him in front of the angels. Absolutely not! God knew how Satan would respond before He ever called upon him to give his report concerning the affairs on Earth. Satan thought himself the victor and thought he would expose God as conquered on the Earth, but we will soon see that this wouldn't be the case.

God says unto Satan, *"Whence comest thou?"*

And Satan says, *"From going to and fro in the Earth, and from walking up and down in it."*

Now, God will ask Satan a question, which will expose him to be a liar. God will ask Satan a question that will expose his fictitious report as being untrue. Satan has boasted before the Glorious God in the presence of the angels. He has declared victory in this celestial council. He has claimed wickedness overcomes righteousness in the Earth.

Yes, Satan makes his boastful claim in this holy gathering. Yes, the brazen Satan makes his boast before the Glorious God. What will become of Satan's claim of victory over God in the Earth? God will ask Satan one question, which will cause his entire house of cards to crumble. God will ask Satan one question. This question will expose Satan's claims to be untrue. God will ask one question, which will turn Satan's boasting into shame, his bragging into embarrassment, his joy into rage (if Satan is even capable of experiencing joy), his rejoicing into sadness, and his self-proclaimed victory party into defeat.

Satan has come into this meeting boasting of his power, dominion, and victory on the Earth, but he will soon be exposed as a liar when God asks him one question. Yes, he will be exposed as the liar he is after God asks him this question. Satan has come into this gathering, suggesting that the heavenly host wave the white flag of surrender concerning the Earth, as he states that he has conquered it. Still, one question from God will expose Satan's claims to be false and show that the Earth hasn't been totally conquered by him, for the heavenly flag of God still flies high in the land of Job.

What is this question God will ask Satan, which will turn his self-proclaimed victory party into an embarrassment? God asks Satan, *"Hast, thou considered my servant Job, that there is none like him in the Earth, a perfect and an upright man, one that feareth God, and escheweth evil?"*

God asks Satan if he has considered Job in the report he has just given. Have you put Job into the equation you used to produce the answer you just gave? Have you not noticed that you haven't conquered the Earth? Have you not noticed that your flag doesn't fly in Job's domain?

God also proves to Satan that his flag doesn't fly at Job's house. He says, Job is My servant; there is none like him in the Earth. He is perfect and upright, one who fears God and eschews evil.

In other words, God is saying to Satan, you claim to have conquered the entire Earth, but you have lied, or you are ignorant concerning Job, or you didn't consider him into your equation. Which is it? Have you considered Job? Are you ignorant of Job, or was it an oversight when you proclaimed yourself to be the victor in the Earth? It is one or the other.

Satan's next response will show us the truth of this matter. Satan says, *"Doth Job fear God for naught? Hast, not thou made an hedge about him, and about his house, and about all that he hath on every side? thou hast blessed the work of his hands, and his substance is increased in the land."*

God willing, we will speak in more detail on this verse later, but I wanted to mention it to bring out some points concerning whether Satan had considered Job or not. When God asks Satan, *"Hast thou considered My servant Job,"* God asks him if he has noticed Job, paid attention to Job, or set his heart on devouring Job. Have you viewed Job's conduct and noticed that he is perfect, upright, fears God, eschews evil, and there is none like him on the Earth? Have you set your heart on trying Job, overcoming Job, or is your demonic will being performed in his domain? Are you going to and fro in the land of Job and encountering no resistance? By asking this question, God reveals a truth that Satan had conveniently left out when he proclaimed himself to be the conqueror of the Earth. What truth did God reveal? There is still resistance against Satan upon the Earth. This proclaims Satan hadn't wholly overrun the Earth. Wickedness hadn't completely covered the Earth. Therefore, by asking Satan if he had considered His servant Job, God is asking Satan if he had overlooked Job when he said he had conquered the Earth. Was he ignorant concerning Job, or was he lying because Job's house is sure evidence that proclaims Satan hasn't conquered the Earth?

We know that (Job 1:9–10) shows us that Satan had considered Job because Satan said that the Lord had placed a hedge about him and all that he has. In other words, Satan is admitting that he hasn't conquered the house of Job and is also admitting that he has considered him.

Satan says God has placed a hedge around Job and all that he has, thus implying that Satan had considered Job for him to know about the hedge. Satan had considered not only Job but also his wealth. This also implies that Satan hasn't conquered Job, and therefore, he hasn't conquered the Earth.

Satan knew he hadn't conquered the Earth when he proclaimed to have done so. Therefore, Job was not an oversight by Satan, which means Satan knowingly lied when he proclaimed himself to be the victor in the Earth. Satan had considered Job but conveniently left that part out of his report.

In Job 1:8, God also proves that Satan hasn't conquered the Earth and that the heavenly flag of the Lord of Hosts still flies high in all the areas of Job. Notice that God doesn't just ask Satan if he has considered Job; He also speaks of who Job is and how he conducts his life. God calls Job His servant and says there is none like him on Earth, for he is perfect and upright, fears God, and eschews evil.

So, we see who Job is (the servant of God) and how he conducts his life (Job is perfect, upright, fears God, and eschews evil). Yet, this isn't the end of it, for God says that Job conducts his life in such a righteous manner that there is none like him on Earth. There is not another person on the Earth as righteous as Job.

Now, think about this: Satan has claimed victory over the Earth, stating that he has conquered it. Yet, Job is the most righteous man on the planet, with the biggest spread in the East, and Satan hasn't conquered him. The flag of righteousness flies high at Job's house, which is a declaration that Satan hasn't conquered the Earth.

Satan's proclamation of victory on the Earth is quickly shot through with the holes of who Job is, how he conducts his life, and, to go without saying, his wealth. Job has the biggest chunk of wealth and probably the largest land spread in the East. Job is not an insignificant person on Earth, for he is the greatest man in the East.

In other words, Job isn't a little minnow in the sea but a huge fish in a pond. Job is very noticeable in the Earth, for he is the greatest man in the East. This shows us how big Satan's lie had to be for him to claim that he goes to and fro in the Earth and walks up and down in it. This shows the magnitude of Satan's lie, when he proclaims he can go anywhere he wants and do anything he wants on Earth.

Satan has no problem with lying, for he is the father of lies, but he often likes to tell little lies that might be more believable and acceptable to those he lies to. Satan often tries to dilute the truth with a little lie here or there, which will cause the power of the truth to be absent from the lives of those who have believed them.

Yes, many times, Satan likes to tell little lies for this purpose, but this one is a whopper. Satan claimed he had conquered the Earth when he couldn't step one foot upon Job's spread, which was the biggest in the East. So, we see, Satan came to brag on his progress on the Earth but was exposed to be a liar before all that were gathered unto this glorious meeting.

Let's examine Job's conduct in the land Satan can't conquer a little more closely. Job is said to be perfect, upright, God-fearing, and one who eschews evil. There is none like him on Earth.

We also find that the Book of Job proclaims Job as being respected so greatly that he had a seat at the gate where the princes, nobles, and great men gathered. Job is also considered wise and influential because the great men stood as a sign of respect when he came to the gate.

The nobles placed their hands over their mouth when and after Job spoke, showing that they esteemed him as wiser than they were. Therefore, they would listen to him and not speak after he spoke, for they acknowledged his wisdom as greater than theirs and wouldn't dare to speak because they would have seemed foolish.

It is hard to follow a master's performance on stage. If the warm-up band is better than the band that closes the show, then the band that closes the show looks worse than if they had played alone. The princes, nobles, and great men would not speak after Job spoke because they knew their wisdom was inferior to his, for even a fool shows himself to be wise when he refrains from speaking (Proverbs 17:28).

In the light of God's wisdom in Job, the others seemed to be flickering candles. In the light of God's wisdom in Job, the others would be very dim. Therefore, they refused to speak while Job spoke or after he spoke because this would have caused their lack of wisdom to appear before all who heard Job speak. They respected Job's God-given wisdom so much that they would not dare speak when Job spoke or after he spoke, for they knew that the wisdom of God was in him.

With the greatness of Job's wealth, the wisdom of God in him, and the respect he had, he would have also been very influential. These attributes were platforms for Job to counsel others he encountered directly or indirectly. The way Job conducted his life and the wisdom of God that proceeded from his lips would have given great testimony unto God. Job clothed himself with righteousness, and his judgment was a robe and a diadem (Job 29:14).

Everywhere Job's feet treaded, or wherever the mention of his name and wealth went, the name of the Lord was glorified. Job would have greatly glorified God on the Earth, for there was none like him in it. Yes, Job was the servant of God, for he was perfect, upright, God-fearing, evil eschewing, and there was none like him in the Earth.

The righteous way Job conducted himself was an open declaration that wickedness hadn't completely overrun the Earth. Job's righteousness was a heavenly flag of God flying high and easily seen, which proclaimed Satan wasn't victorious, for he hadn't conquered the Earth, as he had stated. The heavenly flag flew high in this stronghold of righteousness.

Satan had seen this flag many times but didn't have the ability to overcome this stronghold and replace it with his hellish flag of wickedness. The flag flying at Job's house is without spot or wrinkle and easily discerned, for Job was righteous, and there wasn't another person like him on Earth.

Yes, there was still a place, a very big place in the Earth where Satan's jackbooted heels hadn't trodden, nor had his fiery darts been shot over the wall. The evidence was very great, which testified that Satan hadn't conquered the Earth as he had proclaimed, and therefore, he was exposed to be a liar amid this heavenly meeting.

O Satan, you have boasted of your great power and conquering abilities as Sennacherib done, yet the virgin daughter of Zion has laughed you to scorn (Isaiah 37:22).

Job's righteous lifestyle proclaims Satan to be a liar, for he said he could go to and fro in the Earth and walk up and down in it. The righteous conduct of Job displayed openly that Satan couldn't walk on any of the acreage of Job. The manifest righteousness of Job showed that wickedness hadn't completely overrun the Earth, for righteousness shined forth as the sun in this dark world from his house.

All one would have to do is consider Job, and Satan would be exposed as a liar. All one had to do was consider Job, and they would know that the proclamation of Satan was false. Satan had lied about his abilities on Earth during this holy gathering. He proclaimed to have the ability to do anything he wanted on Earth, anytime he wanted. Yet, he has been exposed to be a liar before the glorious angels and the Holy God, for the Lord said unto Satan, *"Hast thou considered My servant Job?"*

# CHAPTER 5
# THE CONVERSATION CONTINUES

Job 1:9-10. *"Then Satan answered the LORD, and said, Doth Job fear God for nought? Hast not thou made an hedge about him, and about his house, and about all that he hath on every side? thou hast blessed the work of his hands, and his substance is increased in the land."*

After God exposes Satan to be a liar before His glorious angels, Satan tries to defend himself and the false report he has uttered in this meeting by crying foul in God's protection of Job. Satan is saying it isn't fair for God to say, *"Hast thou considered My servant Job?"* when he can't get to him because the Lord protects him. Satan says, "It isn't fair to say I haven't conquered the Earth if the Lord won't remove the hedge about Job so that I can war against him." Satan says unto God, "It's not right to expose me as a liar when I proclaimed to have free rein on Earth because Your hedge keeps me from getting close enough to Job to set the battle in array. You are saying I'm not victorious on Earth because I haven't conquered righteous Job, but Your protection of him doesn't even allow me an opportunity to do so." Satan is implying that God hasn't given him the chance to conquer Job, and therefore, his report of complete victory is accurate because he can't conquer what God protects. Satan takes offense to God using Job to prove that he hasn't conquered the Earth because he implies God's personal protection of Job is unfair. Satan is saying unto God, "My report of complete victory is valid, and me not conquering Job shouldn't even be considered, for You have hedged him in and blessed him greatly, and I can't touch him or anything he has." Therefore, Satan says, "Job shouldn't be considered unless I have the right to touch him and his stuff." God says, *"Hast thou considered My servant Job?"* Yet, Satan says, "Job shouldn't be considered."

So, the validity of Satan's report, which proclaims him to be victorious on Earth, rests on this: Should Job be considered or not? God says Job should be considered in Satan's report, but Satan says that Job shouldn't be considered in his report.

So, Satan comes up with a plan to prove whether he is or isn't victorious on Earth, but before he reveals his plan, he slanders both God and Job by saying, "Job is not really Your servant, for he is nothing more than a hired hand. Job doesn't serve You for Who You are but serves You for the things You give him."

This slanders God because Satan is now proclaiming God's statement of Job being His servant to be untrue, for God has previously said that Job was His servant. Satan may be saying that God only mentioned Job to combat his report of being victorious on Earth. Satan is calling God undiscerning, for he states that God doesn't know the difference between a hypocrite and a servant. Satan is claiming that Job has duped the Lord into thinking he is His servant when all Job really wants is God's stuff. Satan is saying that God proclaims Job to be His servant to contend against my report, but he really isn't. God knows this to be true, but He is simply using this false evidence to cast a cloud over my report. Or Job has deceived God, for Job isn't really a servant of the Lord. Satan says to the Lord, "Job doesn't serve You for Who You are or because he loves You, but because of what You give him. You must bribe Job to serve You, for humanity wants nothing to do with You. All mankind wants from You are Your things because they surely don't want You."

Satan slanders Job by saying he is a liar and everything about him is a lie, for Satan implies that Job acts as if he worships and loves God, but it is only an act, for he only does this to get things from God. Satan accuses Job of being a hypocrite who is simply using God for the wealth he receives from Him. So, Satan accuses Job of being a con man and God of being conned.

Satan has been exposed as a liar in this heavenly gathering, but he defends his report by saying God and Job are liars, and it was unfair for God to consider Job in this report, seeing he can't touch him because God protects him.

God is the Judge in this matter, Satan is the defense attorney, and Job is the evidence. The docket reads, *God v Satan*. Satan will represent himself in this case. In the audience of the glorious angels, Satan presents his defense of the report he had previously given, which proclaimed him victorious on Earth. After Satan gave his report in this great gathering of the glorious God and His holy angels, God points at the evidence, which proves Satan's report to be false, as the Lord says, *"Hast thou considered My servant Job, that there is none like him in the earth, a perfect and upright man, one that feareth God, and escheweth evil?"* Considering Job to be God's servant, perfect, upright, and one who fears God and eschews evil proves Satan's proclamation of earth domination to be false.

Satan argues his case but quickly sees there is no way he can win if Job is considered. All the while this court acknowledges Job as evidence, Satan knows he can't win this litigation. Therefore, Satan petitions the Judge, asking the court to throw the evidence of Job out, for he says it doesn't belong in this case. Satan argues that the evidence of Job shouldn't be considered in this case. Satan then gives the reasons why the evidence of Job should be thrown out, as he states, "I couldn't conquer the house of Job because the circumstances weren't fair or lawful, for God Himself placed a hedge about him, and it was impossible for me to wage war against him." Therefore, Satan proclaimed the evidence of Job to be unlawful and unlawfully obtained, considering the circumstances, which he proclaimed as being unfair. "Job shouldn't be considered!" exclaims Satan, "for it is unfair to say I'm not victorious on Earth because I haven't conquered the house of Job, for God protects him." Satan proclaims Job shouldn't even be considered in his report because of the circumstances. "The circumstances are unfair," cries the old serpent, "for God has placed a hedge about Job."

Satan's conclusion is that Job shouldn't be considered in his report because of the unfair circumstances; therefore, he's not a liar, and his report is accurate, for he is the victor on Earth.

So, what will the conclusion be? What determines whether Job should be considered in Satan's report or not? Satan has protested the evidence of Job being allowed in this case, citing what he felt to be unfair circumstances. Now, it's up to the

Judge to decide what evidence should be allowed in this case. Well, we know the answer: God said that Job should be considered, but Satan refused to acknowledge it. Yes, the Judge of all the Earth, Who always does what is right, declares that the evidence of Job is lawful and belongs in this case.

After the evidence is declared lawful, fair, and legal, it is submitted in this trial and declared relevant. Satan knows that the evidence of Job will soon sink his case into the lowest abyss. He has already tried to have this evidence thrown out of court, but the Judge of the Earth, Who always does what is right, wouldn't allow the evidence of Job to be dismissed and declared it relevant and valid.

So, what will Satan do? How will he combat the evidence of Job? How will he seek to keep this evidence from sinking his case?

Satan comes up with a defense. A lie, of course, but Satan has never been concerned about perjuring himself.

Satan must find a way to discredit the evidence against him if he is going to have any chance of winning this case. So, Satan takes to the floor and claims, "The evidence doesn't proclaim I haven't overcome Earth, but instead proclaims that I am the conqueror of Earth, for Job isn't a true servant of God; therefore, I've actually conquered all that belongs to Job. If Job isn't a servant of God, then God's heavenly flag doesn't fly there, which would mean mine does." Now, Satan knew that the evidence of Job would contest his claim, but he had made this lie his defense, and therefore, he went forward in this line of defense with all his might.

The court could see the evidence lying before their eyes. They could see the proof, which declared Job to be a servant of God. This was easily seen in this great gathering of angels. It was as manifest as the sun in an unclouded sky, but Satan would try to cause the light to look like darkness, as he is so adept at doing.

Yes, Satan is a master of illusions. Illusions that cause light to look like darkness and darkness to look like light. Such illusions are no marvel for him to perform, for Satan often transforms himself into an angel of light (2 Corinthians 11:14).

The proof was right before them. It proved Job to be a servant of God. God had proclaimed Job to be His servant, but not without evidence to prove it, for God said Job was perfect, upright, feared God, and eschewed evil in such a fashion that there was none like him on Earth. The way Job conducted his life was a true token, which proved that he was a servant of God, for this was the heavenly flag which flew so high in the land of Job.

Well, Satan knows he will also have to try and discredit this part of the evidence. So, he slanders Job and God. Satan has no problem using false accusations to slander someone, for he is the chief of slanderers. Satan slanders God by saying, "Job really doesn't serve you but serves You for the things You give him." God had previously said Job was His servant, but Satan says he is more like a hired hand. Satan also slanders Job in the same way; as he says, "Job is a hypocrite who only serves God because of the things He gives him, not for Who He is."

Satan revealed his strategy as he began his litigation. Satan will try to paint Job as a hypocrite and accuse God of bribery before this gathering. Satan claims that Job only worships God for stuff, and therefore, God is guilty of bribery because He gives Job stuff in return for his worship. Satan will also accuse Job of being a hypocrite who doesn't really worship God for Who He is but for what He gives him. Satan is saying that Job worships God because of what He has in His hand, not for Who He is.

If Job isn't really the servant of God but a hypocrite who worships God for the things He gives him, as Satan proclaims, then Satan claims that he is victorious on Earth, because these actions aren't godly, but rather, satanic. Therefore, Satan proclaims Job to be his servant, not the servant of the Lord. Again, if Job really isn't a servant of God but a hypocrite who worships God for stuff, then Satan claims he has conquered Earth because Job isn't really a servant of God. If Job really isn't a servant of God, then there is no evidence submitted against Satan's report, and Satan has already conquered the area of Job. If Job isn't really the servant of God, then Satan claims he has already conquered the house of Job, and therefore, his report was accurate, in which he proclaimed himself as the victor on Earth.

There is no evidence to support Satan's claims, but Satan has never allowed that to stop him from falsely proclaiming something to be true. Therefore, Satan manufactures his own evidence based on lies, but he will not let that stop him, for he will use all his litigation skills to prove his falsehoods to be the truth.

Satan says, "I'm not making this up, for I can prove my claims to be true. I can prove Job is a hypocrite and God is guilty of bribery. I can prove it, for Job only worships God for the things He gives him, and the Lord continually bribes him in return for his worship. I can prove it, says Satan. If the court would allow me some leniency, I can prove it. If the court would only allow me the opportunity to do a demonstration, I can prove that Job is a hypocrite and God is guilty of bribery."

Satan comes up with a plan. A demonstration, in which he says that he will prove his claims to be true. A plan God doesn't have to go along with, for God doesn't have to prove anything, but he will hear Satan's plea.

Satan petitions the court and says, "I have an idea that will prove my report to be valid or invalid, to be true or false. This will prove or disprove this case beyond all doubt."

God will entertain Satan's plan, not because He's trying to pacify him, but because He knows where this will lead. Satan's plan is for God to take the hedge away from Job so that he may touch his stuff. Satan is saying this would make the contest fair, for it's not fair to say I haven't conquered Earth because I haven't conquered Job when it is impossible for me to wage war against him, seeing that God protects him. The contest, so to speak, was already fair, for the ways of God are always righteous. Yet, God will entertain Satan's challenge, remove the hedge that surrounds everything Job has, and allow Satan to touch his stuff.

Satan thinks that his plan is foolproof. Satan thinks that there is no way he can lose in this demonstration. Satan's plan is twofold. First, Satan believes he can conquer Job without any problem after God removes the hedge, for he has full confidence that he can destroy all that Job has. Secondly, Satan believes he can prove Job to be a hypocrite.

Satan may think he only has to accomplish one of the two to be successful. Sure, his greatest desire in this plan is for Job to be proven to be a hypocrite and curse God to His face. Satan feels this would immediately cause him to be declared as the conqueror of Earth. Yet, if he can take Job's stuff in such a devilish manner, although Job isn't proven to be a hypocrite, then Job will lose his respect and influence on Earth, which would increase the power of Satan on Earth. So, by decreasing the power of Job on Earth, Satan's power would be increased therein.

Satan knows that Job is no hypocrite, yet he thinks if he can apply enough pressure on him, then he will break. Satan believes he can overcome the grace of God in Job's life if he is allowed to touch his stuff. Satan knows Job is no hypocrite but believes he is powerful enough to make him one. The question is, can the dark prince hit Job so hard that it will knock the grace of God out of him? Satan's plan is deceptive, as is his manner.

The deception in Satan's plan is this. Satan feels that he will win either way. Even if Satan can't prove Job to be a hypocrite, he feels that he will increase in power if the hedge is removed from Job. Satan feels that if he can take away Job's stuff, then Job will decrease in power, which means Satan will increase in power, and this will bring Satan closer to becoming the conqueror on Earth. Satan believes with all his heart that he will conquer Job if God removes the hedge. This is Satan trying to bend the rules to benefit himself. God knows this, of course;

Satan hasn't pulled the wool over His flaming eyes, which pierce through all of Satan's deceptive schemes, for the fiery eyes of the Lord always behold the truth. Yet, the Lord will allow it. He will permit Satan this demonstration; the Judge of all the Earth will grant Satan this leniency because God also has a plan—a plan Satan can't see, but a great plan indeed.

Satan is blinded by rage and hate as he thinks about taking hold of Job and sifting him like wheat. His cruelty and rage blind him. Satan can't even fathom the thought of not being able to conquer Job, nor does he have any comprehension of how this could harm him. Satan thinks his plan is foolproof and is so blinded by pride, anger, and rage that he can't even see the plan of God, though it lies right under his nose.

Oh, Satan, you are about to throw a brick up into the air, never considering that it will come down and hit you on your own head (to paraphrase Spurgeon). You see no risks, only rewards in this plan of yours, but you will soon suffer self-inflicted wounds. You will try to break Job like a potter's vessel but never succeed. You will find your condition worsened after the tribulation of Job is over. Yes, worse than it was before it began. Brutus betrayed Caesar, but someone closer to Satan will betray him. Brutus stabbed Caesar in the groin, but someone closer to Satan will stab him in the loins. Yes, Satan, you will betray yourself, for your wounds will be self-inflicted.

(Though I've stated that Satan knew Job was no hypocrite, it is possible that Satan believed what he said about Job, for spiritual things may be somewhat of a mystery unto him, as they are unto this world. Satan may have really believed Job worshipped God for stuff and possibly couldn't see any reason for Job worshipping God if these things were taken from him. Satan may not understand love, the miracle of a person being a child of God, or what it means to be a servant of the Lord. These things may be a mystery unto him. Therefore, the statements he made about Job may have been his true feelings, for the spirit of Satan is the spirit of the world, and we know that we can find some worldly thinkers that would have drawn the same conclusion, for spiritual things are mysteries unto this world. Although I feel it is very probable that he knew better, it also seems to be apparent that Satan feels that he can cause Job to turn from God by taking away his stuff.)

Satan's plan is to conquer Job. He is so focused on this that he can't see anything else. He is like a bird that hastens to the snare, not knowing it will cost him his life (Proverbs 7:23). His pride has been hurt, he has been taken down a few notches, he has fallen from the lofty perch he built right in front of all who are gathered at this celestial meeting, and now he desires to prove that he is the victorious power on Earth. Satan desires to prove God wrong and prove that Job really doesn't worship God for Who He is but for the things He gives him. So, the plan of Satan is to prove God wrong concerning Job. He plans to expose Job to be a hypocrite, and in so doing, he will conquer the area of Job.

Satan is like Haman. Although Haman was the second most powerful man on the face of the earth, had enormous wealth, many children, &, etc., he couldn't be happy all the while Mordecai refused to bow unto him. Haman had everything a person could want but couldn't enjoy it all the while Mordecai was alive and refusing to bow in his presence.

Sure, there is some validity to Satan's report, for he had great power on Earth, but now he can't focus on anything but Job. Although Satan has succeeded in many areas on Earth, he can't enjoy them all the while Job refuses to bow unto him. It is the unconquered land that Satan is so obsessed over that he can no longer enjoy or boast about the land he has conquered. Although Satan has great power on Earth, it avails him nothing; all the while Job refuses to bow before him. The mere thought of Job's godly integrity enrages Satan. Everything he has on Earth means nothing unto him, while Job refuses to fall on his knees before him. Satan is marching his army to Waterloo, but little does he know that the Battle of Waterloo will get the best of him.

The great Napoleon lost the Battle of Waterloo and was forced into exile. While in exile, Napoleon looked at a map, and Waterloo was marked in red. He then loudly exclaimed, "Sirs, if it were not for that one red spot, I would have conquered the world!!!"

During the time of this conversation between Satan and God concerning Job, Satan looks at the map of the Earth and says, "If it weren't for Job, I would have completely conquered the Earth." Satan sees Job as the only one standing between him and his complete dominion on Earth.

Satan's demonstration, which he claims will prove Job to be a hypocrite who only serves God because of the things He gives him, is for the Lord to allow him to touch Job's stuff. Satan says, "If I can touch Job's stuff, it will become evident that Job isn't the servant of God, but a hypocrite that only serves the Lord because of what He gives him." Satan says, "If

I can touch Job's stuff, then it will become clear before the eyes of everyone that Job is a hypocrite, for he will curse God to His face. This will prove my report of victory on Earth to be true, for Job isn't really a servant of God, and his actions aren't a means of worship unto God, but a means in which he receives the blessings of God." Satan implies that Job will not serve the Lord if He doesn't give him things, and when the things God has given him are taken away, it will be apparent, for Job will curse God to His face.

God agrees to Satan's demonstration but places one stipulation upon it. God says that Satan can touch all that Job has, but he can't touch him. God sets the scope of this demonstration to be all that Satan requested, but no more. God has given Satan everything he desired to perform his demonstration, for Satan never asked to touch Job, nor did he say Job served God for good health. Satan only claimed that Job served God for stuff, not anything else. Therefore, God will allow Satan to do all he wishes, yet God also knows Satan. God knows Satan may not only stop with Job's possessions but will seek to touch him as well. This is the reason God placed this stipulation in His agreement to allow Satan to touch Job's stuff. God is allowing Satan to do all that he had asked for, for this stipulation doesn't stop Satan from having anything he requested, but it does stop him from going beyond his request.

# CHAPTER 6
# GOD'S PERMISSION

Job 1:12. *"And the LORD said unto Satan, Behold, all that he hath is in thy power; only upon himself put not forth thine hand. So Satan went forth from the presence of the LORD."*

Let's take a moment and look at God permitting Satan to touch Job's stuff, and let's also notice that God didn't allow him to do so without a stipulation. It is important to notice that Satan couldn't touch Job's stuff without permission, and this permission had to come from God. In other words, Satan couldn't just touch Job's stuff because he wanted to; he had to have God's permission; nor could Satan touch Job's stuff anytime he wanted to, or he would have already done it before this heavenly gathering ever took place. Satan had to have God's permission.

This truth should strengthen the hearts of all Saints. Satan cannot touch God's Saints or anything they have without permission from God. Satan can't touch us or our stuff anytime he wants; he must have God's permission.

We can also see that Satan doesn't have free rein even when he does have permission to touch us or our stuff, for God still has him on a leash, and it's God Who decides how long or short the leash is. Yes, God has Satan on a chain, and it is God Who decides how many links are in it. Martin Luther said, "Even the devil is God's devil". This means that Satan isn't sovereign, and although God may allow him some leeway concerning

Saints and the affairs on the earth, God only allows them to produce His godly desires. Sometimes, God permits Satan to do the things he desires, but God only allows this because He knows it will work out His desires in the lives of the Saints that He allows the devil to touch.

Though permission to touch the Saints may come verbally, as seen here, it may also come in other ways, for Satan had already considered Job, but couldn't touch him because a hedge was about him. If the hedge wasn't about Job and his stuff, then it seems that Satan would have already touched him and his stuff before this conversation between God and Satan ever took place. God may indirectly grant Satan permission to touch the Saints by partially removing the hedge about them or their stuff. God may shrink it slightly or greatly according to His wisdom and desire, which would allow Satan certain liberties concerning the Saints. Yet, God would still have stipulations upon Satan by the things Satan could or couldn't touch based upon the dimensions of the hedge.

God permits Satan to touch Job's possessions, but with the stipulation that he cannot harm Job himself. In other words, God set the scope of this demonstration, and Satan must only work inside of these parameters. God sets the parameters Satan must work in. Satan can only touch Job's stuff, nothing more. There is only a certain area in Job's life that Satan can touch. God permits Satan to touch all that Job has, but no more, for Satan is not allowed to touch Job. In the Book of Job, we will see that God grants Satan permission to touch Job and his stuff twice, but never without stipulations, and I'm convinced that this is a common thing when Satan is granted permission to touch God's Saints. I'm convinced that Satan is regularly or always given a stipulation or stipulations when God permits him to touch one of His Saints.

Now that we have established that Satan has to ask God's permission before he can touch one of His Saints, we also see that God grants Satan permission sometimes. We can also see that the Lord determines the scope in which the devil must work, for God sets boundaries that Satan cannot cross when touching the Saints.

Why would God grant Satan permission to touch His Saints? God has a plan. God never permits Satan to touch His Saints unnecessarily. God decides when and where Satan can touch His Saints, and He does permit Satan to touch us sometimes. This is evident from the two times God allows Satan to touch Job and his stuff, and it is also evident in other portions of scripture as well. So, what can we learn from this? If God allows it, then it is necessary. If God allows it, then it is proper. If God allows it, then it is right. If God allows it, then there is a purpose. If God allows it, then there is a plan.

Romans 8:26-29. *"Likewise the Spirit also helpeth our infirmities: for we know not what we should pray for as we ought: but the Spirit itself maketh intercession for us with groanings which cannot be uttered. And he that searcheth the hearts knoweth what is the mind of the Spirit, because he maketh intercession for the saints according to the will of God. And we know that all things work together for good to them that love God, to them who are the called according to his purpose. For whom he did foreknow, he also did predestinate to be conformed to the image of his Son, that he might be the firstborn among many brethren."*

As we look at these four verses, it is likely that we've quoted verse 28 (*"And we know that all things work together for good to them that love God, to them who are the called according to his purpose."*) unto ourselves and others many times, but we rarely put all these verses together. We usually quote Romans 8:28 and stop, but if we continue to read the next verse and look at the two previous verses to get the context and purpose of this verse, we will see a greater revelation of verse 28. We will have a better understanding of it.

(It is always important to read scripture in context. So often, scripture is misinterpreted because it isn't read in context, and so often, we don't get the purpose of a verse because we don't read it in context. I believe this is one of the greatest reasons why the scriptures are misinterpreted.)

Let's look at these four verses in conjunction with the question of why God grants Satan permission to touch the Saints. If God allows Satan to touch us, it will be to our good and God's glory, for we can see that *"All things work together for good to them that love God, to them who are the called according to his purpose."*

Let's notice a couple of things about this verse to begin with. All things work together for good - for whom? For those who *"love God"* and are *"the called according to His purpose."* It is the Saints who *"love God,"* the ones who are lost don't, and the Saints are *"the called"* according to God's purpose. Every Saint has a calling upon his/her life. We are not here to simply take up space and breathe air. We aren't taken straight to glory after salvation for a reason. God has a purpose for our lives on Earth.

Think of the Gadarene man who was possessed with a legion of demons. A standard Roman legion during the time of Jesus consisted of six thousand men. This would show that this man was possessed by thousands of demons. He lived in tombs, ran around naked, cutting himself and crying, and no one could bind him. He was miserable, a nuisance unto himself and a nuisance unto the community where he lived. When Jesus came unto him, He cast the demons out of him and into a herd of swine. Then, the swine ran violently into the lake and drowned. The keepers of the swine went and told the community what had happened. When the people of the community came, they saw the man who was previously possessed by a legion of demons sitting at the feet of Jesus, clothed and in his right mind. The Gadarene people asked Jesus to leave. So, Jesus left, for the Lord will not abide where He isn't wanted, but as He was leaving, the man previously possessed by demons asked Jesus if he could go with Him. Jesus told him he couldn't but told him to go and tell his friends what great things the Lord had done for him and how He had had mercy upon him. The man did what Jesus told him, and the people marveled (Mark 5:1-20).

Notice that the man wanted to go with Jesus, and Jesus told him he couldn't, but not without giving him a mission. When we are saved, for the most part, God doesn't take us straight to heaven. We don't immediately go with Him into glory, for the Lord has a plan for our lives. Although we may desire to be where Christ is, God doesn't allow it immediately for the most part. Yet, He tells us to go and tell the people what great things the Lord has done for us and how He has had mercy upon us. The community asked Jesus to leave, and He left, but by not allowing the man formerly possessed by the legion of demons to go with Him, Jesus left a witness of Himself in the community He left. When we are saved, we don't immediately go to heaven for the most part but live on the earth as a witness of Jesus.

When Jesus was on Earth, many people didn't want Jesus to be among them, and therefore, they crucified Him. Jesus has now ascended to heaven, but not without leaving a witness of Himself on the earth. The church is a witness of Christ on Earth. This is our calling. We are to tell the people on Earth what great things God has done for us and how He has had mercy upon us. All Saints have a calling. We are called to be witnesses of Jesus Christ. Although we all have different callings, they work for the same purpose. We are to be witnesses of Christ on this earth, for we are all called to be Saints (Romans 1:7; 1 Corinthians 1:2).

Now, let's return to the four verses we previously mentioned (Romans 8:26-29). Notice how these verses start. They begin by saying that we don't know what we should pray for as we should because of our infirmities. So, why don't we understand what we should pray for? Our infirmities keep us from understanding what we should pray for. So, is this saying that only those who aren't sick know what to pray for? No, it is saying that all Saints have infirmities, and therefore, we have problems understanding what we should pray for.

Let's define infirmities. Infirmities mean weakness, sickness, frailty, and disease. If we look at Romans 6:19, we should get a better understand of this word.

Romans 6:19. *"I speak after the manner of men because of the infirmity of your flesh: for as ye have yielded your members servants to uncleanness and to iniquity unto iniquity; even so now yield your members servants to righteousness unto holiness."*

Notice that Paul couldn't speak spiritually to the Romans but had to speak carnally (*"after the manner of men"*) to them because of the infirmity of their flesh. The infirmity of the flesh causes Saints to think, act, and live carnally instead of spiritually. In previous chapters, we have already described what the flesh is, which consists of the lust of the eyes, the lust of the flesh, and the pride of life. The flesh is an infirmity unto the Saints, and it causes us not to have the ability to understand the things of God as we should. It causes Saints to be weak, frail, sick, and diseased spiritually. This is the infirmity we see in Romans 8:26-29.

The flesh hinders us from being the spiritual Saints God has called us to be. The lust and pride of the flesh cause Saints not to think or understand as we spiritually should. The flesh causes Saints not to be as spiritually sound as God has called us to be. The flesh causes Saints not to act as the very Saints God has called us to be. The flesh is an infirmity unto the Saints of God. It is a hindrance unto our walk with the Lord.

Saints are called to be spiritual people, but the flesh weakens us in many ways, and it's as if we are made spiritually sick by it. Many sicknesses and diseases have limited or kept people from doing certain things. The flesh also limits the Saints and keeps us from doing certain godly things (Galatians 5:17).

Now that we have established the infirmity mentioned in Romans 8:26-29 let's move on to what this infirmity does unto us in these four verses. The infirmity of the flesh causes Saints to lack understanding in their prayer life. Why? The flesh is an enemy of God, and its desires and understandings are opposite unto God (Romans 8:7; 1 Corinthians 2:14). The infirmity of the flesh causes Saints not to understand what they should pray for because the flesh weakens us spiritually. Therefore, our weakened understanding doesn't pray spiritually. In these instances, Saints pray carnally, although they may be ignorant of it. Yet, amid all of this, Saints have the Holy Spirit abiding within them. The Spirit of Truth, Who knows all things and Who isn't influenced, enticed, or hindered by the flesh. The Holy Spirit, Who dwells in all Saints, always understands spiritual things perfectly. Saints have the infirmity of the flesh, and because of this, we often misunderstand how we should pray; but thank God, the Holy Spirit is in our midst, and He is not only in our midst but also makes intercession for us in our prayers. The Holy Spirit knows when we aren't praying spiritually because of the infirmity of our flesh, and He begins to intercede on our behalf. The Holy Spirit desires the spiritual things that need to happen in our lives when we so often pray for the carnal things we want to happen in our lives because of the infirmity of our flesh.

How could the Saints get so far off base? How could we not understand that we are praying prayers that aren't for our good, the good of our calling, or the glory of God? The infirmity of the flesh is how. The infirmity of the flesh often influences us to pray for things that aren't spiritual. Therefore, our prayers are often carnal (fleshly).

We are sort of like a child that has a contagious cold. The child doesn't want to take medicine because it tastes bad. The child doesn't want to stay in the house out of the cold because of boredom. The child wants to play with his friends, even though it could cause others to be sick, because he wants to have fun. Therefore, the child says to his mother, "Please don't give me the medicine; please let me go outside; please let me go and play with my friends." The child has no concept of what he is asking for, yet his fleshly desires cause him to plead with his mother to allow such things. We know the responsible mother will not grant such requests. She will cause the child to take the medicine, stay out of the cold, and not go around his friends. The child may cry and try his very best to accomplish his desires, but the mother will force him to do what is best for him and others. Sure, the child will make his requests known to his mother with many tears, but she will not budge in the matter, for the child's requests are foolish, guided by the flesh, and not according to knowledge.

This is how Saints often are. We don't know what we should pray for because of the infirmity of the flesh. Therefore, the Holy Spirit is the responsible One in our lives, and He will pray the proper prayer. The Holy Spirit makes intercession for us when our prayers are like this, for He is the responsible One Who understands what is best for us, our calling, and the glory of God.

Now that we have established this point let's move on to the prayer of the Spirit. What does the Spirit pray for on our behalf that we don't understand that we should be praying for because of the infirmity of the flesh? The Holy Spirit always prays spiritually, while Saints so often pray carnally. The infirmity of the flesh causes Christians to pray for carnal things. Things that are desired by the flesh. Things that promote the flesh. We are like the sick child; often, we only see the desires of the flesh. We see it hurting, and we want it strengthened, and when it is so strong in our life that it hinders our calling, we don't pray for it to be weakened but rather rejoice in it. The Holy Spirit prays for our spiritual growth, which is opposite to the growth of the flesh.

One may say, I always pray that God would cause me to be more spiritual and less carnal. Yes, you may, but that doesn't mean you do, or it doesn't mean it is your desire, although you may think it is.

So often, we ignorantly take pride in our fleshly growth. So often, we think certain things of the flesh are necessary for our spiritual success. So often, we lean upon the flesh and think it is how we succeed in our calling. Are we not prone to lean on our willpower, education, finances, worldly wisdom, oratory skills, influence, etc.? We think we need them to be successful in our calling. God may use them, but our faith shouldn't be in them. Our faith should solely be in the finished work of Christ to walk in our calling, not our fleshly abilities. Will we worship willpower, saying, I was able to do the call of God upon my life because of my great willpower? Think about this.

God called Moses to go to Egypt and speak to Pharaoh, saying, *"Thus saith the Lord God of the Hebrews, Let My people go"* (Exodus 9:1). Moses wasn't called to wage war with Pharaoh but to speak the word of the Lord unto him.

Moses' speaking ability was the weakest part of him, and we know he had great bodily strength, for he killed the

Egyptian and stood up for the daughters of Jethro at a well when others tried to deny them access. Moses prevailed over the Egyptian and those who withstood Jethro's daughters by his physical strength and abilities. Moses was a strong man, and the Bible also says he was mighty in word and deed, but he couldn't speak well. He seemed to have a speech impediment of some sort. Yet, the tongue of Moses, not his physical strength or abilities, was what God would use to accomplish his calling. Moses was called to speak the word of the Lord to Pharaoh and unto the children of Israel.

Moses couldn't see how this could work, as he pleaded with God at the burning bush. Moses told the Lord, *"I am not eloquent, neither heretofore, nor since thou hast spoken unto thy servant: but I am slow of speech, and of a slow tongue"* (Exodus 4:10). In other words, Moses says unto the Lord, I can't speak well, and I still can't speak well after you called me to speak to Pharaoh. Moses felt that God would or should have given him a silver tongue if He was going to call him to speak to Pharaoh, but God didn't. After God spoke to Moses out of the burning bush and told him to go and speak to Pharaoh, Moses felt that God should have fixed his tongue after He placed this call upon his life. Yet, God left Moses' tongue exactly as it was. God had called Moses to speak to Pharaoh, but Moses couldn't understand how his stammering tongue or lack of oratory skills would be sufficient to do so. This was exactly the point.

If Moses had a silver tongue, then he would have felt his fleshly abilities were sufficient for the call of God on his life. He wouldn't have trusted in God to perform his calling or completely trusted in God to perform it. God took Moses' weakness and manifested His strength (2 Corinthians 12:9). Therefore, the children of Israel didn't come out of Egypt praising the diplomatic oratory skills of Moses but praising God.

Moses pleaded with God to give him an eloquent tongue, but Moses didn't understand that he shouldn't have been praying for that or concentrating on it, for Moses was concentrating more upon his tongue than on the One speaking unto him out of the burning bush. Moses concentrated more on his lack of fleshly abilities than on God's spiritual abilities. Sure, Moses felt his lack of eloquence disqualified him from the call of God upon his life, but it didn't, for all Saints are qualified for their calling by the abilities of God, not their own (fleshly) abilities.

God told Moses He was the One Who created the tongue and that He would also be with Moses' tongue, but Moses had a hard time understanding this, which would show that he was looking more at his own abilities, or the lack thereof, than the abilities of God.

If God had healed Moses' tongue; it seems that Moses would have leaned upon it to some degree. However, God didn't heal his tongue, so Moses would have to lean on someone else. First, he leaned upon God and Aaron, as God allowed Aaron to speak on Moses' behalf, but eventually, Moses learned to lean solely upon God, as he boldly spoke the word of the Lord unto Pharaoh and the Israelites.

Saints often pray for a silver tongue, but the Holy Spirit makes intercession for us. So often, Saints don't understand how they should pray, and therefore, we are blessed to have the

Holy Spirit intercede in prayer for us unto God. So often, Saints unknowingly pray for fleshly things instead of spiritual things, as did Moses when he desired God to heal his tongue, but the Holy Spirit makes intercession for us. So often, Saints pray for the strengthening of the flesh, as did Moses, but the Holy Spirit makes intercession for us.

Thanks be to God for the intercessory work of the Holy Spirit in our prayers, for we often pray prayers that would cause us to lean upon the flesh instead of God, and so often pray prayers that would strengthen the flesh instead of killing it, for we don't understand what we should pray for, but the Holy Spirit makes intercession for us.

The Holy Spirit makes intercession for us by praying spiritual prayers for our lives when we don't understand what we should pray for.

We also see what the prayer of the Spirit is. Saints have an infirmity, which is the flesh, and so often, we aren't praying for this infirmity to be removed but rather strengthened. Therefore, the Holy Spirit intercedes for us in prayer and prays that the flesh will be killed in our lives.

The infirmity of the flesh causes us to be spiritually sick, but we misdiagnose ourselves as we pray for fleshly things. Yet, the Great Physician has sent the Holy Spirit unto the Saints, and He doesn't misdiagnose us but prays for God to destroy the flesh so that we may be spiritually sound.

Notice that the Holy Spirit makes intercession for us with unuttered groanings (sighs). When we read this in context, looking at some previous portions of this chapter (Romans chapter 8), we see that creation was made subject unto vanity because of Adam's sin, but not without hope. Creation will lie in this condition until the sons of God are manifest (resurrected and glorified). Creation is under the dominion of man, and therefore, it is subject to vanity because mankind is in a fallen state. This is why creation can't be changed until the Saints are glorified, for creation is subjected to the condition of the ones who have dominion over it. Yet, when the Saints are glorified, creation will be made new. When the Saints are glorified, creation will no longer be subjected to vanity because the Saints will no longer be in a fallen condition. The meek shall inherit the earth, and therefore, creation will be released from the curse of sin it was subjected to through the fall of Adam. Creation has borne the burden of humanity's sin since the fall of Adam in the Garden, but when the Saints are glorified, creation will be also. So, when the resurrection occurs, creation will be redeemed from the vanity it is subjected to. Therefore, creation groans (sighs) as it awaits the manifestation of the sons of God. Creation groans in its fallen condition and will do so until the time the manifestation of the sons of God comes to pass. Creation groans because of its fallen condition, desiring to be changed. Creation groans and will groan until it is changed, which will occur after the resurrection of the Saints.

Here, we see the Holy Spirit groaning in the same context as creation. The Spirit is groaning because of the sinful state of the children of God. Though we have been saved, we still have much of the flesh remaining. Spurgeon put it something like this: though Dagon has fallen, and his head and hands have been broken in our lives, the stump remains. This is a grief unto the Holy Spirit, and therefore, He groans (sighs) as He too awaits the redemption of our bodies, but while we are here in this life, the Spirit makes intercession for the Saints in prayer, desiring the flesh to be killed. So, it is the flesh that causes the Holy Spirit to sigh, as the groaning of creation is produced because of the vanity it has been made subject unto. Therefore, the sighs of the Holy Spirit are because of the flesh of the Saints, and the mind of the Spirit is for the flesh to be killed.

The Holy Spirit prays according unto the will of God; although He may not be speaking words, He is sighing, and God knows the mind of the Spirit. Though the Spirit doesn't speak words, God understands His sighs. God knows the Holy Spirit is groaning because of the flesh in our lives. The infirmity of the flesh influences our prayers in the wrong direction. This would mean that these infirmities cause us to pray for fleshly things instead of spiritual things, but glory be to God, for the Holy Spirit makes intercession for us in such times as this!

Now, the flesh isn't destroyed all at once in our lives, nor will we ever be completely rid of it in this lifetime, but piece-by-piece, the flesh is decreased in our lives. Maybe a small slice of pride here or a small slice of lust there, but the flesh must decrease so that God may increase in our lives (John 3:30). As Saints move along in God's call upon them, God must increase in their lives before they can go further in their calling; therefore, it is necessary for more of the flesh to die. Yet, more than likely, we don't understand this truth, which would cause us to pray for it in a proper manner. Sadly, we so often pray for the flesh to be increased in our lives because that is what we think we need to proceed further in our calling, as did Moses, or because we desire comfort, worldly success, or carnal praise. Yet, the Spirit knows what is needed, and therefore, He makes intercession for us. The Spirit makes intercession for the Saints as He prays for this piece or that piece of the flesh to be killed so that we may grow in our calling. Again, our infirmity is the flesh, and it will hinder our growth as a disease hinders our health. Therefore, the Holy Spirit makes intercession for us because the infirmity of the flesh influences us to pray carnally.

The Holy Spirit makes intercession for us, and God answers the request of the Spirit. Now we come to verse 28, which says, *"And we know that all things work together for good to them that love God, to them who are the called according to his purpose."* Now that the Holy Spirit has made intercession for our ignorant prayers, we know that all things will work together for good. God will answer the prayers of the Spirit on our behalf, and we are guaranteed that all things will work together for good.

Why do we need this encouragement? Why would we need to be assured that all things will work together for good in our lives when the intercessory prayer of the Spirit is answered? Shouldn't this be something that we already know? Sure, it is something we already know, but we must be assured. Why? Many times, it won't look like it in our eyes. It won't look like it in our sight or understanding because of the infirmity of the flesh. So often we see the flesh being killed and think this isn't a good thing. We often see the flesh shrinking in our lives and think this is doing us harm. Again, this goes to our understanding of God's ways. Our understanding isn't always clear regarding spiritual matters, because of the infirmity of the flesh. When we see the flesh being killed, we think it isn't what we need; therefore, we need assurance that it is. Notice the last of these four verses.

Romans 8:29. *"For whom he did foreknow, he also did predestinate to be conformed to the image of his Son, that he might be the firstborn among many brethren."*

Now, we see the purpose of the intercessory work of the Spirit. The intercessory work of the Spirit is to cause us to be more like Christ. It is to pray for things in our lives that we would never pray for so that we may be more like Christ. Then, we are told that all things work together for our good.

Why would we need this assurance after the Spirit prays for us? The things the Spirit prays for in our lives don't align with our limited knowledge, for we are ignorant of it because of the infirmity of the flesh. The Spirit always prays for the right thing, not the easy thing. Through the intercession of the Spirit, we sometimes receive things we don't want because they go against our carnal thinking and abilities. Sometimes, we receive things we despise. Sometimes, we receive things we don't understand. The intercessory work of the Spirit prays for things that we would never pray for because of the infirmity of our flesh.

Remember, the Spirit is groaning because of our fallen fleshly condition, and the Spirit's groaning is what makes intercession for us. God knows the Spirit's mind, for He understands why the Spirit is groaning. Again, the Spirit is groaning because of the flesh in the Saints—the vanity we are subjected to.

So, what does the Spirit pray for in our lives? To simply bring this to a point: the Spirit prays for the cross in our lives.

The Spirit prays for the flesh to be killed; therefore, the answer to the Spirit's prayer is to allow things that will kill the flesh to come into our lives. We would never pray for that; when we receive it, we often think it is a curse rather than a blessing. We think it is bad rather than good. We despise it rather than embrace it. The cross is meant to kill the flesh, and the more of the flesh that is killed, the more we will look like Jesus. This is why the scripture says that all things work together for good to those who love God and those who are the called according to God's purpose. God has a predestinated calling for all Saints, and that calling is to be conformed to the image of His Son.

Saints may think they are praying for this conformation, but most of the time, we don't understand what it takes for us to be conformed to the image of Christ. We pray for the easy road and sometimes feel that strengthening the flesh is necessary for us to advance in our calling, but the Spirit prays for the cross in our lives that we may be conformed into the image of Christ. The image of Christ is glorious unto God in this world. The image of Christ is good for the Saints, but so often, we don't understand that it takes the cross to conform us to Christ's image. Oh, how off base we so often are in prayer. So often, we miss the mark as we ask amiss. Notice these scriptures.

James 4:2-3. *"Ye lust, and have not: ye kill, and desire to have, and cannot obtain: ye fight and war, yet ye have not, because ye ask not. Ye ask, and receive not, because ye ask amiss, that ye may consume it upon your lusts."*

There are times when we don't receive what we desire. Why? We either try to accomplish the things we want through our own abilities and never ask God for them or when we do ask Him, we miss the mark because we are asking prayers according to our lusts, which aren't spiritual prayers.

So often, we want a conformation into the image of Christ without the cross. Sometimes, we say the right things in prayer but don't understand what we are saying. The more our lives are emptied of the flesh, the more they will be filled with Christ, but we often misunderstand the process in which we are emptied, for we are emptied of the flesh on the cross.

On the cross, the old man dies more and more every minute so that the new man may be manifested more in our lives. Christ does tell us to take up our cross daily and follow Him, doesn't He? Those who desire to be Christ's disciples are told that they can't love anyone more than Jesus, not even themselves, and be His disciple. They are also told to take up their cross and follow Him.

The cross is hard to bear because it exposes us to pain and shame. Even the greatest of us have run from it. Remember our dear brother Peter? He told the Lord the very night Judas betrayed Him that he would die for Him. Peter told the Lord, though all men deny You, I will never deny You, for I will die before I deny You. Peter speaks unto Jesus and says, not even imprisonment or death can cause me to deny You. We can see that Peter meant what he said, but we can also see that Peter didn't understand what he was saying either.

To show that Peter meant what he said, we only need to look at the events that happened in the Garden of Gethsemane that night. When Judas betrayed Jesus and brought the temple guards to take Him, Peter single-handedly took up a sword and began to fight with them, even to the point of cutting off the ear of the high priest's servant. Think of this for a moment. Was Peter willing to go to prison for Christ? Was Peter willing to die for Christ? This certainly states that he was. He took up a sword to fight the trained temple guards. This was a suicide mission. Peter fought with the temple guards all by himself.

We must also state that the temple guards weren't ordinary people when it came to fighting. They were trained guards and would have been some of the best fighters in all of Israel.

The temple guards were trained fighters, yet Peter was willing to engage them in a sword fight alone. The only thing that stopped Peter from fighting was the words of Jesus. Jesus told Peter to put down his sword. Peter was willing to be imprisoned and die for the Lord, but we will also see that the night wouldn't be over before the rooster would crow after he denied Christ three times, according to the words Jesus spoke to him beforehand, which said, before the cock crows twice, you will deny me thrice (Mark 14:72).

Later that night, as Jesus was being tried at Caiaphas's palace, Peter was confronted three times concerning his relationship with Jesus. These people weren't of the same fighting caliber as the temple guards. They weren't trained soldiers but ordinary people, and they would confront Peter three times at Caiaphas' palace.

The first confrontation was by a damsel (by definition, a girl, a bondmaid, or a slave). The second confrontation says that a maid recognized him and told others who stood by that Peter was one of Jesus' disciples. The third confrontation was by the servant and kinsman of the high priest, whose ear Peter had previously cut off in the Garden of Gethsemane, which Jesus healed.

These people didn't have the power or fighting skills of the temple guards. For the most part, they didn't have the authority of the temple guards. Yet, they confronted Peter with a question, not swords. The question was, aren't you one of the disciples of Jesus?

Though Peter was willing to fight to the death for Jesus in the Garden of Gethsemane, he was not willing to be condemned to the cross at Caiaphas' palace. Yes, Peter was willing to die for the Lord in a sword fight but wasn't willing to be condemned to the cross at Caiaphas' palace. Peter was willing to fight with all his strength in the Garden but wasn't willing to voluntarily be nailed to the cross at Caiaphas' palace. Peter was willing to go down in a blaze of glory at Gethsemane but not willing to endure the shame and pain of the cross at Caiaphas' palace. Peter was willing to be killed by one blow of the temple guard's sword at Gethsemane but wasn't willing to die slowly, painfully, and shamefully on a cross at Caiaphas' palace. There is a difference.

For the most part, we aren't as good as Peter. We may turn tail and run in the Garden, but there are some who wouldn't. Some Saints would use all their fleshly power to fight for the Lord, but most of the time, we will not willingly embrace the cross. This is why the Spirit must make intercession for us. We pray for the Lord to give us the fleshly strength to fight for Jesus in the Garden, but never or hardly ever pray that the Lord would bless us to embrace the cross. There is a difference. Most Saints want to do right or think they understand what is right, but we run from the cross when it comes down to it. Sure, we openly say we are soldiers of the cross or proclaim our love for the cross, and rightly so, but we do everything we can to keep from being nailed to it. We may despise the flesh, according to our limited knowledge, but for the most part, we don't run to the cross to see it killed. We pray this way and that way to be more like Christ, but we don't truly pray for the cross in most instances. This is the intercessory work of the Spirit. The Holy Spirit prays for the cross in our lives so that we may be conformed to the image of Christ, but we rarely, if ever, pray for the cross.

It is important for us to understand what the image of Jesus is, and although I don't have the ability to portray it fully, I think this should give us somewhat of an idea. Jesus wasn't carnal, and we are. Jesus wasn't shapen in iniquity and conceived in sin, and we are. Jesus didn't have a sinful nature, and we do. Jesus was spiritual, and we, by nature, aren't.

Therefore, for us to be conformed further to the image of Christ, more of the flesh must die, and the cross is designed to kill it. This is why those who desire to be the disciples of Christ are told that they can't love anyone, not even themselves, more than they love Jesus, and then are told to take up their cross and follow Him daily (Luke 9:23; 14:26-27). The path of Jesus is a spiritual path, and for us to follow Him, we must do it by bearing the cross. The flesh must continually die all the while we follow Jesus, for the flesh cannot tread down this path. The further we follow Jesus, the more the flesh must die. Therefore, we must bear the cross because it continually kills the flesh minute by minute, hour by hour, and day by day.

The more the flesh dies, the more the Spirit is manifest in our lives. Yes, we bear the glory of God in the person of the Holy Spirit. Remember, it was the cross that killed Jesus, but the Holy Spirit raised Him from the dead. Jesus humbled Himself unto the cross and died. Now, He sits on the highest of all thrones. The more we die, the more the Spirit shines in our lives, and the more we are humbled on the cross, the more God exalts us.

Remember, God has predestinated Saints to be conformed to Christ's image. This means Christ is the mold God pours us into. Think of the process of molding for a moment. How are things molded into shape? They are heated in a fire, and when they have reached their melting point, they are poured into the mold, which causes them to take the mold's shape. So often, Saints want to be conformed to the image of Christ without a fire. We want to be conformed to Christ's image but don't desire or see the necessity of the fire. We must be placed in the fire so that we would become malleable. We must reach our melting point as the fire softens our hard hearts. Then, we are poured into the mold of Christ. This doesn't happen all at once, for the cross doesn't kill all at once. We die a little here and a little there, but every minute we hang on the cross, we become more like Christ because more of the flesh has died. Every minute we hang on the cross, more of the flesh dies, and the more the flesh dies, the more the Spirit shines in our lives as we take on more of the image of Christ.

After the Holy Spirit makes intercession for us, God grants His desire by allowing the cross to come into our lives so that more of our flesh will die. God allows the cross to find us, for we don't go looking for it. It has sought us out, though we have run from it. Remember, the cross is a slow, painful, and shameful death. It is a death that causes a person to die little by little over the course of time. Not all at once, but little by little. Not one swing of a temple guard's sword, but very slowly, little by little, one's life leaves them upon the cross. There is no pride in the cross, although we would find a way to be prideful fighting the temple guards in the Garden of Gethsemane in defense of our Lord, for the cross is shameful in the eyes of the world. Life dwindles away slowly on the cross; little by little, life leaves the person, and so, it is with the Saints. The flesh doesn't just die out of our life all at once, but little by little over a painful and shameful amount of time. Very seldom does a person stretch their arms and legs out and allow their hands and feet to be nailed to a cross without any resistance; no more than a Saint truly prays for the cross in their lives; therefore, the Spirit makes intercession for us in prayer.

Yes, the Spirit prays for the cross to come into our lives so that we may be conformed to the image of Christ, but in these times, we must be assured of the purpose of the cross which has come into our lives, because we so often don't understand why it has come unto us. We don't understand it and are praying for deliverance from it; therefore, we must be forced into bearing it. We cry unto the Lord as the two thieves crucified on each side of Jesus, saying, "Deliver us from the cross," although our words may not be as contemptuous as theirs.

Yet, when the cross comes, the words of Romans 8:28 must be forged into our lives. We must believe and trust in them, or we may find ourselves in greater despair. We must learn to allow these beautiful words to sing unto us while nailed to the cross. We have never doubted these words in the past, but now we can't even remember them, nor are we trusting in them. Words that seem so far away, though they are very nigh unto us, for they are the very words of God. We must learn to listen to their melody, although our cries and screams seem to drown them out. We must learn to allow them to become a beautiful song unto us all the while we are bound to the cross. Sure, before the cross, we held these words up high and shouted them from the rooftops, but while on the cross, we must learn to trust them. They must become our meat and drink, for we have come to a place where our own strength is being drained, and when we are given a steady dose of vinegar and gall, we must learn to sweeten them with these beautiful words. They must be our strength; we must trust them, for they are sent unto those who are nailed to the cross. Our own strength isn't sufficient to bear the cross because it is stronger than we are. It is designed to take away our strength little by little as every minute passes. The cross drains us more and more, and the more the cross drains us, the louder these words become. Then, they are forged in the fires of our souls as we begin to trust them, for we can no longer rely on our own strength because the cross has taken it from us. These words assure us that the cross is not the end, for the cross only kills the flesh so that the resurrection we received by the Holy Spirit might shine brighter in our lives. These words assure us that the cross is only killing the flesh, not the spiritual things in our lives. The cross is causing the flesh to die a little more every minute so that the Spirit may become more and more manifest in our lives. On the cross, we see these beautiful words differently than we ever saw them before. We understand that God has allowed this in our lives so that we may be conformed into the image of Christ. We understand what we didn't understand before, as the Spirit had to make intercession for us, but now we know that all things work together for good to those who love God and are the called according to His purpose.

God allowed this to come into our lives for a spiritual purpose, not a fleshly one. God allowed this to come into our lives so that more of the flesh would die, which would cause the Spirit to become more manifest in our lives. We have a call of God upon our lives, and for us to take the next step in this heavenly calling, we must die a little more. Therefore, God allowed the cross to find us, for "*All things work together for good to them that love God, to them who are the called according to his purpose*" (Romans 8:28).

Job had a great call of God upon his life. This is apparent, but now it is time for Job to take the next step in his heavenly calling. Therefore, God permitted Satan to touch all that he had.

Before we go on to the next chapter, let's ask ourselves: is it worth it? Is it worth it to have our flesh killed more and more so that we may excel in the call of God upon our lives? Is it worth it to become more like Christ? That is the question, isn't it? Jesus said that if we are truly going to be His disciples, we must love Him above father, mother, sister, brother, spouse, child, or even ourselves (Luke 14:26). We must love Him above all things. Jesus went on to say that if we are going to be His disciples, then we must count the cost (Luke 14:28-30). There is a cost in moving closer to God and being more like Christ. This cost is that the flesh must die a little more. Every bit that the flesh dies, the closer to God we become, and the more like Christ we are made. Those who truly desire to be Christ's disciples must understand this truth, for there is a cost. There are times that we truly wonder if it's worth it, but if we are going to be the disciples of Christ, the answer will be yes. Yes, Lord, it is worth it! Yes, Lord, it is worth my dying so that I might be more like Christ! Christ's disciples will all come to this same conclusion, although we may waver as Peter did at Caiaphas' palace.

Job may not understand what will happen to him, may despise it, and indeed didn't pray for it, but in the end, he will say it is worth it! I promise you, dear brothers and sisters in Christ, it is always worth it, and although we may waver in this understanding, we will eventually say it is worth it! Oh, how priceless it is to hear one word from God or to move one inch closer to Him; is it not more valuable than rubies or diamonds? Yes, when our minds are spiritually sound, we would surely count all that Job possesses as dung compared to it. Therefore, the Spirit makes intercession for us when we aren't in our right minds spiritually, and God allows Satan to touch Job's stuff, and eventually Job that he may move closer unto the Lord.

God permitted Satan to touch Job's stuff, although Job didn't desire it or pray for it. Job prayed for the opposite. Remember what Job said after all of this fell upon him? Job said, *"For the thing which I greatly feared is come upon me, and that which I was afraid of is come unto me"* (Job 3:25).

This isn't what Job was praying for, but it is what God saw necessary. God saw that it was necessary for Job to be tried like this because God wanted him to take the next step in his heavenly calling. Oh, what a glorious calling it was, yet Job would have never realized it if Satan wasn't allowed to touch his stuff and eventually him. Job was flourishing in a comfortable place, but God had bigger plans for his life than he could ever realize, yet before God would manifest this next step in Job's heavenly calling, more of God would have to be manifest in him. Therefore, God gives Satan permission to touch him and his stuff because God knows what is best, even if the wealthy and wise Job doesn't.

# CHAPTER 7
# SATAN TOUCHES JOB'S STUFF

Job 1:13-22. *"And there was a day when his sons and his daughters were eating and drinking wine in their eldest brother's house: And there came a messenger unto Job, and said, The oxen were plowing, and the asses feeding beside them: And the Sabeans fell upon them and took them away; yea, they have slain the servants with the edge of the sword; and I only am escaped alone to tell thee. While he was yet speaking, there came also another, and said, The fire of God is fallen from heaven, and hath burned up the sheep, and the servants, and consumed them; and I only am escaped alone to tell thee. While he was yet speaking, there came also another, and said, The Chaldeans made out three bands, and fell upon the camels, and have carried them away, yea, and slain the servants with the edge of the sword; and I only am escaped alone to tell thee. While he was yet speaking, there came also another, and said, Thy sons and thy daughters were eating and drinking wine in their eldest brother's house: And, behold, there came a great wind from the wilderness, and smote the four corners of the house, and it fell upon the young men, and they are dead; and I only am escaped alone to tell thee. Then Job arose, and rent his mantle, and shaved his head, and fell down upon the ground, and worshipped, And said, Naked came I out of my mother's womb, and naked shall I return thither: the LORD gave, and the LORD hath taken away; blessed be the name of the LORD. In all this, Job sinned not, nor charged God foolishly."*

In these verses, we see that Satan was granted every one of his wishes. He was given everything he had requested, which he claimed would expose Job as a hypocrite and prove his assertion that he was victorious on Earth.

Earlier in this book, I stated that Satan had proclaimed himself as being the victor on Earth. He declared that he could do anything he wanted, anytime he desired. He claimed to have this ability in the entire earth. He proclaimed evil to have overcome good and himself as the victor over God. God quickly put Satan to shame, putting him in his place, when the Lord said unto him, *"Hast thou considered My servant Job, that there is none like him in the earth, a perfect and an upright man, one that feareth God, and echeweth evil?"* (Job 1:8)

God asks Satan if he has considered Job. In other words, God asks Satan if he has set his heart on Job. What does this mean? Is this saying, have you set your heart on trying Job? Have you sought to devour him, seeing you go about as a roaring lion? Of course, Satan had, but because of God's hedge about Job, he couldn't touch him. Yet, this question would have been layered.

So, God responds to Satan's statement by asking him a layered question. When God asked Satan if he had considered Job, it would have brought Job to the forefront of the conversation. It would have implied that Satan hadn't conquered Job. It would have implied that Job was a servant of God. It would have implied that wickedness hadn't wholly overrun the Earth. Therefore, by asking Satan if he has considered His servant Job, God is telling Satan that his report is false and his claims are untrue.

Basically, God is saying unto Satan, if you really had control on Earth as you claim, then Job wouldn't be behaving so righteously. Furthermore, you cannot consider Job an insignificant person on Earth, seeing he is the greatest man in the East. You aren't the victor, nor has evil conquered therein, for all one must do is look at Job to see your report isn't accurate. God is saying unto Satan, have you considered Job in your report? If you had, you wouldn't have made the statements you have made.

Now, I also stated that Satan cried foul, as he contended that Job shouldn't be considered in his report because the Lord had put a hedge around him and all that he had, and therefore, it was impossible for him to triumph over Job. I also stated that God's ruling was that Job should be considered, which would make the prideful report of Satan untrue. Therefore, Satan, desiring to prove that he is the victor on Earth and that evil had conquered good, slanderously reported Job to be a hypocrite who is being bribed into worshipping God because of the things the Lord gave him. Satan accused Job of not really being a servant of God. He also proclaimed that Job's righteous lifestyle wasn't sincere, saying he only walked righteously to receive things from the Lord. Satan also said that he could prove this if the Lord would take away the hedge from Job's stuff. Satan said, "if I'm allowed to touch all that Job has, then he will curse You to Your face, and thus, prove that I am the victor on the Earth and my evil has overcome Your good." God permitted Satan to touch Job's stuff, which brings us to these verses at the beginning of this chapter.

Satan was permitted to touch all that Job had, and so he did. Satan hit Job's stuff as hard as possible, as seen in these verses.

Satan didn't take Job's possessions little by little, but all at once, in the most horrific manner he could envision. Notice that Satan not only takes Job's things but also kills his children and all his servants except four. Satan sends the Sabeans, fire, the Chaldeans, and a wind from the wilderness to destroy everyone and everything Job has, except for four servants and his wife. So, Job remained, but nothing from his household or stuff remained except for five people.

Notice how Job's wealth, posterity, and household were violently removed. Again, Satan didn't take it away little by little, but all at once, in a way that Job would have to examine the spiritual implications of this great loss. Job's stuff wasn't taken in a manner in which some of his livestock had caught some disease, his children had gotten sick, or some of his household had fallen on hard times. This wasn't a case in which some cattle rustlers had stolen a few of his livestock, his household had trouble, or his children had problems. Therefore, Job's stuff wasn't taken in a way that would suggest it to be a natural event. Also, this wasn't something that Job could remedy. This was something supernatural; therefore, Job would have had to look at it spiritually.

This is how Satan wanted Job to view this, for this is how Satan desired him to understand this calamity. Satan wanted Job to look at this spiritually, not as though it was some natural occurrence. Why? Why would Satan want Job to look at this spiritually instead of it being a natural occurrence? Satan wanted Job to see this as God removing His blessings and protection from him. Satan wanted Job to look at this as God disapproving of him. Satan wanted Job to see this as God's hand against him. Satan didn't want Job to have the slightest thought that this horrific event in his life could be chalked up to chance. Satan knows that humanity is prone to blame God in times of loss or lack of success. Therefore, he wants Job to understand this to be a spiritual event, not a natural one, that surely didn't happen by chance. Satan wants Job to see this as the hand of God against him, nothing else. Satan wants Job to think that he can't trust God. Satan wants Job to see God as untrustworthy and unpredictable. Satan wants Job to view God as being unfair in his dealings with him. Satan wants Job to think that all his service to God is worthless. Satan wants Job to lay this event at the feet of God. Satan wants Job to see God as his enemy, not his friend. Satan wants Job to know that this is a spiritual occurrence, not a natural one, and therefore, he touches Job's stuff in this horrific manner.

We should also notice that Satan took all that Job had in four steps, not one huge blow. The Sabeans didn't take it all, the fire didn't consume it all, the Chaldeans didn't overtake it all, and the wind didn't destroy it all. This was a calculated move on Satan's part. Satan didn't want one event to take all that Job had but wanted it to come from different directions in different ways. This, too, would show this to be a spiritual event and not a natural occurrence. One may chalk up one occurrence as chance, but four different events that are not connected to each other are much harder to view as coincidental. Can the fire from heaven and the Chaldeans collaborate with each other, or do the Sabeans and the wind from the wilderness confine in each other? These four circumstances, which took all that Job had, couldn't be confederate with each other. Sure, a hurricane may destroy all you have, but how unlikely is it for a tornado, fire from heaven, the Chaldeans, and the Sabeans to take all you have in one day or in a single hour? This could not be chalked up to chance or to any natural occurrence, and Satan wanted Job to know this.

We also see that all of this happened in one day, and to be more precise, all at once or successively. This would also have been a calculated move by Satan. This would also show Job that these were spiritual events. What are the chances of two separate armies taking your stuff in one day, or what are the chances of fire falling from heaven and a wind from the wilderness destroying all you have at the same time? The odds against all these things happening at once are astronomical. Therefore, these events couldn't be looked at as chance but rather understood to be spiritual occurrences. Satan wanted Job to know that there wasn't any possibility that this was a natural occurrence but a spiritual one. Satan wanted Job to think this was God doing this to him, and at the very least, he wanted Job to know that this had to be approved in the heavens by the Lord.

Satan hits Job with everything he can hit him with all at once. Satan doesn't come into this boxing ring and throw a few jabs here and there but hits Job with one haymaker after another. Satan doesn't want Job to be able to get his footing after being hit, nor does he want him to be able to go to his corner and get his bearings. Satan is trying to crush Job all at once; he is trying to overwhelm him, and he wants him to know this is spiritual, not a natural occurrence.

Now, let's look at the five people Satan didn't kill in Job's household. Satan left four of Job's servants and his wife alive. Let's look at the four servants first, and God willing, we will look at Job's wife later in this book. One may say, why didn't Satan kill them as well? Well, Satan had a reason for not killing them. Satan is very calculating, for this was no oversight. Satan knew what he was doing. It was a strategic move on his part.

Satan left four servants alive, one for each catastrophic event. Four separate events took place, which took Job's wealth, household, and posterity. Satan left one servant alive for each event. Why? Satan wanted someone to report these horrific events to Job. Job's wealth was so vast that he couldn't have seen all these events occur; in fact, he didn't see any of them occur. It would have taken some time for Job to be able to find out or survey the damage, and therefore, Satan leaves four servants alive so that they may report this heart-wrenching news to him. Not only did Satan leave them alive to report the terrifying news to Job, but they did it in such a manner that they all reported it one after another. There wasn't a minute of delay between one report and the other. The scriptures teach us that while one was reporting, another came to report. While one was still talking, another servant came to report another disaster. This would have not only drawn out or lengthened the reporting but would have also caused Job to understand that this was spiritual. One servant didn't come unto Job and say all you have is gone, but one came right after another, reporting in detail. Before Job could digest the first report, another was given to him, and so on.

There is something about multiple calamities that causes us greater confusion. Multiple calamities also cause us to look at them spiritually instead of naturally. We try to catch our footing, but the next report comes before we can. Job is hit with a terrible body blow, which knocks the wind out of him, but before he can catch his breath, he is hit just as hard again. This was a powerful combination by hell's champion, which was meant to knock the grace of God out of Job, but we will soon see that the grace of God remains, and Job, the vessel of clay, is still standing.

There is something about multiple calamities that crushes us and breaks our will. One comes, and we try to figure out how to cope with it, then another, then another, and then another. Multiple calamities seem to drive us into submission quicker than one. Satan wanted to overwhelm Job. Satan wanted to hit him with all of this at once. Satan didn't want Job to have any time in between reports, which may allow him to come to grips with one calamity before the next was reported. Satan wanted to place all the weight of these calamities upon Job all at once, with multiple reports. Satan wanted Job to be crushed under the weight of it all at the same time. Satan wanted Job to be like an ox unaccustomed to the yoke (Jeremiah 31:18), as he was laden with all of this at once. Satan didn't want Job to have any time to get accustomed to this heavy load he would have to bear. This is why Satan left these four servants of Job alive.

So, what will Job do now that all he possesses has been so violently taken away? Will Job do as Satan had proclaimed he would do before God and the celestial gathering and curse the Lord to His face? Does Job only worship God for the things He gives, or is there more to the relationship between God and Job than possessions? This is the question. Now, let's see the answer.

Job 1:20-22. *"Then Job arose, and rent his mantle, and shaved his head, and fell down upon the ground, and worshipped, And said, Naked came I out of my mother's womb, and naked shall I return thither: the LORD gave, and the LORD hath taken away; blessed be the name of the LORD. In all this, Job sinned not, nor charged God foolishly."*

There are a few things I would like to point out in these verses, God willing. Before we speak about Job worshipping God instead of cursing Him, let's look at Who Job said all these things belonged to. Job ascribes all that he had to have been owned by the Lord, not him. Job says these are God's blessings, not my possessions. They are God's; therefore, God has the right to do with them as He pleases. God is the owner of them, and therefore, He has the right to do with them as He will. There is nothing wrong with God giving or taking what is His. There is no wickedness in the Lord using what is His in any manner He desires. Job didn't see these things as belonging unto himself but unto God, and Job also understood that God had the right of ownership and could do with them as He wished. Job doesn't become angry with God for doing what He wishes with what He owns; Job knows this is God's right. Job says the Lord gave and the Lord has taken away; blessed be the name of the Lord. It was the Lord that gave Job all that he had for all the time he had it. Job didn't earn these things on his own; they were gifts from the Lord. Will we get angry with someone who has loaned us their car when they take it back? No, we thank them for allowing us to use it. Job knows all these things belong to God and is thankful for the time he was allowed to enjoy them. Job could have spent his entire life without them, yet God allowed him to enjoy them for a certain amount of time. Job is thankful for all the things God allowed him to enjoy and knows he would have never gotten to experience such things if God hadn't blessed him to do so. All those years of comfort and happiness were blessings from God. They were God's blessings, and now, God has chosen to take them away. No, Job won't be angry with God for taking away these blessings, for Job never owned them to begin with. These are God's things, and He has the right to do with them as He wishes. Job refuses to be angry with God for doing what He will with what is His, but rather thanks Him for sharing them with him. Sure, Job was thankful for them and blessed God for giving them to him, even when they were taken away, which shows Job's relationship with God wasn't about stuff.

(There is a lesson to be learned in how we view God's blessings. These things are God's, and therefore, we should use them accordingly when we have them. We should treat our blessings as God's possessions, and therefore, we should use them in a manner that would glorify Him. They are God's blessings; therefore, we should try our very best to use them as God would.)

Job knew all these things came from God. Job always knew these things weren't the works of his own hands. Job knew it wasn't his own might and wisdom that caused him to be the greatest man in the East. Job knew all of this came from God. Job wasn't prideful because of all his wealth, but humble, as he gave glory to God for it all. It was evident to Job that the Lord had blessed him, for how else could he have come to such a great estate if God hadn't? Job didn't hold himself in such high regard that he thought he could have done all of this on his own, for he easily saw that the Lord had blessed him.

Now, all of this has come to pass in Job's life. Job has lost everything, and it is apparent that this wasn't a natural occurrence but a spiritual one, for as certain as Job is that God blessed him with all these possessions, he is also certain that God allowed them to be taken from him. Yet, through all this, Job doesn't curse God unto his face but does exactly the opposite, for he worships the Lord amid this catastrophe. Amid this horrific calamity, Job worships God; amid the ashes, Job worships God; and amid the bones of his children and household, Job worships God. Oh, how Job's heart must have been broken, yet, out of this brokenness, he looked up through his teary eyes and worshipped God. "God gave me everything I had and took it away," says Job. "It was all God's to begin with; He didn't have to give it to me, and He also has the right to take it away, for it is His." Job may have spoken to God something like this. "Thank You for allowing me to have had pleasure in those things for the time You gave them to me. You didn't have to give them to me, but You chose to, and now, You have chosen to take them away, and I will not question You in this matter, for they are Yours, and You have the right to do with them as You will. Therefore, I bless Your holy name for all the blessings You have given me, and I bless Your holy name now with all being taken from Me. Our relationship is still the same. I didn't worship You because of what You gave me but for Who You are. All those things You blessed me with are gone, for You saw fit to take them away, which is Your right, for they belong to You. Yet, with all these blessings gone, I still worship You, for You are God, and I have never worshipped You for what You gave me, but I have always worshipped You for Who You are. Now, with all Your blessings stripped from me, I worship You as I did while I was blessed with them. I was thankful for all Your blessings, but I have always worshipped You for Who You are. You have not changed, and although all that I have is gone, my worship of You has not changed, for I never worshipped You for the things You gave me, but for Who You are. You are still the same, though my wealth, household, and posterity are gone. You, my only object of worship, remains, though all my earthly possessions have perished; therefore, my worship of You remains."

O, how these must have been some of the hardest words Satan ever had to listen to. O, how these words must have been like icepicks in his dark ears. O, how this would have caused Satan's rejoicing to come to a screeching halt. O, the anger he must have felt at this moment, and then confusion would have set in shortly afterward.

Think of the confusion Satan must have felt at this time. Think of how baffling this must have been to him. Satan was certain that Job would break, and he would have been proclaimed the victor on Earth, yet this small clay pot (Job) stands between him and victory. Satan was sure he could break Job into shivers, yet he remained intact. "Job still worships God amid all that I've brought on him," ponders Satan. "This one clay pot is still whole. How did it not break", cries Satan? "How could this mere human withstand all that I have brought upon him? I was sure he would curse God to his face. I was sure I would have been proven right before heaven and earth. I was sure this clay pot would break into a million pieces, yet it remains shining like the sun, although I have taken everything from him. How could Job withstand me?" Satan ponders. "How could I have been so wrong in this matter? I was so sure of this, and I have pridefully addressed the heavenly counsel with all confidence, proclaiming that Job would curse God to His face. I said this was a reality, not a possibility. I staked all my credibility on this, and now it has blown up in my face. All that the Lord said concerning my false report has been proven to be right, and I have been proven to be a liar before everyone in the celestial gathering. My pride proclaimed victory over God in front of them all, and all the charges I brought against the Lord have been proven to be false. All of Job's possessions have turned to smoldering ashes, yet I am left disgraced. How could this be? How could this clay pot remain intact? I hit him with enough force to break nations and topple kingdoms, yet he remains unbroken and continues to worship God. I couldn't even cause an interruption in his worship of the Lord, for after he heard of his great calamity, he immediately fell upon the ground and worshipped Him. How did this happen? My condition is worse after I touched Job's stuff than before. God has been proven to be right, and I have been proven to be a liar. Job not only hasn't cursed God, but he continues to worship Him. God proclaimed Job to be His servant beforehand, and now this greatly magnifies it before heaven and earth."

Oh, Satan, you will again stand before the celestial counsel. What will you say after all of this? Will you hang your head in shame or bow your prideful heart before the Almighty God? Well, we all know you feel that is beneath you. So, what will you do? How will you hope to save face when you appear before the great God and the celestial counsel again? You have made your accusations against God and Job. Your slanders have been witnessed in their presence. Your erroneous report has been proven false by your own standards. You are the one who suggested this demonstration. You have said the removal of all that Job possessed would prove that he isn't a true servant of God. You said this would be evident, for you said he would curse the Lord to His face if you were allowed to touch all that he had. You are the one who has crowned yourself victor in the Earth. You are the one who said this trying of Job would prove that you are all you say you are. Now, you will face a second summons just like Haman did. You will be humiliated in the presence of the King and His holy angels. Yet, we know you're full of pride, and pride is never willing to admit defeat though it is clearly beaten. Your pride will still claim victory, although the battlefield declares the opposite. Your pride will not allow you to accept your place of defeat. You are confused but still scheming. You don't understand how Job didn't break, and you are still trying to find an angle to argue before the great God and the celestial counsel.

There! You have it, or so you think! I know what the problem is, you will argue. Possessions cannot be a means to measure whether one is truly a servant of God or not; it must be one's life. You feel that most will break when it comes to possessions, but those who don't will break when it comes to choosing between themselves and God. No, Job didn't break when I touched everything he had, but he would break if I could touch him. You think you have it, and this will be your argument before the Lord and His holy angels at the next gathering.

# CHAPTER 8
# ANOTHER CONVERSATION BETWEEN GOD AND SATAN

Job 2:1-6. *"Again there was a day when the sons of God came to present themselves before the LORD, and Satan came also among them to present himself before the LORD. And the LORD said unto Satan, From whence comest thou? And Satan answered the LORD, and said, From going to and fro in the earth, and from walking up and down in it. And the LORD said unto Satan, Hast thou considered my servant Job, that there is none like him in the earth, a perfect and an upright man, one that feareth God, and escheweth evil? And still he holdeth fast his integrity, although thou movedst me against him, to destroy him without cause. And Satan answered the LORD, and said, Skin for skin, yea, all that a man hath will he give for his life. But put forth thine hand now, and touch his bone and his flesh, and he will curse thee to thy face. And the LORD said unto Satan, Behold, he is in thine hand; but save his life."*

Here, we see another gathering of the sons of God, in which they present themselves before the Lord, and Satan is also present. Earlier in this book, we spoke somewhat about the first gathering, and although we can't be certain of its purpose, we gave some thoughts on what it could be in accordance with other scriptures. Here, we see the second celestial gathering mentioned in the first two chapters of the Book of Job. This second gathering seems to be the same as the first, or at least very similar. They seem identical, although the conversation between God and Satan will end differently, even though it begins in the same manner as the first meeting.

In this gathering, God will ask Satan the same question He asked him in the first gathering, as He says unto Satan, *"From whence comest thou?"* Satan answers the Lord in the same manner as he had answered Him in the first meeting, saying, *"From going to and fro in the earth, and from walking up and down in it."*

Now, I know we should never put anything past Satan, for his pride has no bounds, but if Satan felt this was the proper report to give to the Lord in the first meeting, surely after his failed trial of Job, he should have adjusted his report. No, not Satan, as bold and as brazen as ever, still full of pride and boasting, although Job's integrity is still intact. Satan reported this same report in the first meeting, as he proclaimed to have full sway in the earth. He proclaimed that evil had conquered good, and therefore, he was victorious over God on earth.

Satan proclaimed himself to be the victor on earth with this very statement in the first meeting, but God rebuked his false report with the mention of Job. In the first meeting, when Satan had said that he went to and fro in the earth and walked up and down in it, the Lord said, *"Hast thou considered my servant Job, that there is none like him in the earth, a perfect and an upright man, one that feareth God, and escheweth evil"* (Job 1:8)? In other words, God is saying to Satan, your report proclaims you to be the victor in the earth, but is Job considered in your report? By saying this, the Lord is saying unto Satan (before the entire celestial gathering) that your report isn't true. Your report can't be true if you don't consider Job, for there is none like him in the earth; he is a perfect and upright man who fears God and eschews evil, and everyone present would have known that Job was the greatest man in the East.

It is apparent that evil hasn't triumphed in the earth, for all one must do is consider Job. Satan has no right to claim victory, nor does he have the right to proclaim that evil has triumphed in the earth because a simple consideration of Job loudly declares such a statement to be false. Job is not evil, for he is a servant of God. One must only look at how he orders his life to realize this. Therefore, Satan is not victorious on the earth, and wickedness hasn't triumphed there, for all one must do is consider Job, and it will become apparent that this isn't the case. Yet, Satan makes the same assertion in this second gathering. Job's integrity is still intact, and Satan continues to boast without considering Job.

Satan may have felt more empowered in the earth, although he failed in his trial of Job, because now, Job seems to be weaker in the earth, and Satan seems to be stronger, for the greatest power for good in the earth at this time may have very well been Job. Now, all of Job's wealth, posterity, household, and influence seem to be smoldering under the hand of Satan. Yet, Job still holds fast his integrity, and all that Satan said he could cause Job to do hasn't come to pass. Therefore, Satan's report in the first meeting has been proven false, but Satan still proclaims victory in the earth at this second gathering.

So, this conversation between God and Satan starts as it did in the first meeting. God asks Satan where he has come from, and Satan replies by pretty much saying, "I have come from the earth, and all my desires are accomplished there." God again asks Satan if he has considered Job, as He says, *"Hast thou considered my servant Job, that there is none like him in the earth, a perfect and an upright man, one that feareth God and escheweth evil? And still he holdeth fast his integrity although thou movedst me against him, to destroy him without cause."* Again, God rebuts Satan's report as having all power in the earth by saying, *"Hast thou considered my servant Job?"* Simply by considering Job, Satan's report is proven to be false. Upon the examination of Job, it becomes clear that evil has not conquered righteousness in the earth, nor have all of Satan's desires been fulfilled. So again, Satan's report is declared to be false before this heavenly gathering by simply considering Job. It may seem that Satan has conquered Job through all that he had done unto him, but the integrity of Job remains, although all that he has is destroyed. Therefore, the integrity of Job is a beaming light on the earth, which shines upon Satan's dark report, proclaiming it to be false. All of Satan's desires aren't accomplished in the earth as his report says, and evil hasn't completely triumphed in the earth as he proclaims. The integrity of Job still stands firm; it stands as a great mountain in the earth, proclaiming Satan isn't victorious, as his report declares.

In the first gathering, Satan insists that Job shouldn't be considered in his report because God supernaturally protected him. God ruled that Job should be considered, and therefore, Satan said Job serves God for nothing; let me touch all that he has, and he will curse the Lord to His face. God gave Satan permission to touch all that Job had, which Satan proclaimed would prove his report to be true. Satan said, if I can touch all that Job has, then it will be proven that he isn't a servant of God, and my report of having my desires accomplished on earth will be verified. If I can touch all that he has, he will curse God to His face, proving my report to be true and accurate.

God gave Satan permission to touch all that Job had, and Satan did, and now we have another gathering in which Satan is proclaiming to be victorious in the earth. Yet, though Satan had destroyed all that Job had, he couldn't prove that Job wasn't the servant of God; rather, the opposite was displayed, for Job still worshipped God. Despite losing everything, Job's unwavering faith remains strong; he continues to worship God amid poverty and sorrow, just as he did when he had great wealth and comfort. Tears stream down Job's face as torrential rain, yet he looks up to heaven through them and worships God. These tears may blur Job's vision, yet he still worships God. Job doesn't understand what is happening but still proclaims God to be righteous and worships Him. Job is confused about why all this has happened to him, but he is not confused about God. Job still knows God is righteous, even when he doesn't understand His ways. Job still loves God, although His blessings have been violently stripped away from him. Satan's first report has been proven false, but he still gives the same report of being victorious in the earth in this second meeting. So, God once again states that Job should be considered, which would prove Satan's report to be false.

In the second meeting, Satan cannot protest Job's insertion because God has already decided to consider him in the first meeting. Satan also cannot argue that Job is only serving God for His blessings because he has already been allowed to take away everything Job has, and yet he continues to worship God. So, how will Satan defend his report this time? Satan will still insist that Job isn't a true servant of God. Satan insisted on this same thing in the first meeting and proclaimed that it would be proven if God allowed him to touch all that Job had. Between these two meetings, Satan has touched all that Job had, and it didn't prove Job wasn't the servant of God, as he said it would, but has had the opposite effect, for Job still worships God. Job still worships God amid this calamity, and upon consideration of this, Satan's report is again proven false. Now, Satan still proclaims Job isn't a true servant of God, and therefore, he still insists that he is victorious in the earth. God again says that Job should be included in your report, for he has held fast to his integrity, even though all he had was destroyed without cause. (Job's actions didn't deserve these things coming upon him). Satan says, let me touch him, and it will be proven that he isn't a true servant of God. Yes, all he has is taken away, and he still worships the Lord, but the truest test is, will he put the Lord above his own life? Satan says to the Lord, "Let me touch him, and he will curse You to Your face. This will prove my report as being true, for all my desires are accomplished in the earth."

# CHAPTER 9
# SATAN IS PERMITTED TO TOUCH JOB

Job 2:6-8. *"And the LORD said unto Satan, Behold, he is in thine hand; but save his life. So went Satan forth from the presence of the LORD, and smote Job with sore boils from the sole of his foot unto his crown. And he took him a potsherd to scrape himself withal; and he sat down among the ashes."*

God once again grants Satan permission to try Job, but again, not without stipulations. God will allow Satan to touch Job, but his life must be spared. God's permission is clear and to the point. Satan is allowed to do anything he desires unto Job, but he can't kill him. So, Satan is again granted everything he desires to prove Job to be a hypocrite, and again, God places stipulations upon Satan as well. Think of this: Satan can do anything he desires unto Job except kill him. Therefore, Satan will bring the greatest suffering upon Job that he can muster. Satan will bring the greatest of miseries upon Job and take him as deeply into pain, shame, and despair as is possible. Satan can't kill him, but he will do everything in his power to make Job wish he were dead. No, Satan can't kill Job, but he will bring him as close to death as he can. There is a variety of fiery darts in the quiver of Satan, and he will choose the very one he feels to be the hottest and hit Job with it, for he will throw Job into the hottest fire he can dream up.

So, Satan chooses out of his vast quiver the very thing that he thinks will cause Job the most suffering. The very thing he thinks will cause Job to curse God to His face. Yes, Satan reaches out his cruel hand and touches Job, which causes Job to be stricken with boils from the top of his head to the soles of his feet. Satan took full advantage of the permission God gave him, and not one inch of Job has been spared from his demonic hand. Job is covered with boils from head to toe. There is no place on the body of Job that the dark hand of Satan hasn't touched. There, Job sits among the ashes, covered with these excruciating boils, scraping himself with broken pieces of pottery. Job only has his wife and his things, which are reduced to ashes. Job sits among these ashes in misery, reaches down, grabs a broken piece of pottery, and scrapes his boils with it. All that Job possesses has been broken to pieces, and now he is broken to pieces. Job was once the greatest man in the East, and now he sets upon the ash heap, scraping himself with a broken piece of pottery. Oh, the misery Job must have felt within and without. Who could weigh it? Job said it was heavier than the sand of the seashore (Job 6:1-3). Yet, this isn't all that Job would have to endure, for his three friends would soon come to speak with him and accuse him of being a secret sinner, insinuating that he is a hypocrite, and his wife would counsel him to cast aside his integrity, *"curse God, and die"*.

We may try to imagine what it would have been like for Job during this fiery trial. I must admit, it is hard even to begin to imagine the place Job found himself in, for our hardest times are probably very small compared to the circumstances he had to endure. I don't believe I have the ability to understand how Job felt during these hard and miserable times, as many times we can't understand what others are going through because we have never experienced what they are experiencing. Still, I feel that it would be appropriate to say that Job had found himself in a place he had never been in before. Job had found himself in the hardest time of his life, and I'm sure that Job would have felt that he was taken beyond his limits.

(We can see Job as a type of Christ in his sufferings. Job seems to have suffered more than anyone else in the Old Testament, and Christ suffered more than anyone else in the New Testament or throughout history. Job wasn't punished for the sins he committed, and Christ didn't suffer for the sins He committed.)

Though we may not be capable of understanding Job's great suffering, we can still draw many things from his fiery trial. There are still things about Job's suffering that apply to us. We may not fully comprehend Job's suffering, but what can we understand about his trial and misery? When we are tried, so often, we may feel that the trial is greater than we are. We may feel that the trial has gone further than we think it should or beyond where it needed to go. Yet, we must be brought to the end of ourselves if the trial is going to perform the godly purpose the Lord has designed it to fulfill. We must remember that although Satan had done this to Job, God gave him permission. Therefore, we know that all things work together for good to those who love God and to those who are called according to His purpose (Romans 8:28). Through this, we should understand that God had a purpose in Job's tribulation, a purpose that Job probably couldn't see, but a godly purpose indeed. This is something we should always understand when we go through trials.

Job had recognized this to be a spiritual occurrence, not a natural one, and it is evident from the conversation Job had with his three friends that he understood God allowed this to happen to him. When we go through trials, we should recognize the same. Although Satan may touch us, we must understand that he couldn't have touched us unless God allowed it, and if God allowed it, then God also has a purpose for it.

Now, to get back to how Job was feeling, we won't try to comment upon it, except to say Job was brought into a trial bigger than himself, which also happens to us. The trial is meant to be bigger than we are, or we would stop it or handle it in our own power. The tribulation is meant to take us to the end of ourselves; therefore, it lasts longer than we think it should and is greater than we think it should be. Why? There are times in which we think we are crushed, but we really aren't. Sometimes we think we have been brought to the end of ourselves when we haven't been brought to that frightful place. Yes, we often look at ourselves in higher esteem than we should, but in tribulation, we sometimes behold ourselves in lower esteem than we are. We think we are crushed, but God knows our pride is only wounded, and we think our lust has been destroyed, but God knows it is only idle. So often, we feel that the tribulation has served its purpose, and therefore, we wonder why it continues, but God knows other things still need to be burned out of our lives. We must be brought to the end of ourselves. Yes, to a place where we no longer have confidence or hope in the flesh, and so often, that place is farther than we think it should be.

This is why the tribulation must be greater than we are. It must be greater than our abilities, or we would stop it short of God's goal in our lives, or we wouldn't even allow it to happen. It must be greater than we are, so we are forced not to trust in ourselves for deliverance, for we must learn to trust in God to deliver us. Our pain, anguish, and misery cry out; this is the end of myself; nothing more is needed, but we often can't see how strong and resilient the flesh is. We can't see that it is in better shape than we realize. We don't understand that it is stronger than we think. Yet, God sees it, and therefore, He allows the tribulation to continue. As the tribulation continues, we, too, see that some other fleshly thing died in our lives that we didn't even know existed or thought the tribulation had already killed. Oh, the end of ourselves is a place none of us wants to go, for it is farther than we want to travel, farther than we think is necessary, and farther than we ever thought it to be. So, why must we come to the end of ourselves? There are things in us that must cease before God will shine brighter in our lives, and many times, they must be killed by tribulation because we don't have the strength or desire to kill them ourselves.

Often, fleshly things in our lives must be identified by tribulation because sometimes, we cannot see them as the vile things they are. When we are brought to the end of ourselves, these things are identified and cease, and we understand them to be the fleshly things they are. These things must be revealed and killed so that we would no longer trust in them but would trust solely in the Lord. We may feel like the tribulation is too extreme and much of it is unnecessary, but as it continues, we are completely broken under its weight. Then we see carnal things in our lives that we didn't even know existed, for the tribulation has revealed them. Often, we can't see the dross because it is buried so deeply inside of the gold, but it is still there, causing the gold to be less valuable, although we can't see it, for it must be revealed and separated from the gold in the fire.

Tribulation also destroys fleshly things in our lives that we think are necessary to fulfill our calling. We would have never identified these things as the flesh but would have considered them to be most useful in the areas God has called us to minister. The dross is revealed to us in the fiery trial, granting us the ability to see it. We now understand that these fleshly things aren't the light we thought them to be but darkness lying within us. We are brought to the end of ourselves so that we may see ourselves. We are broken so that certain things may be shattered in our lives and discarded. We must be brought to the end of ourselves because we would have never identified and killed the things in us that God is using the tribulation to burn out of our lives. In many cases, we would have protected certain parts of our lives that the tribulation has destroyed, for we see them as profitable to our ministries.

Therefore, we must be brought to a place where we can no longer protect or trust in these fleshly things. We find ourselves marred and hopeless in the fire and understand that we have no viable strength to trust in. There, we see ourselves for who we are and turn loose of the things that must go, for the fiery trial has caused them to become less valuable in our eyes. The fleshly things we treasured before the fire have become as dung to us, for we only glory in Christ. There, in tribulation, Christ is revealed unto us as the Morning Star and the flesh as the dung it is. There, in the fire, when all fleshly hope is lost, we look and see that we are not alone, for there is One likened unto the Son of God walking among us (Dan 3:25). Then we see that we are free, for the fire was never designed to burn us; it was only designed to burn the things that bound us. The fire was never meant to destroy us; it was only meant to reveal Christ to us in a greater manner. We must be brought to the end of ourselves so that we may get a better and closer view of Christ, for the Lord said He would dwell in the thick darkness (1 Kings 8:12). We must be brought to the end of ourselves so that our pride may bow down before the Thrice Holy God.

What do we do with unyielding things that refuse to bend? We throw them in the fire, and at a certain temperature, they become malleable. Sure, different materials have different melting points, for aluminum becomes malleable at a lower temperature than steel, and pride may have the highest melting point of all. Therefore, the Saints of God must be brought to the end of themselves. Yes, the fire will have to be hotter than ever before, for it is essential that pride bows down.

I've often wondered what it would take to kill pride, which is present in my life. How many times hotter would the furnace have to be heated to destroy my pride? I have often shuddered to think of what it would take to rid myself of this pride, and yet, every time some pride is removed, I find other parts of pride in me that I didn't even know existed—yes, revealed in the fires of tribulation. I've often feared, as I thought, what it would take for pride to be removed from me, for I have often thought that after I die, pride would breathe another breath. Yes, the tribulation needs to be greater than we are because it is essential that we be brought unto the end of ourselves, for there, lust shrinks, and pride bows down that we may get a closer look at ourselves and of God as well.

This is why the tribulation had to be so hard on Job, for the perfect and upright man must be brought unto the end of himself to get a clearer view of himself and a greater revelation of God. It will take a great tribulation to reveal these things unto Job, for the fleshly things that remain in him are hidden deep, so deep that he can't see them. It will take a bright light for Job to see them; therefore, he must be cast into a great fire. The view of God Job must get is unique, and the path very dark, for Solomon said, the Lord dwells in the thick darkness (1 Kings 8:12). There, in the darkness, the light shines the brightest. It's not that the glory of God doesn't always shine brightly, but sometimes it takes darkness for us to be able to see and comprehend it. This is why Satan is permitted to hit Job so hard. This is why God permits such suffering to come into Job's life. Job must be brought unto the end of himself so that God may shine brighter in his life. This is where Job is. He is being brought unto the end of himself. To the very brink of death so that he may see the glory of God. This is why God will allow it. This is why God permits Satan to touch Job.

(I've often thought of Moses desiring to see the glory of God. God told him no man could see His glory and live [Exodus 33:20]. Yet, it seems that the closer we come to death, or the more we are broken, the clearer the view of God becomes. Spurgeon said, "In prosperity God is heard, and that is a blessing; but in adversity God is seen, and that is a greater blessing." I believe that Saints will see the glory of God in the land of the living, although it may only be for a very brief moment. One may say the scripture you just referred to proves we won't, but I do believe that we will, for I believe that on our deathbeds, as the last few moments of life remain, the glory of God will appear in the Valley of the Shadow of Death, and God will take us out of this life with the kiss of His glory. At that moment, we will be as dead as we have ever been during this life, and I believe the glory of God will shine brighter unto us than we could ever imagine. Sure, no one can see the glory of God and live, but when it comes time to die, I believe God will snatch us from the Valley of the Shadow of Death with the kiss of His glory. When Stephen was being stoned, he saw the heavens opened and Jesus and the Glory of God standing on the Father's right hand [Acts 7:55]. No, we can't see the glory of God and live, but at that time, it will be time to die, and I believe God will take us out of this life by showing us His glory, as the shadow of death is overcome by the glory of God.)

The loss of Job's health and wealth wouldn't be all that he would have to contend with, for there are still people in Job's life who don't have the understanding to counsel him in his painful situation, although they think they do. Job's wife is still with him, and Job has three friends that will come to him.

Now, regarding Job's wife. Why did Satan allow her to live? I must admit, this isn't completely clear to me. Firstly, I think that Satan couldn't kill her, but secondly, I think that Satan left her to counsel Job to cast aside his integrity, curse God, and die.

Let's look at the first point. Why would Satan not be able to kill her when he was first allowed to touch Job's stuff? Didn't Satan have the right to touch all that Job had? Yes, he did, but we also know that Satan wasn't allowed to touch Job.

The Bible teaches that when a man and a woman are married, they become one flesh. Therefore, Satan may not have had the right to kill her, seeing God told Satan he couldn't touch Job.

Secondly, Satan may have spared her life to do exactly what she had done. Satan is very calculating, and he has studied humanity extensively. Satan knows how humanity will act under certain circumstances for the most part, although the spiritual man seems to be somewhat of a mystery to him. Therefore, Satan would have left her alive so that she may counsel or influence Job to forsake his integrity, curse God, and die. This is the very thing Satan wanted Job to do, and the closest person to him would have carried these very instructions unto him. Remember, Satan had Eve carry the forbidden fruit unto Adam, and Satan will have Job's wife carry these instructions unto him. Satan wanted Job to curse God, and although the thought may have never crossed Job's mind, nor have been in his vocabulary, Satan would be sure to cause him to hear these very words from a person who shared a life with him.

It is also noteworthy to notice that Satan wanted Job to know that others saw this calamity as coming from God. This would have been Satan making sure that Job saw this horrific event as coming from the Lord. Satan didn't want to leave any doubt in Job's mind and heart that this event was spiritual, not chance. So, Satan would have spared Job's wife to testify that the calamity came from God and to try to influence Job into cursing God.

Who is more influential to a man on earth than his wife? It was Eve who influenced Adam to eat the forbidden fruit when

Satan didn't have the ability to do so, and it was Job's wife who would instruct Job to cast aside his integrity, curse God, and die. Therefore, Satan leaves Job's wife for this purpose.

(One's spouse is usually the most influential person in their life, whether it be the husband or the wife. This is why God commanded the Israelites to marry other Israelites, not strangers. This is why the Bible teaches us that Christians should marry Christians, not the unsaved. God gives this command because the unsaved spouse may move the saved spouse away from God and cause them to embrace the sins the unsaved spouse embraces. God warns us of this in the Old Testament and the New Testament.

The serpent couldn't influence Adam to eat of the Tree of the Knowledge of Good and Evil, but Eve could. The Bible implies that Adam would have never eaten of the Tree of the Knowledge of Good and Evil if it was up to the serpent's temptation and influence alone. If the serpent had reached the forbidden fruit unto Adam, he would have never eaten it, but because Eve gave it to him, he did eat it. It wouldn't have been as great of a temptation if Satan personally told Job to curse God and die as it was when Job's wife told him to do so. The unsaved spouse may be able to cause the saved spouse to partake in sin when many people, powers, and circumstances on earth couldn't.

Now, I'm not saying Job's wife was an unbeliever, nor am I throwing rocks at Eve, for many husbands have tried to influence their wives in an ungodly manner, but I'm trying to show how great of a temptation this was, for the wife of Job would have been the most influential person in Job's life on earth.)

Whether Satan could have killed Job's wife or not is uncertain to me, but what is apparent is that Satan used or influenced her to try and get to Job in four different ways.

First, Job's wife tells him to cast aside his integrity; second, she states this calamity came from God; third, she counsels Job to curse God; and fourth, she tells Job there is nothing left to live for. Throw aside your integrity, says Job's wife, curse God, and die.

These were the very words Satan wanted Job to hear, and he used the most influential person Job had left on earth to speak them to him. She asks Job, *"Doest thou still retain thine integrity"* (Job 2:9)? She asks Job: will you still worship God after it is evident that He has done this to you? Why would you still do this, seeing He has done this to you? Why would you still worship God when he has taken all that you had, including your servants, children, and health? How is it profitable to serve God when he has brought you to sickness and turned everything you have into ashes? There is no profit in serving God, for it is evident that he has brought you to nothing. Why continue in your service to Him? Can't you see there is no advantage in it? You would be better served not to worship Him at all, for it could be no worse for you. Then, she counsels him to curse God and die.

Notice these four words, *"Curse God, and die"* (Job 1:9). Curse God and give up. There is nothing left to live for. Yet, before you die, you should do one last thing and curse God, seeing He has brought this destruction and misery upon you.

So often, this is the advice of Satan. Not only should you curse God, but you should also give up, for there is no hope in life, nor is there anything left to live for. God has abandoned you, and your entire life is wrapped up in Him. Therefore, there is nothing left to live for; it is hopeless, seeing you can't see a life without Him, and it is evident that He has abandoned you. Look around you Job; can't you see what is happening? God has become your enemy, and you have nothing left to live for. Your wealth is gone, your health is gone, your children are dead, and your servants have been slaughtered, and if that isn't enough, can't you see that God is your enemy and has done all of this unto you? Cast off your integrity with your last words, and just give up and die. Are these not the very words of the enemy being spoken by Job's wife?

Sure, Job was confused, for he didn't understand why all of this happened to him. Job knew this couldn't have occurred unless God saw fit that it should, but he was confused about why. Job couldn't understand what was happening, but he wasn't so confused that he would agree with his wife. Job still knew God was righteous, although he didn't understand why He would choose to allow this. Job not only refuses the counsel of his wife but also rebukes her, saying, *"Thou speakest as one of the foolish women speaketh. What?* shall *we receive good at the hand of God, and not receive evil"* (Job 2:10)?

Does Job serve God for His earthly blessings alone, or does he serve Him for Who He is? Job will not cast aside his integrity because of earthly circumstances, for Job doesn't serve God for health and wealth but for Who He is.

Should we only worship God when His blessings are displayed in our lives, or should we always worship Him? Is the Christian life based upon a quid pro quo? We are thankful for all the blessings of God and praise the Lord for them, but Christianity isn't about worshipping the Lord in return for blessing, but because of our relationship with God through Jesus Christ our Lord. We are so thankful to the Lord for making us His children. Oh, what love the Father has bestowed upon us that we should be called the children of God (1 John 3:1). We are so grateful because we know the Lord has redeemed us from this earth, and eternal bliss awaits us in heaven. We praise God for who He has made us and for the eternal life He has given us, rejoicing because our names are written in heaven. Sure, blessings will come, but the Christian life still sings praises unto God after being beaten and chained in a dungeon (Acts 16:23-25). Job may be confused, but he isn't confused enough to follow his wife's counsel.

The timing of this is also something we should look at. Job was at his life's lowest, weakest, and most confusing point. He would have felt very vulnerable and longed for counsel to help him understand this matter. The only person left in his life was his wife, and we know how greatly God blesses wives to comfort, encourage, and strengthen their husbands. Job may have longed for this, but when he refused her counsel, he may have known she wouldn't comfort or strengthen him during this trial. It may have also been apparent that he couldn't expect her help during this time. Rebuking her as he did may have been a line drawn in the sand that guaranteed she wouldn't be there for him in his life's weakest and hardest moments. Job needed her now, more than ever before, but he would not choose her over God, even during this time of great calamity and sorrow unto his soul. Job would rather wallow in the ashes alone than accept her at this price. Job desperately needed her strength, but not at the expense of turning from God. Yes, he was so committed unto God that he wouldn't even entertain his wife's counsel but rebuked her for speaking as a foolish woman.

It also seems to be apparent and increasingly evident that Satan wanted Job's wife to say these things to him. Satan wanted Job to cast aside his integrity and curse God. This was Satan's plan all along, but we also see a little bit more in these words concerning Satan's desires. Satan couldn't kill Job, but he did want him dead. Therefore, the counsel is for Job to kill himself. When possible, Satan tries to place us in great despair. He uses despair to try and cause us to do unto ourselves the very thing he can't do unto us, though he greatly desires to, for God forbids him from doing it. Satan uses despair in this way. He uses despair to try and cause us to move in a direction he can't move us. Satan wants Job dead but doesn't have permission from God to kill him, and therefore, he counsels Job through his wife to kill himself or to just give up on life and die, for many people die because of a loss of purpose or hope. Although Satan wants Job dead, there is something he wants more. Therefore, the instructions come in this order, *"curse God and die."* Satan wants Job dead, but not before he curses God. Therefore, the instructions are in this order, for they instruct Job to curse God with his last breath and then commit suicide or die because of a lack of purpose or hope. Though Satan would delight in the death of Job, his main goal is for Job to curse God; therefore, he doesn't want Job to die until he first curses Him. This is why the instructions come in this order, for Satan wanted Job dead, but not before he cursed God. This is why these four words are arranged in this manner, *"curse God and die."*

(Satan wanted Job to curse God above all, but the death of Job would also be a victory unto him, for if Job is dead, then God couldn't say, *"Hast thou considered my servant Job, that there is none like him in the earth, a perfect and an upright man, one that feareth God, and escheweth evil"* (Job 2:3), when Satan gives his report of being victorious in the earth in the next celestial gathering. Satan feels that the death of Job would be a victory as well, although he desperately wants Job to curse God before he dies.)

It is also important to understand that Job's life was completely wrapped up in God, and without God, Job would have no reason to live. The counsel of Job's wife suggests that God has forsaken you. God has become your enemy. God is no longer your friend; therefore, you have nothing left to live for. You can never hope to have comfort in this life. All you can expect is more misery, for God has become your enemy, and He will continue to cause you great suffering and pain all the while you are alive. Your wealth is gone, your children are gone, your servants are gone, your health is gone, and God is gone. Therefore, there is nothing left to live for. How is it profitable to hold fast to your integrity? Just curse God and die.

There are times in which Christians, whose lives are wrapped up in God, feel as though God has abandoned them. They may feel like they have sinned so greatly that the Lord will no longer have anything to do with them. They may feel they have destroyed their calling and have no purpose in life. They may be experiencing great tribulation and think this is a sign of God being displeased with them. There may be various other reasons Christians feel this way, for Satan is a master at counseling the Saints that God has abandoned them or has become their enemy. During these times, Saints feel they have nothing left to live for, and therefore, Satan whispers in their ears and says, what is the point of you living any longer? Just die. In these moments, Satan wants these Saints dead, yet he doesn't have the ability to kill them; therefore, he tries to bring so much despair into their lives that they kill themselves, die for lack of purpose, or live a purposeless life.

My dear brothers and sisters, God hasn't abandoned you; you have been bought at a great price. You are not your own but belong to God, for it is the very blood of Christ which has purchased you (1 Corinthians 6:20). You may be in despair at the moment and feel as though you can't find God, but let the Book of Job be an encouragement unto you, for you too will come forth as tried gold (Job 23:10). The glory of God will also shine brighter in your life after the tribulation has run its course, for all things work together for good, to them who love God, to them who are the called according to His purpose (Romans 8:28).

The Book of Job is a source of encouragement to us during these times, for the book doesn't end with Job sitting amongst the ashes, scraping his boils with broken pieces of pottery. The last few chapters of this great book proclaim that Job had the privilege to speak unto the Almighty God in the whirlwind and was also greatly increased in the earth. As sure as you find yourself in the middle of the Book of Job, the day will come in which you will find yourself in the latter pages of the book as well, and there, you will see God's love and wisdom in all of this tribulation, for as sure as the tribulation comes, the comfort of God is also guaranteed, as the scriptures declare by saying, *"And our hope of you is stedfast, knowing, that as ye are partakers of the sufferings, so shall ye be also of the consolation"* (2 Corinthians 1:7).

Sometimes, Saints find themselves in the fires of tribulation and are confused. Often, we don't understand what is happening, as we wonder why God allowed such things to come into our lives. Tribulation can be very confusing because we often don't understand its purpose. Think of Job's situation. Job is a perfect and upright man who fears God and eschews evil. Job can't see the work that needs to be done in his life; he can't see that this will lead to him being increased in the earth, nor can he see that this will bring him closer to God than he has ever been. Job has no clue as to why this has come upon him. Job doesn't know because he can't see what God sees. Can Job see the work that needs to be done in his life? Can Job see that God will use this tribulation to increase his position in the earth? No, he can't. Yet, he knows that this had to be allowed by God, or it couldn't have happened unto him. Although Job is confident that he will come out of this tribulation better than he went in, proclaiming that he will come forth as tried gold (Job 23:10), he doesn't understand the purpose, and as we read the Book of Job, we can see that Job feels that the Lord is against him, even though he doesn't know why. Again, Job is confident that he will come forth as tried gold, which shows us that Job had some understanding of why God allowed this, but he can't see the dross in his life, nor can he imagine the revelation of God that will come unto him through this tribulation.

Saints may become very confused during tribulation because we often don't understand its purpose. We can't see the work that needs to be done in our lives, nor can we see how this tribulation will increase us in the earth. We know that it is spiritual, and if it is spiritual, then God had to allow it, yet we don't understand its purpose. Job couldn't see the evil that lurked within him, nor could he understand that it was important for him to increase in the earth.

Again, try to think like Job for a moment. He is the greatest man in the East, and the Lord even says there is none like him in the entire earth, for he is perfect, upright, fears God, and eschews evil. How could Job see the importance of being increased in the earth or the evil that lurked within him? Job may have been the most righteous man on earth during his day, yet evil was still within him. Job can't see this, or he would have already sought to get it out of his life. Job is a very righteous man, but he can't see the evil lurking within him. Think about this. How often have we read the Book of Job, trying to figure out what had to be burned out of his life? Job was so upright that it is hard for us to see any flaw in him. Job couldn't see the evil that lurked within him, nor did he understand the revelation of God that must be worked in his life, and therefore, Job didn't understand the purpose of this tribulation.

So often, this is the case with us. We can't see what God sees. Sure, our spirit is the candle of the Lord, which searches the innermost parts of the belly (Proverbs 20:27). Yes, we are spiritual. Nevertheless, the flesh still distorts our vision in many cases (Romans 8:26). However, God is a Spirit (John 4:24). His eyes are flames of fire (Revelation 19:12). Therefore, we don't always see as God sees. We don't understand as God understands, for His ways are higher than ours (Isaiah 55:8-9). We don't see the necessary work that must be done in our lives. Therefore, we find ourselves confused in such circumstances. We know this isn't a chastisement for known sin, yet we don't see the evil lurking within us, and therefore, we can't see the purpose of God in this matter.

Job is confused but not so confused that he would hearken unto the counsel of his wife. Job knows God is righteous, and all that He does is right, and although he can't understand why God allowed this to come upon him, he still knows God is just.

This is very important for us to understand. Regardless of how many times the fiery furnace of tribulation is heated up in our lives, we still know that God is righteous. This can bring us some understanding while in the fire, although we may not understand the purpose of it. We know that God is just, and because of this knowledge, we know God has a righteous reason for allowing the tribulation to come. We may not understand the purpose of the tribulation and may also be confused as to why it must be so difficult, but we can always rest in this: the Judge of all the earth will do right. Although we can't see it, there must be a godly reason for this. We must hold on to this through these trying times. We must not let the tribulation blind us from seeing this truth. Sure, the tribulation is great, and all we can see is the fire, but we must remember that everything God does or allows is right. There is a purpose in this harsh environment, and fruit will come forth in this seemingly barren wasteland, for we will come forth from this tribulation as tried gold. This is what Job said, although he didn't understand much more about his trial than this. He knew God would use this to burn something bad out of his life so that he may be purer than before the tribulation came. Job knew this, although he probably didn't understand much more, and we can also know this, for the scriptures teach all Saints this very same truth.

Now, in continuance of our discussion on the lack of understanding and confusion Saints sometimes feel during tribulation, I'd like to bring your attention to Shadrach, Meshach, and Abednego (Daniel chapter 3), God willing. Could they have ever seen any godly purpose coming from being cast into the fiery furnace at the commandment of Nebuchadnezzar? Think about it. King Nebuchadnezzar had a huge idol built and commanded everyone to worship it. The punishment for not worshipping it was to be thrown into the fiery furnace. These three men were godly Jews, and as the music played and a sea of people bowed and worshipped the idol, they refused to do so. They refused because they didn't want to sin against God. They would rather have their lives taken away than worship anything or anyone other than God. Therefore, they refused to bow down, and because of this, Nebuchadnezzar was going to kill them by throwing them into the fiery furnace. Not just any fiery furnace, but into a fiery furnace that was heated seven times hotter than it was normally heated.

When they were about to be thrown into this fiery furnace, it would have been impossible for them to see the godly purpose behind this. All they could see was the fire. They couldn't see what God would do for them in the furnace or what God would do in the Babylonian Empire through this fire. All they knew was that they were going to be faithful unto God if it meant losing their lives, but other than that, they probably couldn't see anything else. They probably felt or knew God would give them the ability and strength to die a martyr's death, but they really didn't see anything beyond the fire in this earthly life. All they could see was the fire, and so often, that's all we can see. So, they were bound and thrown into the fire without knowing the godly purpose of it. All they could see was the fire, but they saw something amazing after being thrown into it.

After Nebuchadnezzar threw them into the fire, something, or Someone (God), strongly urged him to investigate the furnace. He may not have known why, but he was strongly inclined to investigate the fire. When he investigated the roaring furnace, he saw something amazing, as he said: didn't we bind three men and throw them into the fire? The people agreed with him and said yes. Then he said, I see four men loosed in the fire and walking around, and the fourth man looks like the Son of God. Christ was with the three Jewish men in the fire, and all the fire could do was burn the things that bound them. They went into the fire bound, but inside the furnace, they were freed from their bonds. When they were cast into the fire, they were bound and fell onto the floor of the furnace, but now they walk around free from their bonds.

Later in this book, we'll discuss the great lesson of their bonds being burned while they remained unscathed by the fire.

The point I'd like to make at this time is what they saw in the fire and the purpose of them being thrown into it. These three Jewish men couldn't see Christ or the purpose of being cast into the fire before they were thrown into it; all they knew was that they weren't going to sin against God by worshipping an idol. They were prepared to die and receive a martyr's crown, but as far as this life goes, they couldn't see anything but the fire. Before being thrown into the fire, all they could see concerning this life was the fire, but they saw something amazing after being thrown into the fire. They saw Christ! They saw a clearer view of Jesus than they had ever seen, and Nebuchadnezzar also saw the same thing. Saints are cast into the fire so things can be revealed to them, which was also true in Job's situation. In the fire, the three Jewish men saw Christ clearer than they had ever seen Him. They had never seen Him like this outside of the fire, but inside, they saw Him in a greater manner than before. So often, we can't see what God wants to show us when we are outside of the fire, but when thrown into the fire, the revelation becomes clear unto us. These Jewish men saw Christ in the fire, but what was the purpose behind this?

While in the fire, the three Jewish men saw Christ, but Nebuchadnezzar also saw Christ working in their lives, and therefore, he called out unto them and commanded them to come out of the fire. Then, the king acknowledges the God of these three men as the greatest of all gods and commands that He be reverenced and worshipped throughout his entire kingdom. Sure, the fire revealed Christ unto these three men, but the purpose was to reveal Christ unto the king as well, and by revealing Christ unto the king, the entire empire was changed, and these three men were promoted to very high positions in the government. The empire would no longer persecute those who worshipped God and would punish all who refused to allow the worship of Him, and these three godly men were promoted to some of the highest positions in the greatest empire on the face of the earth at that time. These three men now had the ability to influence the empire in ways they had never had before, for they were increased in the earth.

The point I'm trying to make is this. These three Jewish men couldn't see Christ outside of the fire, nor could they see the purpose of the fire. Outside of the fire, all they saw was the fire, but Christ was revealed unto them inside of it, and when they came out of the fire, they could see the purpose of the fire. These three men already had great positions in the Babylonian Empire, but God had a greater purpose for their lives. However, they had to be thrown into the fire before this could take place. Nebuchadnezzar had to see Christ in the fire before he would promote them or change the laws of the Babylonian Empire. Still, the three men also had to see what they saw in the fire to prepare them before being promoted. So often, all we can see is the fire, and we don't understand what God wants to reveal unto us in it, nor do we see the purpose of it.

This was the case with Job. Job didn't understand that he needed to see something, nor did he understand the purpose of the fire, for he was already perfect, upright, feared God, eschewed evil, and was the greatest man in the East. The three Jewish men were already living godly lives and held great positions in the Babylonian Empire, but they still needed to see something. God also wanted them promoted to more prestigious positions of influence, which all came about in the fire. Job was the greatest man in the East, but God wanted him to be greater than he was. Therefore, he had to be placed in the fire. These three Jewish men were confused before entering the fire (Daniel 3:17-18) but understood when they came out. The same was true of Job's tribulation and ours as well. Job was confused, for the fire was all around him, but he still retained his integrity because he knew God was righteous, even if he didn't understand.

# CHAPTER 10
# CONVERSATION BETWEEN JOB AND HIS FRIENDS

Job 2:11-3:1. *"Now when Job's three friends heard of all of this evil that was come upon him, they came every one from his own place, Eliphaz the Temanite, and Bildad the Shuhite, and Zophar the Naamathite: for they had made an appointment together to come to mourn with him and to comfort him. And when they lifted up their eyes afar off, and knew him not, they lifted up their voice, and wept; and they rent every one his mantle, and sprinkled dust upon their heads toward heaven. So they sat down with him upon the ground seven days and seven nights, and none spake a word unto him: for they saw that his grief was very great. After this opened Job his mouth, and cursed his day."*

Let's take a moment and look at the friends of Job. Job's friends, three mainly, although we know there were at least four, heard what had happened unto him, and came to see him. Before we consider Job's conversation with his friends, I'd like to point out that they were true friends. They truly cared about Job. When they saw Job's estate smoldering, saw him covered with boils, and saw him sitting among the ashes, it brought them to tears, for they truly cared about him.

Every word of the Bible is very valuable, and we should always understand that. Every subject in the Bible is significant, and we should always value them. Therefore, we shouldn't disregard any subject of the Bible, regardless of how many words are recorded about the topic. We should view every word of the Bible as a great treasure and of the utmost importance. Yet, I'd like to point out the amount of space the conversation between Job and his friends takes up in the Bible. However, this shouldn't be used as a way for us to decide what part of the Bible is more important than the other, for every word of the Bible is pure, important, and a great blessing to anyone who has the opportunity or desire to read it. Yet, I'd still like to point out the amount of space this conversation takes up in the Bible and the detail in which it is recorded. Though many conversations are recorded in the Bible, few, if any, are recorded to this length and detail. Therefore, I feel it is noteworthy to point this out.

The Book of Job is 42 chapters long, and the conversation he has with his friends starts at the end of chapter 2 and ends at the end of chapter 37. The overwhelming portion of the Book of Job is the conversation he has with his friends. Therefore, it is important for us to understand that God wanted us to know about this conversation. The amount of room this subject takes up in the Bible is huge compared to many other subjects. The amount of space the Bible gives to this conversation between Job and his friends is greater than that of Adam and Eve, the life of Abraham, Issac, Jacob, Melchizedek, or most of the kings of Israel and Judah. Not one epistle takes up this much space in the Bible, and many of the other books of the Bible don't either. Therefore, it is evident that God wants us to read this conversation, as the amount of space given to it in the Bible exhibits its importance.

What is this conversation about? Why is it so important? The conversation is about why God would allow this to happen to Job. This conversation also tries to touch on the nature of God and what causes Him to move in certain ways in the lives of people. Job and his three friends converse about this throughout these chapters. They lack understanding and disagree as to why God would allow this. Job's speech in this conversation is wiser than theirs, but that still doesn't mean Job completely understands, for he also lacks understanding on this subject as well, for he admits to being confused.

When Job's friends hear of the things that had befallen him, they make an appointment with each other to come and mourn with him, desiring to comfort him (Job 2:11). When Job's friends arrive, they see his sad condition. When they viewed Job from afar, they couldn't even recognize him, for his situation was so apparent that they could see it from a great distance. They were so moved by what they saw that they wept, tore their mantles, and sprinkled dust upon their heads. Then, they sat down with Job but didn't say anything for seven days because they saw how great his grief was. They had never seen anyone brought down in this manner. They had never seen anyone suffer the calamity Job suffered. They had never seen anything like this before, for they had never seen anyone suffer all the things Job suffered. They had never seen anyone so grief-stricken. Therefore, they sat with Job because they were his friends but had no words for him.

They didn't have any words for Job because they saw his grief was very great. Their conclusion and the advice they gave Job afterwards may be why they didn't speak to him for these seven days. It might be why they didn't speak until Job first spoke unto them. They concluded that Job brought all of this upon himself. Their advice was for him to repent. Therefore, they may not have spoken to him immediately because they felt his grief was too great to bear it.

After seven days, Job began speaking, saying he abhorred the day he was born. Why Job started the conversation isn't clear to me, although he may have wanted to portray his grief to his friends. He may have wanted to try to cause them to understand how hard this calamity was on him. Job may have felt sorry for himself, although I can't say that for certain. Job may have also sought comfort from his friends in this matter, for it is evident through this conversation that Job felt they should have used their words to assuage his grief, but they didn't.

Sometimes, we want others to understand how we feel and hope they can sympathize with us. We want them to understand our condition and what we are going through. We want them to grasp what we are feeling. Job tries to portray that unto them as he begins this conversation, saying, I despise the day of my birth. How much grief must one be in to say they wish they had never been born? This is what Job is trying to convey to his friends. He is trying to show them how great his grief is.

So, after seven days, Job begins this conversation. Job's friends may have never spoken a word if Job hadn't spoken first. After Job begins the conversation by speaking of his grief, they will join in. The conversation goes something like this. Job says he doesn't understand why this came upon him. Job's friends say that there is no way God would allow all of this to come upon you unless you had sinned in some form or fashion, and their counsel is for Job to repent, which will cause God to bless him again. Job says that he isn't entirely just before God but insists that sin isn't what brought his calamity on. Job's friends contend with him on this subject, and Job continues to insist that he didn't sin to bring this on.

We must also state that a person's counsel in any given circumstance is according to their understanding. This conversation is about God, His holiness, and what He will or won't do on earth. Therefore, the statements in this conversation are made according to their understanding of God, for the subject is, why would God allow this to happen to Job? Their statements are made according to their understanding of God in this matter.

Now, it is evident that no one completely understands God, but we are granted some knowledge of Him. According to our understanding of God, we speak about Him. It is essential that we know this as we look at this conversation.

The people in this conversation are godly and wise, but that doesn't mean they understand everything about God. When we read this conversation in the Bible, we must understand this truth because many of the things said by Job's friends are true regarding other circumstances but not in Job's situation.

I like to say it like this: Doctors are very smart people, but none are all-knowing. Every word they speak isn't always correct.

There was a time when my daughter was sick, and my wife and I took her to the emergency room. There, they ran some tests on her. The doctor diagnosed her and gave her a shot. However, the doctor misdiagnosed her, and the medicine made her condition worse.

Now, let's ask this question. Was the medicine the doctor gave my daughter bad or good? The medicine was good, and if my daughter had had the sickness the doctor thought she had, it would have been good for her, but because the doctor misdiagnosed my daughter, the medicine didn't help her; it hurt her. There was nothing wrong with the medicine; it was only used for the wrong illness. The medicine was good and has probably helped many people, but in my daughter's situation, it didn't help her; it harmed her.

Now, let's ask this question. Why did the doctor give my daughter the wrong medicine? Was he trying to hurt her or help her? He was trying to help her. So, why did he give her the wrong medicine, which hurt her? Was it because he hated her? No! He wanted to help her. So, why did he give her the wrong medicine? It was because he misdiagnosed her illness. He had a lack of understanding concerning her sickness. Therefore, he prescribed her the wrong medicine, which hurt her, instead of helping her. Things like this happen from time to time. When these things happen, we know the doctors aren't trying to hurt their patients. We also know that the medicine isn't bad. The doctor made a mistake because he didn't fully understand the situation.

This was the case with Job's friends. Much of the advice (medicine) they gave Job was good, but not in Job's situation. They aren't giving Job this advice because they want to hurt him, for they truly want to help him, but because of their lack of understanding, they give Job the wrong advice. Their advice would have been helpful in other situations, but because they misdiagnosed Job, they gave him the wrong counsel.

Job's friends are convinced that sin in Job's life has brought this catastrophe upon him, for they see it as a chastisement, not a tribulation. So, how have they misdiagnosed Job? Why did they come to this diagnosis? It was because of a lack of understanding. They can't understand how God would allow this to come upon Job if he didn't have sin in his life. They see God only from this viewpoint regarding Job's situation. They see it as punishment for sin and nothing more.

Many still hold this viewpoint today, though some hold to it tighter than others. Some in the church have a really hard time diagnosing tribulation but very quickly diagnose chastisement.

Let's take a moment to define chastisement and tribulation. What are the differences between them? This may help us better understand them and arrive at the proper diagnosis when we see them. Although tribulation and chastisement do the same work in our lives, they come into our lives for different reasons.

Chastisement is a punishment God allows to come upon Saints because of known sins in their lives. It is sort of like a parent punishing a child for wrongdoing. Why does the parent punish the child for wrongdoing? The parent tries to drive the wrongdoing out of the child's life. The same is true with the Saints of God. God is our Father, and He has instructed us in the ways of righteousness. When we sin, the Holy Spirit convicts us of it, which grants us the ability and opportunity to judge ourselves.

How do we judge ourselves? When we see sin in our lives, we ask God's forgiveness, repent, and forsake it. If we ask

God's forgiveness, repent, and forsake it, there is no need for punishment, yet God chastens us if we refuse to forsake known sins in our lives.

God chastens us to drive the known sin out of us. God punishes His children to cause them to forsake their known sins. God does this because we are His children, whom He loves, for the scriptures say the Lord chastens those He loves (Hebrews 12:6-7). Therefore, chastisement is a punishment from God because of sin in the lives of His Saints. This is what chastisement is.

Tribulation comes for a different reason but has the same effect on us. Tribulation doesn't come because we have known sin in our lives, but because of unknown sin in our lives. Tribulation doesn't come because we have committed a known sin, but tribulation comes when we haven't committed a known sin. Tribulation comes to grow us. Tribulations are growing pains Saints go through, which causes them to grow spiritually and be increased on the earth. God wants to grow us in grace and in the knowledge of the Lord. There are things God wants to remove from our lives and things He wants to place in our lives. Therefore, we are placed in the fires of tribulation so that the dross may be removed and our hearts softened so that the things God wants to add to our lives may be placed in them. The sinful flesh abides in all Saints, and although we may not be walking in known sin, these sinful things are within us. Again, the sinful and twisted flesh abides within all Saints of God, and although it may not be manifest at present, it is there. Therefore, before God increases us on the earth, tribulations may come to kill certain parts of the flesh, which lie within us, so that it wouldn't be manifest after we are increased and have more godly responsibility. These parts of the flesh may not be manifest at present, but God knows that they will be after we are increased in the earth. Therefore, He deals with them ahead of time. We may not be able to see them, but God does. God sees them and knows they must be dealt with before He increases us, for if they are not dealt with beforehand, we may do more harm than good after we are increased.

God knows when and how to remove these wicked things from our lives. God knows whether it should be beforehand or afterward. God's wisdom is qualified to make this decision. Therefore, chastisement comes upon us because of known sins in our lives and tribulation for unknown sins in our lives. Chastisement is a punishment for committing known sin, and tribulation deals with unknown sin in us before it is manifest. God will grow Job, but the unknown sin in his life must be dealt with before He does. Job will have to be prepared before God increases him in the earth. A greater responsibility comes with this increase. Therefore, Job must be prepared for it.

Think of this for a moment. As a child grows, he is given greater responsibilities, and with these greater responsibilities come greater consequences. Therefore, it is very important for the child to be prepared ahead of time.

There is a difference between crashing a toy truck and a real truck. There are greater consequences. This is why we don't give a five-year-old the keys to our truck. We wait until he is more mature and has passed his driver's examination. After passing his driver's examination, he receives his driver's license, which proclaims that he is now prepared and certified to drive a vehicle on the roadway. This is a simple concept for us to grasp, although the five-year-old may not understand it at the time.

The five-year-old may feel like he is ready to drive, but the parent knows he isn't. Yet, when the child has become properly prepared, the parent gives him the keys to the vehicle. We get this concept very easily, but we often miss it when God does it in our lives or the lives of others.

God has placed a great calling on Job, which is already evident in his life, but before God further increases him, Job must be prepared for the responsibility. This is why God allows this tribulation to come upon Job. It isn't because of known sin in his life or ignorance concerning God, for Job has a great knowledge of God and has lived a life in which God says he is perfect, upright, fears God, and eschews evil. Yet, God has a greater calling on the life of Job than he has previously experienced, and the time has now come for it to come to pass. Therefore, Job must be prepared through the fires of tribulation. Job is telling his friends that he didn't commit a known sin that brought this misery upon him, but they just can't agree with him on the matter, for they are convinced that it is the chastisement of God. In this conversation, it seems that the concept of tribulation has never crossed their minds because their understanding of God is limited.

Again, many in the church today hold tightly to the view of Job's friends, although some are stauncher than others concerning it. They feel as though every hard circumstance is the judgment of God upon Saints for their sin. They feel that every car wreck is a divine judgment or every house fire is the chastisement of God on sinning Saints. Their understanding of

God is limited; therefore, they continue to declare that every hard circumstance in the lives of Saints is the judgment of God. They rarely think of tribulation, and some don't even have the word in their vocabulary. Jesus knocks this type of thinking down in Luke 13:1-5, which says,

*"There were present at that season some that told him of the Galileans, whose blood Pilate had mingled with their sacrifices. And Jesus answering said unto them, Suppose ye that these Galileans were sinners above all the Galileans, because they suffered such things? I tell you, Nay: but, except ye repent, ye shall all likewise perish. Or those eighteen, upon whom the tower in Siloam fell, and slew them, think ye that they were sinners above all men that dwelt in Jerusalem? I tell you, Nay: but, except ye repent, ye shall all likewise perish."*

We will also see God knock this thought process down at the end of the Book of Job, as God says his three friends didn't speak right concerning Him (Job 42:8). So often, Christians misdiagnose the circumstances other Christians go through because of their lack of understanding concerning God, for they think every hard situation is a chastisement, and never consider that it could be tribulation. Sure, there are chastisements, but there are also tribulations, and we should be careful not to label every fire as arson, for some aren't. Every wound in life isn't self-inflicted, nor is every hardship in the Christian's life a chastisement.

So, how do we distinguish between the two (chastisement and tribulation) since they look the same and work the same things in our lives? We must examine the patient carefully so that there is no misdiagnosis. How do we do that? The same way we would examine ourselves. When fires come into our lives, we must ask what caused them. We must ask ourselves if this results from known sins in our lives. Did we sin against God to bring this upon us? Is this the result of us embracing sin? We should always go before the Lord in prayer concerning this as well.

This is what I do. When I see fires in my life, I examine myself, and then, if I see no known sin, I go to the Lord in prayer and ask Him, have I done something wrong? If no sin is revealed unto me, then I chalk it up as a tribulation, not a chastisement, for God doesn't chasten His children without them knowing why, no more than a parent does. Knowing why a person is being chastened is as important as the chastisement itself because if a person doesn't know why they are being chastened, how will they repent of it?

I also understand that sometimes chastening reveals our sin unto us or causes us to be reminded of our sin, but somehow or the other, the sin will be made known unto the one being chastened.

Israel sinned against God in many ways, and He had previously told them that if they sinned, certain chastisements would come upon them. Sometimes, Israel had so hardened their hearts towards God that they didn't even think of their sins, but when the chastisement came, they were reminded. Sometimes, they would continue in their sins after chastisement came, but God would send a prophet to tell them why the chastisement had come.

Sure, chastisement can come upon a person who doesn't understand why it has come, for David saw a famine in the land of Israel and didn't know why, but when he prayed about it, God told him it was because of the way Saul had treated the Gibeonites. This chastisement came upon the kingdom of David, but David didn't understand why it came. So, what did David do? David asked God about it, and the Lord showed him why his kingdom was being chastened. Therefore, David understood how to repent, and the famine ceased after repentance.

So, again, I say unto the Saints, when you see fires in your life, examine yourself. If you see no known sin in your life, ask God to show you if you have sinned to bring this upon yourself. If it is revealed unto you that you have sinned, ask God to forgive you and repent, but if no sin is revealed unto you, then chalk it up as tribulation, understanding that God is doing a work in your life.

The fires of tribulation will purify you, causing your life to become purer, killing more of the flesh so that the Spirit may shine brighter in your life. These tribulations also soften our hearts to receive a greater revelation of God.

So, what should we do when advising others concerning fires in their lives? Ask them the same questions we previously stated that we should ask ourselves. The purpose of asking these questions is to cause them to ask themselves these questions. Remember, the diagnosis isn't for us; it is for the patient. Ask them if there is a known sin in their lives. If they reply no, ask them if they have asked the Lord if this results from sin in their life. Listen to them. Be careful not to immediately diagnose them as being chastened for sin in their lives. If they are honest, then you will be able to help them with the diagnosis.

Before advising on such matters, it is important to listen to the patient. Ask them these questions. Is there sin in your life? Be careful not to accuse them of sin because of what they are going through. Ask them if there is sin in their life. If their answer is no, there isn't any known sin in my life, and I have approached the Lord in prayer, and He has not revealed any sin in my life, then you may help diagnose them. You will be able to tell them that this is a tribulation in their life. God is growing you for the next step in your calling. It will be hard but understand that God is doing a work in your life, for He is going to increase you in the earth.

If their answer is yes, there is sin in my life, then you should diagnose them as being chastened. Your advice for them should be to ask God for forgiveness and repent, and the chastening will be removed, for the entire purpose of chastisement is to cause you to repent.

Remember, your diagnosis of them isn't important; their diagnosis of themselves is what is important. You may be blessed to help them with this diagnosis and advise them on it, but the whole purpose is for them to see it for themselves. Also, their diagnosis of themselves will only be as true as they are truthful to themselves, and your diagnosis of them is based upon their honesty. Yet, the diagnosis isn't for the ones advising but for the ones being advised. The advisor should only try to cause the patients to diagnose themselves. The advisor is simply trying to show the patient how to do that.

It is important not to diagnose the patient wrongly because we will prescribe them the wrong medicine. Though the medicine we prescribe is good under the right circumstances, it is not good under the wrong circumstances. The wrong medicine can do more harm than good. If someone is going through tribulation and we diagnose him or her as experiencing chastisement, we can cause his or her spirit to become weaker. We can cause them to feel condemned before God. We will weaken them as they go through this tribulation. This misdiagnosis can weaken them as they are under this heavy burden. Surely, we don't want to do that; we want to encourage them. If we diagnose someone being chastened as going through tribulation, they will feel as though they are living properly before God when they aren't, and they will see no need to ask the Lord's forgiveness and repent. As advisors, it is better to say we don't know than to misdiagnose someone, and it is worse to misdiagnose someone than to give them no diagnosis.

So, chastisement is punishment for sin in our lives. Tribulation is a hard time that comes upon us when we haven't sinned. Tribulation burns fleshly things out of our lives before they come to fruition, while chastisement burns sin out of our lives that have come to fruition. Chastisement and tribulation burn fleshly things out of our lives, but the difference is that chastisement comes after we have sinned, while tribulation comes when we haven't sinned. Tribulation is not a punishment for sin but rather a means of purging the fleshly things from our lives before they lead us into sin. On the other hand, chastisement is a punishment for our sin aimed at purging it from our lives.

Again, many in the church desire to be advisors, but they only have one diagnosis when fires come into the lives of Saints. Their diagnosis is always chastisement for sin. I've heard members of the church speak about other members whose houses burned down, who were in car wrecks, or who were in the hospital sick, saying they will learn not to miss church again. Sure, Saints should attend church, but every car wreck, every sickness, or every house fire isn't always chastisement for sin.

Now, back to Job's friends. They were convinced that this calamity came upon Job because he had sinned against God. They felt Job must have had a secret sin in his life. They felt he was hypocritical in his lifestyle. Job insisted this wasn't the case, but they contended with him on this matter repeatedly. Job continued to insist that this wasn't true, but they continued to imply that it was. This conversation eventually reached a place where they felt Job was saying he was 100% just before God concerning all things. They told him he wasn't just before God, and Job agreed that no one could be completely just before God, but he still proclaimed this hadn't come upon him because of known sin in his life. Job's friends refused to accept this statement from him because of their lack of understanding concerning God. They just couldn't see God allowing this if Job hadn't sinned, and repeatedly, they accused him of having known sin in his life because that was their understanding of God. They misdiagnosed Job and thought they had given him the proper diagnosis. They just couldn't understand why Job wouldn't accept it and take the medicine they prescribed. They were confident they were right and Job was wrong. They thought they understood Job's situation better than he did.

They truly thought they understood Job's circumstances. Yet, they didn't, and I believe this conversation eventually came to the point where it was more about proving they were right than helping Job with his situation. They thought they were representing God in their speech, as one of them even said that he was in the place of God to speak unto Job (Job 33:6). Job saw that they truly felt they were 100% right, and he also saw that they thought they had great wisdom, as he said unto them, *"No doubt but ye are the people, and wisdom shall die with you"* (Job 12:2).

It is important to stand on the truth of God, but it is also important to understand that we don't know everything. Job is sarcastically saying unto them that they are the only ones who possess wisdom, and when they die, wisdom will cease from the earth. Why would Job say this unto them? Job said this unto them because that is how they were acting. They believed they understood Job's situation and God's ways completely. Job's friends were so confident in their diagnosis of Job that they refused to hear anything that said otherwise.

It is important for those who advise to know that their advice is correct. This isn't about driving someone into submission by causing him or her to acknowledge us as being right, for every man must be persuaded in his own mind (Romans 14:5). This is not a game of pride in which we try to show ourselves as being correct at all costs. This isn't about who is right and who is wrong. This is about helping Job, nothing more and nothing less.

Job's three friends misdiagnosed Job because they didn't understand God's ways concerning his situation. They felt they were experts on the subject, but they weren't, and this fact will be proven at the end of the Book of Job by God Himself. Job's friends came to him with the best of intentions, but their misdiagnosis of his situation didn't help him; it only added to his misery.

# CHAPTER 11
# THOSE WHO WILL BE GREAT IN THEOLOGY MUST ALSO BE GREAT IN SUFFERING

2 Corinthians 12:1-10. *"It is not expedient for me doubtless to glory. I will come to visions and revelations of the Lord. I knew a man in Christ above fourteen years ago, (whether in the body, I cannot tell; or whether out of the body, I cannot tell: God knoweth;) such an one caught up to the third heaven. And I knew such a man (whether in the body or out of the body, I cannot tell: God knoweth;) How that he was caught up into paradise and heard unspeakable words, which it is not lawful for a man to utter. Of such an one will I glory: yet of myself I will not glory, but in mine infirmities. For though I would desire to glory, I shall not be a fool; for I will say the truth: but now I forbear, lest any man should think of me above that which he seeth me to be, or that he heareth of me. And lest I should be exalted above measure through the abundance of the revelations, there was given to me a thorn in the flesh, the messenger of Satan to buffet me, lest I should be exalted above measure. For this thing I besought the Lord thrice, that it might depart from me. And he said unto me, My grace is sufficient for thee: for my strength is made perfect in weakness. Most gladly therefore, will I rather glory in my infirmities, that the power of Christ may rest upon me. Therefore I take pleasure in*

*infirmities, in reproaches, in necessities, in persecutions, in distresses for Christ's sake: for when I am weak, then am I strong."*

2 Corinthians 1:3-10. *"Blessed be God, even the Father of our Lord Jesus Christ, the Father of mercies, and the God of all comfort; Who comforteth us in all our tribulation, that we may be able to comfort them which are in any trouble, by the comfort wherewith we ourselves are comforted of God. For as the sufferings of Christ abound in us, so our consolation also aboundeth by Christ. And whether we be afflicted, it is for your consolation and salvation, which is effectual in the enduring of the same sufferings which we also suffer: or whether we be comforted, it is for your consolation and salvation. And our hope of you is stedfast, knowing, that as ye are partakers of the sufferings, so shall ye be also of the consolation. For we would not, brethren, have you ignorant of our trouble which came to us in Asia, that we were pressed out of measure, above strength, insomuch that we despaired even of life: But we had the sentence of death in ourselves, that we should not trust in ourselves, but in God which raiseth the dead: Who delivered us from so great a death, and doth deliver: in whom we trust that he will yet deliver us;"*

The title of this chapter is paraphrased from a statement that Charles Spurgeon once made. Yet, I don't hold it as truth because Charles Spurgeon said it, but because it has its foundation in the scriptures.

In the first set of verses of this chapter, we see that a messenger of Satan buffeted Paul. We also see the purpose for this buffeting. God blessed Paul to say that the messenger of

Satan was sent to buffet him because of the abundant revelations he had received. This messenger of Satan would keep Paul from being exalted any higher than he should have been. In other words, Paul had been blessed with so much from God that his exaltation would have been beyond what was appropriate for him.

Before we explore these scriptures further, let's consider what Paul meant when he said he would have been exalted above measure if the messenger of Satan hadn't buffeted him.

At first glance, it seems this is speaking of Paul's pride, implying that he would have been exalted above measure because of all God gave him. Therefore, a messenger of Satan was sent to buffet him so he wouldn't become exceedingly prideful.

Although this may hold true for many of us and seemed to have been the case with Hezekiah and Uzziah, when we read the previous two chapters (2 Corinthians 10 and 11), we will see the context in which these verses were written. The context will show us that this isn't about Paul becoming prideful but about how he would have been viewed by others. If this messenger of Satan hadn't beaten Paul, then others would have held him in higher esteem than they should have.

One may say, shouldn't they have held Paul in high esteem? Sure, they should have, but not in higher esteem than he should have been held. Paul was a great apostle of Jesus Christ and should have been esteemed as such, but he shouldn't have been revered to have been any greater than that. The Lord had given Paul so much that he said he wasn't *"a whit behind the very chiefest* [greatest] *apostles"* (2 Corinthians 11:5). This was true, and this is how the church should have viewed Paul, but if they had viewed him to be greater than that, then it would have been counterproductive in his ministry.

Sometimes, people ascribe too much glory to human beings. Many times, humanity trusts in mortals more than it should. When we do this, we place them on a pedestal they shouldn't be placed upon. We are holding them in higher esteem than they should be held. There is a highly esteemed place for the great apostle Paul, but there is also a place that is too high for even him. There is a place of rarified air that only belongs to God, and sometimes, man tries to intrude into that place, or sometimes, others hold people in such high esteem that they place them there (Acts 12:20-23). This is what the first part of our text is speaking of.

God had given Paul so much revelation as the great apostle unto the Gentiles that others would have held him in higher esteem than they should have. There is an esteemed place for the great apostle and a place of highest esteem for God. When we view any man in such high esteem that they take a place in our lives reserved only for God, we have exalted them too high, for we have exalted them above measure. This is detrimental to us and to them as well. The scriptures say, *"A man that flattereth his neighbour spreadeth a net for his feet"* (Proverbs 29:5).

This causes us to place too much faith in them. We place faith in them when that faith should be placed in God, and this also hinders their ministry because God will not work through them in a manner that brings glory unto them, whether that is their desire or not. The church is not called to praise and glorify

Paul, as great as he is, for the church is called to glorify and praise the Lord. The church's faith should be in the gospel, not the great apostle. The purpose of Paul's ministry is to bring praise and glory unto God, but if the people esteem Paul too highly, exalting him to a place that is too high, they will be praising and glorifying Paul in areas that are only reserved for God. This is what is meant when Paul says that a messenger of Satan was sent to buffet him, which kept him from being exalted above measure. The people would have placed Paul on a pedestal he shouldn't have been placed on.

Paul had to be humbled in the eyes of those he preached to because he was given so much that the people would have exalted him above measure (the measure given unto him by God). Therefore, a messenger of Satan was sent to buffet him. A messenger of Satan was sent to beat Paul so that he wouldn't be exalted above measure in the eyes of the people.

What would have exalted Paul above measure in the eyes of the people? It was the abundance of revelation God had given him. I'm convinced that revelation is the greatest of all gifts from God. To know more about Him and His ways is a gift that can't be measured. It is a revelation from God that must work in people's lives before they can be saved. God must supernaturally reveal Christ unto a person before they can place faith in Him (Matthew 16:13-17; John 6:44). A person can't come to this revelation of Christ on their own, for it must be revealed unto them by God. When Peter said that Jesus was the Christ, the Son of the living God, Jesus told him that flesh and blood didn't reveal this to you, but My Father Who is in heaven (Matthew 16:13-17). It was God Who revealed this mighty revelation to Peter. One can't see Jesus as the Christ and

Savior of the world if God doesn't reveal Him to us. One will never see or understand the gospel if God doesn't reveal it to us. We may read or hear it, but until God reveals it to us, we will not be able to see what we need to see in it, for we cannot understand the gospel unless God opens it up to us.

Divine revelations teach us the things God will do for us and has done for us. Divine revelations teach us about God. The Bible teaches us that grace and peace are multiplied in our lives through the knowledge of God and His Son, Jesus Christ. Life, godliness, glory, and virtue come into our lives through that knowledge, and we are also a partaker of the divine nature through this same knowledge (2 Peter 1:2-4).

With this being the case, revelation is also the thing Satan fights hardest against. In the parable of the Sower, we see that Satan is the bird that eats up the seed of the word that falls by the wayside (Luke 8:4-15). Satan also seeks to persecute and hinder all who proclaim God's word. The Prince of Persia (a demonic power) tried to stop the angel from bringing Daniel a revelation concerning a prophecy of future kingdoms, Israel during those times, and Israel during The Great Tribulation Period (Daniel 10:11-14). Satan is a great enemy of revelation and fights with all his might to stop it in the earth.

Satan fights ferociously against revelation, for it is no wonder that the word of God has come unto us on the blood-soaked path of the martyrs. Satan tries to keep revelation from coming to a person or being received by them, but when he can't stop it from coming, he then tries to corrupt it by having teachers pervert it (Galatians 1:6-7). Satan will do all that he can to cause people to misunderstand the word of God, as he promotes a legalistic doctrine to try and pervert the doctrine of grace or promotes an insufficient God instead of an all-sufficient God, &, etc.

Revelation is also a great enemy of Satan, for revelation teaches us about God and His promises. Revelation teaches us that we are saved by grace through faith; revelation teaches us that through faith in the cross of Christ, His blood cleanses us of all our sins; revelation teaches us to trust in Christ's work (death on the cross, burial, and resurrection) for salvation, sanctification, and blessing, revelation teaches us that the power of God keeps us, revelation teaches us that Christ's work is a finished work, revelation teaches us to trust in Christ that we may have peace and power in the earth, revelation teaches us all the great doctrines of the Bible, and revelation also exposes Satan as a defeated foe, etc.

Paul was given great revelation, possibly more than any of the apostles, and because of this, there was a danger of him being exalted above measure in the eyes of the people. Satan is a master at this as well. So often Satan tries to stand on our heads to keep us from climbing up the ladder, but when he sees God blessing us and understands that he can't stop us from climbing it, he will soon get on the other end of us and push us up with all his might. He tries to push us up to an exalted position. He tries to cause us to lift ourselves up in pride, or in Paul's case, to be exalted above measure in the eyes of the people.

Why does he do this? If he can't hold us down, he knows that our pride, or the pride of others in us, will hinder our calling. Sure, he would rather have us pinned down at the bottom of the ladder, but if he can't pin us down, he will try to exalt us above measure, for Satan tries to hinder us on both ends of the ladder.

Paul has been given an abundance of revelation, which came directly from God. Now, he needs to be humbled in the eyes of the people. Others have been given much revelation, and it is also important that they be humbled. Though Saints are blessed by God and granted an esteemed place by the Lord Jesus, we are not the Lord, nor should we think we are, or be viewed as Him by others.

I have been on both sides of this coin. God has given me some revelation, and I have been exalted in my own eyes through pride, and I also have been exalted above measure by others. In both instances, I had to be brought down. I had to be humbled in my own eyes and in the eyes of others. It is a painful thing to be humbled. It is also a painful thing to be humbled in the sight of others. I feel through my experience that it is more painful to be humbled in the sight of others than to be humbled in my own sight. Yet, both are extremely important and necessary. My experience should not be compared to Paul's, for Paul's would have been on a far greater scale.

Paul must be humbled in the sight of men because God has given him such great revelation. As previously stated, Paul needs to be humbled in the sight of men because it will hinder his ministry if he isn't. The power of Christ won't rest upon Paul if it results in others glorifying him. Therefore, this suffering comes unto him, not because of something he has done wrong but because of all the things God has given him.

Revelation has a price, so to speak, a price for learning and a price for humility.

Think of what it meant for Paul to be humbled in the sight of men. Paul's bodily presence was viewed as weak. His speech was said to be contemptible (2 Corinthians 10:10). We also see, in the aforementioned scripture, other things Paul suffered to be humbled in the sight of men, as he said, *"Therefore I take pleasure in infirmities, in reproaches, in necessities, in persecutions, in distresses for Christ's sake: for when I am weak, then am I strong"* (2 Corinthians 12:10).

Why must Paul experience such things as this? To keep him from being exalted above measure in the eyes of the people he preached to. Humanity will speak highly of a boxer who has just won the championship belt but not of one who is knocked out repeatedly. Paul was publicly shamed for his faith time after time, and his speech and bodily presence weren't something the natural man would boast about or desire.

Isn't this how our glorious Christ came unto us? The scriptures say, *"For he shall grow up before him as a tender plant, and as a root out of a dry ground: he hath no form nor comeliness; and when we shall see him, there is no beauty that we should desire him."* (Isaiah 53:2). Jesus didn't come unto us crowned with natural glory. Jesus didn't come unto us in a manner that the natural man would desire. Jesus came unto us crowned with heaven's glory, not the glory of men. Paul would have to be brought low naturally so that he could shine spiritually.

Notice that this messenger of Satan buffeted Paul, which means to rap with the fist. This messenger of Satan beat upon

Paul, and we know from the portion of scripture at the beginning of this chapter that this caused Paul much suffering. This wasn't easy on Paul, for this hurt him greatly; therefore, he prayed unto the Lord to remove this thorn in his flesh, which was the messenger of Satan sent to buffet him.

Paul asked God to remove this thorn, not once, not twice, but three times. Yet, we still see that God didn't remove the thorn. Therefore, one may conclude that God didn't answer Paul's prayer, but did He? Notice how the scripture reads. Paul prayed three times for the thorn to be removed, but it wasn't. Though the thorn wasn't removed, we do see that God spoke to Paul about his prayer request.

Let's look at some of the things we can glean from what God said unto Paul concerning his prayer request. First, we see that God says His grace is sufficient. In other words, though a messenger of Satan beats upon you, I have given you enough grace to bear it. We can learn a lot from this. Nothing is ever allowed to come upon the child of God in which God hasn't given us sufficient grace to bear it. If Satan is permitted to hit you with the forces of hell, God will make sure that you possess the forces of heaven. God's grace will always be sufficient for anything we face. God only allows Satan to harm the flesh, and although we must suffer for it to be so, in the second set of scriptures at the beginning of this chapter, we are guaranteed the comfort of God when these sufferings come. So, we must always remember that God's grace in our lives is sufficient for any thorn that may be placed in our flesh. Sometimes, we don't see it that way, but it is so, and we must always remember that. Sometimes, it is hard for us to identify God's grace, but it is always there. God's grace may show up as the jawbone of an ass lying on the ground when the Philistines attack Samson or even a broken piece of pottery amongst the ashes to scrape Job's boils. Yet, we must remember it is there, for it is certain that God's grace is sufficient.

We can also see that God says unto Paul that His strength is made perfect in weakness. God's grace shines brighter in our lives when we are weak. This doesn't mean we must be sick or persecuted for God's grace to shine in our lives, but the flesh must be weakened for God's strength to be perfected in us. God's glory shines the brightest in our lives when we are the weakest in the flesh. The weaker the flesh is, the less we lean on it, and the more we lean upon Christ. This causes God's glory to shine brighter in our lives. This causes the power of Christ to rest upon us. Also, the weaker others perceive us to be, the more God's grace shines in our lives, for then God will be glorified through His grace, not ourselves.

(Though there is a fine line in how others view us, it is apparent that they shouldn't exalt us above measure, but they shouldn't look at us below our measure either, for this can also cause the congregation problems. There were times that the church viewed Paul so lowly that they were dangerously close to replacing him with others who appealed more unto the flesh. It even came to the point where Paul had to defend his apostleship.)

It is important to understand that the flesh doesn't mean the body. When we are weak in the flesh, the glory of God shines brighter in our lives. This doesn't necessarily mean that our body must be weak, although many times, the way the flesh is weakened is through the weakness of the body. To be strong in the flesh is to trust in our fleshly abilities as the means by which we live for God, and to be weak in the flesh is to trust in the finished work of Christ to perform godliness in our lives rather than trusting in ourselves to accomplish these things. Sometimes, the body must suffer to keep us from trusting in ourselves. Sometimes, we must go through trials so the flesh would be weakened. Sometimes, we must be placed in a situation bigger than we are so that we will forsake confidence in ourselves and look unto the finished work of Christ. When we see that our fleshly abilities aren't sufficient for the godly task at hand, then we trust in the finished work of Christ to perform godliness in our lives. This is when the power of Christ will rest upon us and cause the godly ministry given unto us by God to prosper. It is evident from these scriptures we are referring to that Paul had to be brought low bodily because this is what others could see, yet this bodily weakening would also cause Paul to be weakened in the flesh so that the power of Christ would rest upon him.

In the two passages of scripture referenced at the beginning of this chapter, it is important to note that tribulation sometimes comes because of revelation and revelation also comes through tribulation. The revelations God had given unto Paul would have caused him to be exalted above measure if the thorn hadn't been placed in his flesh; therefore, the power of Christ wouldn't have been as manifest in his life without the thorn. Tribulation humbles us that we may trust in Christ's finished work instead of our own abilities, and in so doing, Christ is revealed unto us in a greater manner. This tribulation came upon Paul to humble him in the eyes of the people; therefore, the power of Christ could rest upon him without it causing him to be exalted above measure.

It is one thing to have revelation and entirely another to communicate it unto the hearts of others. We can only speak to a person's ear; it takes God to speak to their hearts (James Gooch). Paul had the revelation but needed the power of Christ to communicate it and perform it. Though God had given Paul great revelation, the power of Christ was essential in spreading the gospel. Our own power isn't sufficient for spreading the gospel, but Christ's power is. Paul's power wasn't sufficient for spreading the gospel, although God had revealed it unto him. It took the power of Christ to give these God-given revelations power in Paul's ministry.

Sometimes, tribulation comes because of revelation, and revelation also comes because of tribulation. Through tribulations, we learn that we are insufficient for the trial. It is then that we see how Jesus delivers us through faith. We learn many of the great truths of the Bible during tribulation because that is when they are burned into our hearts. There, in the fires of tribulation, we learn so many of the truths and promises of God. We also learn how to trust in Christ for them so that the tribulation will no longer have dominion over us. We are freed from the tribulations by faith in the finished work of Christ for the promises of God. These promises are revealed unto us in times of tribulation so that we may learn to trust in them, which causes the tribulation to no longer have power over us. Yet, after the tribulation is finished, we still have these revelations so that we may walk in them and communicate them to others. In the fires of tribulation, we learn more about ourselves, and we also learn more about Christ. We often see how small we really are, we see sin in our lives that we previously haven't seen, and we also see how righteous and powerful God is. Tribulation humbles us! I don't know what God is calling you for, but I'm confident that it will require a certain degree of humility (Zeke Stepp). In the fires of tribulation, we learn to trust in the finished work of Christ and not in ourselves. We learn that we are nothing outside of Christ, but we also learn Christ is everything. In these two sections of scripture at the beginning of this chapter, we can see that tribulation came unto Paul because of revelation and revelation came unto him because of tribulation.

Although I'm not certain about this, it may be possible that Paul thought that if the thorn were removed from his flesh, it would help him in the ministry, for many times, the churches thought of forsaking Paul for others who were more appealing unto the flesh. Paul's bodily weakness and contemptible speech were a means by which others sought to take over the churches God blessed him to plant. Some churches, or some of the members at that time, were in danger of accepting those more appealing to the flesh rather than those more necessary to the Spirit. Paul may have felt that the thorn was holding him back, for there were occasions when the churches or some of the members didn't respect him as they should have because of this thorn. Paul may have felt that if this thorn had been removed, it would have opened more doors for him and made his ministry more effective.

How many times do we feel like this? How many times must things that we feel are needful and necessary to fulfill the ministry God has given us be broken out of our lives? So often, we can't see the flesh or understand that God's strength is made perfect through weakness. We think these things are necessary for our success in the gospel ministry, yet God kills them. God knows they are hindrances, but we think they are complimentary helpers in our calling. So often, God must break things out of our lives that we think are necessary for our calling. We must be brought unto a place of weakness so that our faith would be solely in the finished work of Jesus, so that the power of Christ may rest upon us. We can't see how this weakness will cause God's strength to be perfected in our lives, but God knows, and therefore, He allows the thorn to be placed in our flesh so that the power of Christ may rest upon us.

Sometimes, we think the thorn in our flesh is holding us back. Paul may have thought I could be spreading the gospel if I wasn't in jail. Yet, we need only to look at the prison epistles of Paul to see that God blessed him to spread the gospel while in prison. Paul possibly spread the gospel more while in prison than at any other time. The letters that God blessed Paul to write while in prison went out to the people of his time and to those of every generation since. These letters were preserved by God and included in the Bible. For almost two thousand years now, people from every nation and country have read and studied them, even though Paul never set foot in those places. Yes, Paul wanted the thorn removed, but the power of Christ rested upon him in his weakness. Yes, Paul wanted to be strong, but God's power is made perfect in weakness.

Now, let's get to Paul's response after God spoke unto him concerning his prayer request. Paul says this,

2 Corinthians 12:9-10. *"...Most gladly therefore will I rather glory in my infirmities, that the power of Christ may rest*

*upon me. Therefore I take pleasure in infirmities, in reproaches, in necessities, in persecutions, in distresses for Christ's sake: for when I am weak, then am I strong."*

Here, we see this isn't so much about God not answering Paul's prayer, for after the Lord explained why the messenger of Satan was allowed to buffet him, Paul changed his prayer request. Paul no longer wants the messenger of Satan removed from him but most gladly accepts anything he is permitted to do unto him. After Paul prayed three times for the thorn to be removed, God spoke to him about it. After God explained why the thorn was allowed to be placed in his flesh, Paul no longer wanted the thorn removed.

Why would Paul change his request? Why would Paul go from desiring the messenger of Satan to be removed from him to desiring that he stay and buffet him? This doesn't seem logical. Because it isn't, it's spiritual. Paul understands that without the messenger of Satan buffeting him, he would become exalted above measure, and the power of Christ wouldn't rest upon him in the great manner that it did. Therefore, Paul changes his prayer request because the revelations of God and the power of Christ are so valuable to him. The revelations of God are more valuable unto him than his comfort. Paul is not only willing to have the messenger of Satan buffet him that the power of Christ may rest upon him, but he is glad of it.

Think of it this way. If a farmer asked you to shovel out his barn, you probably wouldn't want to, would you? You have no desire to shovel dung all day. You have no desire to feel the soreness in your body that this chore would bring. You have no desire to smell all the smells within the barn. You have no desire to sweat in the hot climate as the stench of manure permeates your nostrils. You have no desire to put yourself in such a predicament, so you would probably refuse to do it. Yet, if the farmer told you he would give you ten million dollars to shovel out his barn, a big smile would come across your face, and you would feel privileged that he asked you to do it and not another, as you gladly take hold of the pitchfork and make haste to shovel animal manure. You would feel privileged that the farmer chose you for this task, would be glad to go and do the work, and would probably be glad to tell others how honored you feel to have been chosen by the farmer to shovel out his barn. Why? Why would your mind change about shoveling out the barn? You didn't want to do it; you despise doing it, but now you are happy to do it. Why? You see the value in it. Ten million dollars is so valuable that you are elated to have been chosen to shovel out the barn.

This is why Paul's mind changed concerning the thorn in his flesh. Paul despised the thorn, but when he understood that this thorn was necessary or the power of Christ wouldn't rest upon him, his thinking changed. The revelations of Christ were so valuable to Paul that he was not only willing to bear the thorn but rather glad to do so. Why? The revelations God gave Paul were so valuable unto him that he considered anything that was permitted to come into his life so that he may have them to be a great blessing. The revelations Paul received would have caused him to be exalted above measure, and therefore, the power of Christ wouldn't rest upon him. Yet, because the thorn in his flesh humbled him in the sight of the people he preached to, Christ's power would rest upon him.

Therefore, Paul became thankful for the thorn. He was not only thankful for it but also gloried in it because he could now have both the revelations of God and the power of Christ resting upon him.

Is it worth it? Is it worth the suffering to receive the revelations? Oh yes, it is more than worth it, for Paul gladly glories in his sufferings that the power of Christ may rest upon him. Is it worth it? Revelation from God and the power of Christ resting upon us is of much greater value than anything we must suffer for it to be revealed in our lives. Whether we must be humbled in our own sight or humbled in the sight of others, it is worth it, for it is a great treasure. If a thorn is required, then we are happy to bear it because it is necessary for the priceless treasure of revelation to be revealed in our lives.

Does this mean this made it easy for Paul to bear this thorn? No, but it made it worth it unto him. He knew this thorn had a godly purpose in his life. Knowing tribulation has a purpose is important. It is important because this causes us to know we aren't going through such tribulations for nothing. We know that God will use it to add more of Himself unto our lives, and although tribulation isn't easy, for it isn't meant to be, knowing there is a godly purpose in it causes us to have more strength to bear it, which causes us to look at it as a blessing instead of a curse. This will cause us to rejoice in tribulation because we know that tribulation will work a godly work in us. Notice these verses.

James 1:2-4. *"My brethren, count it all joy when ye fall into divers temptations; Knowing this, that the trying of your faith worketh patience. But let patience have her perfect work, that ye may be perfect and entire, wanting nothing."*

How do we look at tribulation as a joyous thing? It is because we know something (*"Knowing this"*). We know that the trying of our faith will work patience in our lives, and when patience has her perfect work, we will be perfect and entire, lacking nothing. Tribulation isn't a joyous thing. Tribulation is a hard thing. Tribulation can be a painful thing. Tribulation can be a depressing and sad thing. Tribulation hurts, but we can count it as joyous when we know something. We know that God uses tribulation to work heavenly things in our earthly lives, and when we value the things of God in our lives to be the treasures that they are, then we can count it all joy when tribulation comes because of the heavenly things that will be revealed in us through it. We value the heavenly things of God so greatly that tribulation becomes a joyous thing, for we know that God will use the tribulation to do marvelous works in our lives. Tribulation causes the flesh to mourn but the Spirit to rejoice. The flesh mourns because the tribulation is killing it, but the Spirit can rejoice because He is increasing in our lives.

So often, I've despised tribulation. How many times have I asked God to remove it? How many times have I wished it to be gone from me? Yet, when I truly think about tribulation and God's work in my life through it, I also say it is worth it! It is worth it a thousand times over! It is worth it! It is worth it! So, we, too, are pained with Paul in tribulation, but we also accept it gladly, as he did when we understand it.

Think of it this way. Most people want to be in shape. Most people want to be physically fit, but many people aren't. It takes a lot of work and dedication to stay in shape. Some people work out, but many don't. Those who work out are usually stronger, healthier, and in better shape than those who don't. It is hard work to exercise, and those who want to be physically fit must continually work at it. There is a lot of sweat and time spent exercising, and muscles must first be torn if they are to grow. When a person works out, their muscles are torn, and when they recover, they become bigger and stronger. This is a scientific fact, and most people know this, yet most people don't work out, although most people wish they were in shape. Why? It isn't worth it to them. The time, effort, and money it takes to work out is too high of a price for most people to pay for physical fitness. This is why most people don't work out, but those who do reap the rewards of being physically fit.

1 Timothy 4:8 *"For bodily exercise profiteth little: but godliness is profitable unto all things, having promise of the life that now is, and of that which is to come."*

God didn't bless Paul to say that bodily exercise was profitless because there are benefits to working out, but he did say it only profits a little bit. Why? God is blessing Paul to compare bodily exercise with godliness. He is comparing natural things to spiritual things. There is nothing natural that can be called big when it is compared to something spiritual.

My cousin's husband (Ray) is six feet and four inches tall. He is almost always taller than everyone in the room. Therefore, most people ask him how tall he is. They speak of how big he is. Yet, no one speaks of his height at a family reunion. Why? He is the smallest person in his family. They call him the runt of the family. His dad is six feet and eight inches tall, and he has cousins who played the center position on college basketball teams. One of his cousins is around seven feet tall. He played center for a college basketball team in the NCAAM Tournament. So, when Ray is around other families, everyone speaks of how big and tall he is, but no one speaks of his height around his family. Why? It is what he is being compared to. Around most families, few are his height. Therefore, he usually stands head and shoulders above all, as did Saul among the Israelites (1 Samuel 10:23). Yet, around his own family, everyone stands head and shoulders above him. Therefore, he is not viewed as being tall by his own family.

Natural things are temporary, but spiritual things are eternal. Natural things are only profitable in the present, but spiritual things are profitable now and for all eternity. God blesses Paul to compare exercise to godliness and proclaims godliness to have a present and eternal benefit. Therefore, bodily exercise is small in comparison to godliness because it only produces a temporary benefit, while godliness produces benefits now and throughout all eternity.

Now, if we asked someone who worked out, is it worth it to exercise like you do? Is it worth spending all this time, money, and effort working out? Is it worth it to sweat and cause your body so much discomfort? They would say, yes, it is. They would say it is worth it to be in shape, to feel good, to be healthy, to be strong, and not to be overweight. If it is worth it to work out, how much more is it worth it to have the flesh weakened so that we may be spiritually strong and effective in the calling of God upon our lives? It is worth it!

Brother Paul says I will gladly accept this thorn, for the revelation of God in my life is a great treasure. I will rejoice in being buffeted by the messenger of Satan, for it is a means by which the power of Christ may rest upon me! My dear brothers and sisters, it is worth it, and it was worth it to Paul and Job as well.

Now, let's look a little closer at the second set of scriptures given at the beginning of this chapter, which are:

2 Corinthians 1:3-10. *"Blessed be God, even the Father of our Lord Jesus Christ, the Father of mercies, and the God of all comfort; Who comforteth us in all our tribulation, that we may be able to comfort them which are in any trouble, by the comfort wherewith we ourselves are comforted of God. For as the sufferings of Christ abound in us, so our consolation also aboundeth by Christ. And whether we be afflicted, it is for your consolation and salvation, which is effectual in the enduring of the same sufferings which we also suffer: or whether we be comforted, it is for your consolation and salvation. And our hope of you is stedfast, knowing that as ye are partakers of the sufferings, so shall ye be also of the consolation. For we would not, brethren, have you ignorant of our trouble which came to us in Asia, that we were pressed out of measure, above strength, insomuch that we despaired even of life: But we had the sentence of death in ourselves, that we should not trust in ourselves, but in God which raiseth the dead: Who delivered us from so great a death, and doth deliver: in whom we trust that he will yet deliver us;"*

Here, we can also see that sometimes, a price must be paid to receive revelation. Remember, revelation is free. God gives it freely, but many times, a price must be paid to learn it.

When I was young, my schooling and books were free. All the information was given to me, but there was a price for learning. Many nights, I stayed up late studying as I tried to memorize the material in the books. Learning isn't always easy or fun, but if we are to benefit from the information, we must learn it.

Paul is speaking about the comfort he and other Saints received from God. This comfort came unto them in their tribulations. What is comfort? Is it a hug or being consoled? Yes, it is in some ways, but we see something more to it in these verses. We see that this comfort is not only something Paul received but also something he possesses; it is not only something he possesses but also something he can use, and not only something he can use but something he can give to others. What is this comfort? It is something he learned in tribulation. We see that Paul and those with him thought they would be killed. They had come to the point where they had resided themselves unto death. In this fearful time, tribulation brought them to a place they had never been to before. A place where it seemed certain that they would die, and there, in that frightening time, they learned to trust God with their deaths. They learned to trust God beyond death. They learned to trust God for the resurrection. This is something they had possibly never experienced before. Sure, they had experienced persecution and the threat of death, but they had never come to a place where they felt there was no other alternative but death. (Paul was stoned and left for dead at Lystra earlier, but that happened at the spur of the moment. Here, we see that Paul and those with him are awaiting their death, and death seems to be a certainty. They must face it over a certain amount of time. They are forced to think about it as they await their impending martyrdom.)

It not only seemed plausible that they would be killed, but death seemed to be certain. They had come to the place where they were sure they would be killed for their faith. It is one thing to think something like this might happen. It is one thing to try and prepare yourself for something like this, but staring martyrdom in the face is entirely different. Paul was certain that he and those with him would be martyred, which was very hard for them to face. Could you imagine the fear they experienced? Could you imagine what their nerves must have felt like? Like fiery whips that tore into their bodies. Could you imagine how their sleep must have fled from them and how this plight would have increased every moment of every day? This was a very tough place for them to be in. This was quite possibly the toughest place they had ever been in up to this point. Yet, God delivered them from this.

If God was going to deliver them from this, and God had already determined that they would live through this, then why did God allow them to be in this fearful place to begin with? There was something God wanted them to learn. God had taught them about the resurrection and His Paradise that comes after death, but it hadn't completely settled into their innermost being, and therefore, it would be burned into them. The fiery trial would be the branding iron that would burn this glorious truth into their very souls. They were brought unto this place where they had the sentence of death in themselves that they might learn to trust in God for the resurrection.

Sometimes, we must face our fears before we learn to trust God with them. Sometimes, we must face our fears before we learn to trust God's word. Sometimes, we must face our fears so that we may learn the information God has already given us. Spurgeon once said: "Most of the grand truths of God have to be learned by trouble; they must be burned into us with the hot iron of affliction. Otherwise, we shall not truly receive them."

Sure, Paul knew about the resurrection and had preached it mightily, but he learned more about it here in this troublesome place. In this fiery trial, Paul saw that he could do nothing to preserve his life, which moved him to trust God in this terrifying situation. There are times when we must be brought to the end of ourselves so that we may learn to trust in God. Paul knew there was nothing he could do to keep from being martyred, and he was certain that he would be killed, but there, in this frightening place, he learned to trust God for the resurrection. Paul had come to a place where he couldn't trust in himself for deliverance; he had come to a place where death seemed certain, and in this place, he learned to trust in God for the resurrection. It is one thing to trust in God for the resurrection when life seems certain, but entirely another when death seems to be the reality. In this fiery furnace, the great apostle learned how to trust more in God and less in himself. This is what tribulation is all about. It strips more of us away so that we may trust more in Christ. The fiery furnace consumed another piece of Paul's flesh; therefore, more of God was revealed in his life.

It is important to understand that Paul didn't come out of this fire the same way he went into it. Paul came out weaker in the flesh and stronger in the Spirit. Paul had gone into this fire with a certain amount of faith in himself concerning his earthly existence but came out of this fire no longer trusting any part of his earthly existence unto himself. Paul went into this fire knowing about the resurrection but came out of this fire as one who was learned in the resurrection. Paul went into this fire with some fear concerning martyrdom but came out of it no longer afraid of it. Paul went into this fire knowing about the resurrection but came out of this fire understanding the resurrection. Yes, Paul went into this fire with the knowledge of the resurrection but came out of this fire completely trusting in the resurrection. Paul went into this fire preaching the resurrection but came out of this fire comforted by the resurrection. Sure, Paul trusted in the resurrection before he went into this fire, but never to the extent he did when he was in it. Paul knew about the resurrection and trusted in it to a certain extent, but still, he was troubled while in this hot flame. Yet, amid this fire, Paul trusted completely in the resurrection and was comforted, although the dark shadow of death seemed to be closing in all around him. God had added more of Himself unto Paul in this hot fire. Yes, a piece of Paul was consumed, but it was replaced with a piece of heaven.

Paul referred to this as God comforting him. Yet, this comfort wasn't temporary, for it would continue with him long after the fiery trial had been quenched. Yes, the comfort of God lasted longer than the fire. This comfort went with Paul after the fiery trial had ceased; this comfort taught Paul how to trust God throughout his life in a greater way, and Paul could also share this comfort with others. Oh yes, this comfort of God in Paul's life shone long after the fiery trial had ceased. This comfort remained long after the fiery trial stopped smoldering. Remember, the fiery trial will cease, but the comfort received in the fire remains. Others would need this comfort, and there, in that trying fire, God would see that it would be worked into the life of Paul. How many people were positively affected by this comfort God produced in Paul's life? It is impossible to know. How much did this comfort help the great apostle throughout the rest of his life? We don't know, but we do know it did, for the comfort God gave Paul in this fiery trial would have prepared him for his future martyrdom and strengthened him in the ministry. The fear of martyrdom wouldn't have the ability to hinder him in the preaching of the gospel, nor would it have the ability to cause him to shrink away from preaching it, although he would preach it in the very face of death. God's comfort in this fiery trial taught him to trust completely in the resurrection, for fear of death would have lost all power over Paul through the comfort of the resurrection, which God gave unto him in this fierce fire.

So often, it is the fire that must strip us away, and here, Paul was stripped unto his very essence, for he was pressed out of measure and above strength. Here in this fire, God gave Paul victory over the fear of death as he learned the victory of the resurrection. Though Paul already knew this, it had never been as real unto him as at that time, for he had preached the resurrection but had never been comforted by the resurrection as greatly as he was in that hot flame. In that fire, Paul faced death, and he didn't have the strength to fight against it, which caused him to trust God completely. In that dark and trying time, the resurrection shone like the sun in its strength, lit up Paul's heart, and gave him victory over the fear of death.

Oh, how God comforted Paul in this time of great trouble! The fire was hot, and the flames tormenting, but faith in Christ for the resurrection caused the fire to have power over Paul no longer. Paul was free, though bound in the fire. Paul was as free as Shadrach, Meshach, and Abednego in Nebuchadnezzar's fiery furnace. In the fire, Paul experienced a freedom he had never experienced before. Death no longer had any dominion over him, although it seemed to be a reality, for faith in Christ for the resurrection had conquered the fear of death in Paul's life. Paul may never have come to this place of freedom had he not been placed in such a fire as this. Therefore, God allowed this to come upon him so that he could be free from the bondage that the fear of death brings, which would allow him to comfort others, strengthen him in the ministry, and prepare him for his future martyrdom.

This brings us to another purpose of tribulation. We have previously mentioned Shadrach, Meshach, and Abednego, who were cast into the fiery furnace by Nebuchadnezzar because they refused to worship the idol he had made. They were bound and cast into the fire, but when Nebuchadnezzar looked into the furnace, he not only saw Jesus walking among them but also saw that these three Hebrews were free from their bonds.

Daniel 3:21-25. *"Then these men were bound in their coats, their hosen, and their hats, and their other garments, and were cast into the midst of the burning fiery furnace. Therefore because the king's commandment was urgent, and the furnace exceeding hot, the flame of the fire slew those men that took up Shadrach, Meshach, and Abednego. And these three men, Shadrach, Meshach, and Abednego, fell down bound into the midst of the burning fiery furnace. Then Nebuchadnezzar the king was astonied, and rose up in haste, and spake, and said unto his counsellors, Did not we cast three men bound into the midst of the fire? They answered and said unto the king, True, O king. He answered and said, Lo, I see four men loose, walking in the midst of the fire, and they have no hurt; and the form of the fourth is like the Son of God."*

We have already stated that we get a clearer view of Christ in the fire, but now I want to point out the unbinding in the fire, by the fire. These three Jewish men were bound when they were cast into the fire, but when Nebuchadnezzar investigates the fiery furnace, he distinctly notices that they are no longer bound. Yes, Nebuchadnezzar saw Jesus walking with them in the fire, which is the greatest thing the fire produces, but he also noticed that they were set free from their bonds in the fire. Christ was revealed unto these three Jewish men in such an amazing manner in the fire, not out of the fire.

Let's, for a moment, concentrate on their freedom in the fire, as they were released from their bonds in the fire, by the fire. The fire couldn't burn them or their clothes, for the smell of smoke wasn't even upon them when they came out of the furnace. Yet, the fire did burn something; it burned the things that bound them. Whatever Nebuchadnezzar used to bind them with was burned in the fire, by the fire. Whether they were bound with chains or ropes, the fire burned what they were bound with.

The fire was extremely hot, for Nebuchadnezzar made them heat up the furnace seven times hotter than they normally did. The fire was so hot that it killed the most honorable of Nebuchadnezzar's soldiers, whom he had charged with the task of throwing these three Jewish men into the furnace. Yes, it burned the mighty soldiers that had power over them. This fire was extremely hot, and it needed to be that hot, but the fire was never meant to burn the three Jewish men, only the things that bound them. Sure, Nebuchadnezzar's desire was to burn these men into ashes, but God's desire was different. God allowed Nebuchadnezzar to heat the furnace up as he did. God also allowed him to bind the three men and cast them into the fire, but God wouldn't allow the fire to burn them, for He only allowed it to burn the things that bound them.

The scripture doesn't say what these three men were bound with. It could have been ropes, chains, or something else, but it is evident that they went into the fire bound and came out of the fire free. They were not only free when they came out, but Nebuchadnezzar noticed they were free while in the midst of the fire.

We know that different materials have different melting points. Different materials burn at different temperatures. For example, lead melts at a lower temperature than steel, and it takes more heat to burn a log than a twig. Again, I don't know what these three men were bound with. It could have been ropes, or it could have been chains, but the fact remains that the fire burned whatever they were bound with. We know it takes a hotter fire to burn chains than ropes, and we also know that the fire was seven times hotter than normal. Now, I'm not trying to use the heat of the fire to determine what these men were bound with, but to make a spiritual point.

We also know that the men were freed from these bonds while in the fire, not after coming out of the fire. The fire must be hot enough to burn what binds us, and we must be freed from the bonds before we can come out of the fire.

God willing, I'd like to make multiple points about this. One concerns the three Jewish men, and another concerns the effect this had upon Nebuchadnezzar and the Babylonian Empire.

Let's first speak about how this affected the three Jewish men before we speak about the effect this event had on Nebuchadnezzar and the Babylonian Empire. Let's point out the facts that we know. Nebuchadnezzar decreed that everyone should worship his golden idol, and all who refused to do so would be thrown into the fiery furnace. The three Jewish men refused to worship the idol. This caused Nebuchadnezzar to become so angry with them that he heated up the furnace seven times hotter than it was normally heated, bound them, and had his most honorable soldiers cast them into the fire. When these men were cast into the flame, the scriptures say they were bound and cast into the midst of the burning fiery furnace. The scriptures say that when these three men were cast into the fiery furnace, they *"fell down bound."* (Daniel 3:23). Eventually, Nebuchadnezzar investigates the furnace and sees four men free and walking around in the fire, and the fourth man looks like the Son of God. Nebuchadnezzar can't believe his eyes, so he asks the people around him two questions. He asks them if they cast three men into the fiery furnace, and if they were bound when they were cast in. They say yes to both questions. Then Nebuchadnezzar says, I see four men loose, walking in the fire and unharmed, and the fourth is like unto the Son of God. Then Nebuchadnezzar tells Shadrach, Meshach, and Abednego to come out of the fire, praises God, promotes them to some of the most prestigious and influential positions in the Babylonian Empire, and makes a decree that no one should speak anything against the God of Shadrach, Meshach, and Abednego or they would be cut in pieces and their houses would be made a dunghill, because there is no other god who can deliver after this manner.

Now, to the three Jewish men cast into the fiery furnace. What was the purpose of the fire for them? They got a greater view of Christ than they had ever gotten before, which we have already spoken of earlier in this book, but they also were preserved in the furnace and freed from their bonds by the fire. Again, we have already stated that we don't know what they were bound with. It could've been ropes or chains. We have already stated that different materials melt or burn at different temperatures. The point is this. The fire couldn't burn the three men, but it did burn their bonds.

The same is true with Saints. Many different things bind the Saints of God. It could be fear, lust, or pride. It could be any number of things, but the fact is, many things bind us. These bonds can cause us to be idle in our calling, as we are paralyzed by fear, or they can hinder our calling, as the power of Christ won't rest upon us because of lust, pride, or being exalted above measure in our own eyes or the eyes of others. So, the flesh binds us.

We are also limited by a lack of understanding and/or revelation. In the book of Job, we see how his friend's counsel was limited because of their lack of understanding concerning God. So, the flesh binds us, and our potential is based upon our view of God.

In this fire, the three Jewish men got a greater view of God, which would expand their potential, but they were also freed from their bonds by the fire. Tribulation serves both purposes. Tribulation grants us a greater view of Christ and frees us from the things that bind us. This is why the fire must be so hot at times. As there are different melting points for different materials, there are different melting points for fleshly bonds. Ropes and iron burn or melt at different temperatures, and certain fleshly bonds in our lives do as well. Some fleshly bonds burn or melt in our lives at higher temperatures than others. It could be pride for me, fear for you, or lust for someone else, but certain fleshly bonds require greater heat to cause us to be freed from them.

This is one of the purposes of tribulation. The fires of tribulation must be hot enough to burn what binds you. They aren't intended to burn you but to give you a greater view of Christ and set you free from fleshly bonds. They are designed to increase your potential in Christ and free you from all that hinders you from walking in it. The fire seems to be a threat unto you, but it is only a threat unto your limited understanding and bonds. Sometimes, the fire seems so hot that it will kill you, and although the martyrdom of these three men would have worked out for their good and God's glory, this was not the purpose of this fire. The purpose of this fire was to give them a greater revelation of Christ and burn their bonds. This is the purpose of tribulation in our lives, for we will exit the fiery furnace with our lives, clothes, comfort, and no smell of smoke (no natural evidence of being in the furnace), but we will not exit without revelation, nor will we exit with our bonds.

We are not only freed by the fire but freed while in the fire. It is important to notice that these three Jewish men were freed in the fire, not out of the fire. They were freed while in the fire, not after they came out of the fire. Why is this so important? What is the lesson of being freed in the fire and not being freed outside of the fire? Why does it matter? This shows that the fire had done what it was meant to do concerning their bonds. Remember the two things the three Jewish men got from the fire. They got a greater revelation of Christ (comfort), and they were freed from their bonds (fleshly bonds). They must also be freed before leaving the fire, not vice versa. Whatever the fleshly cord is that binds us when we are thrown into the fire must be dissolved before we can come out of the fire.

The fire is so great and fearful that it brings us to a place where we understand that we can't overcome it. We, with Paul, are pressed out of measure and above strength. In other words, we are brought to the end of ourselves. Paul had come to a place where he also learned more about himself, for he knew he wasn't sufficient to handle what had come upon him. There is nothing we can do to stop or fix this tribulation. What could these three Hebrew men do when they faced the fiery furnace? Absolutely nothing!

This is where tribulation brings us. This is the design of tribulation. It is bigger than we are by design, for we must be brought to the end of ourselves. Once we are brought to the end of ourselves, we are forced to trust in the Lord. We are forced to trust in His word. There is nothing else left for us to trust in. We have no strength in this situation. What can these three Jewish men do? We are pressed out of measure as we are taken beyond our limits. What can we do? Is there a fleshly crutch left to lean on? No, the fire has consumed them all. Nothing of the flesh is useful, and according to our own strength, the situation is hopeless, seeing there is no natural remedy, but there, in this darkness, Christ shines the brightest, and God becomes our only hope. Then, we completely trust Christ's finished work and are set free from the fleshly bonds that bound us before we were cast into the fire. We must be taken to a place where we are no longer afraid of the fire. By trusting in God and His word, the fear of the fire ceases, and now we are ready to come out of the furnace. We must have victory over the fire before we can come out of the fire, and this victory comes through faith in Christ, and sometimes, this faith must be forged over time.

The fire is also good for forging. Many swords would have never pierced through the enemy without the fire to forge them. The sword, forged in the fire, has won many battles. It is important to understand that steel isn't placed into the fire and immediately turned into a sword. The sword goes in and out of the fire repeatedly. Every time it comes out, it is beaten and shaped by a heavy hammer, and when it begins to cool, it is placed back into the fire. This process takes a long time, but it is necessary if you want a properly forged and strong sword.

In the furnace, we eventually give up on our own abilities to resist the fire and understand that if we are to be delivered from the fire, God alone must do it. Though we are pressed out of measure and above strength, knowing God is our only hope, we don't always trust in the Lord in the manner we must that we may be delivered from the fire. We are still afraid of the fire and lack the power to resist it. We try to look to God, but our faith is weak. In these moments, God takes the hammer in His hand and begins to forge us. We can't see it all at once, as one can't see the sword immediately, but God forges more of Himself into us blow by blow. Blow by blow, God forces the word into our now malleable hearts.

Often, faith must be forged, for it doesn't always come as quickly as we would like, but it sometimes comes over time in the fiery furnace. One blow after another blow, but we see very little change because we often don't understand that revelation comes line upon line, precept upon precept, here a little and there a little (Isaiah 28:10;13). We must remain in the fire until our hearts become soft enough to receive what God is placing in us. We must remain in the fire until we learn all that God desires us to learn. Time passes, and we are changing, although it is like looking at the clock's hour hand. It's hard to see the movement the hammer is creating in our lives, but we are moving. Yes, we are moving closer and closer to the cross of Christ. Faith is being forged in our lives, and eventually, we are brought to the place where we trust God in the fire. We aren't just trusting God to bring us out of the fire, but we are trusting God in the fire. There, we see that God is sufficient in the fire, and whether we stay in the fire or not, God's promises will sustain us. Therefore, we are set free from our bonds by the fire before we walk out of the fire. We are free either way but must be free in the fire before walking out of it. We must have victory in the fire before it is time to step out of it, and the victory (comfort) we receive in the fire will accompany us when we step out of the fire. We have come to the place where we are no longer concerned whether we are in the fire or out of the fire, for we trust that God's grace is sufficient either way. Therefore, we are free, regardless of the fire, for the fire has burned our bonds. We no longer fear the fire because we know that God's promises are bigger than the fire, for we have seen Christ walking in it with us.

The life of a Saint is a continual forging process as well. The course of our Christian lives is a continual forging process as God continues to place more revelation and more of Himself into us. We become stronger and stronger with each tribulation. Every blow of the hammer shapes us a little bit more into the image of Christ. The life of a Christian is a continual crucifixion, as we are called to die more and more every day. Remember, Jesus tells us to take up our cross daily and follow Him (Luke 9:23). There will always be fires for the Christian. There is no escaping them. As sure as we have come out of one fire, we are marching towards another. Yet, over time, we can see how God has shaped us in the fires of tribulation, and we are thankful for them, for we see the work of the hammer in our lives.

Let's look at it like this. Let's say you had a crippling fear of death (although it could be anything that binds us), and this fear has hindered you in your calling. So, you are bound by this fear. It affects everything you do. You can't be all that God has called you to be all the while you are bound by this fear. Sure, you have read the Bible. You have read all the scriptures that say fear not and all the verses that speak of the resurrection.

Yet, this fear remains like handcuffs on your hands and shackles on your feet.

Many times, such circumstances call for inoculation. What is inoculation? Inoculation is a process of vaccination. Many of us have been vaccinated because of certain diseases. Whether it is smallpox or other diseases, vaccination protects us from them. How does vaccination work? I'm not a doctor, but from my limited understanding of the matter, it works something like this. We are given a shot containing a small amount of the virus we are vaccinated against. This sounds foolish and was truly looked at as such when vaccination was first experimented with and eventually discovered. Why is it important to give us a small amount of the virus we are being vaccinated against? We are given a non-fatal amount of the virus so that a fatal amount won't kill us. When we are given a small amount of the virus we are being vaccinated against, our bodies build up immunity to the virus. Our immune system learns how to fight it. Therefore, the virus can no longer harm us. Through being exposed somewhat to the virus, we become immune to the virus.

So, the fear of death has crippled us, and therefore, it may be necessary for us to face death so that we would have victory over this crippling fear. This doesn't mean we have to die, nor does it necessarily mean that we must be sick, but in some form or the other, a non-lethal dose of death must be placed into our lives so that we may build up an immunity against it and overcome it. We must face the fear of death until we build up an immunity of faith against it. By facing death, we will have victory over death. Not that we must literally face it upon our deathbeds, through sickness, or in war, but face it we must.

God may allow the devil to show you a mirage, which He has previously not allowed the devil to manifest unto you. This mirage isn't real, but a situation can be as real unto us as we believe it to be.

Many people have thought they were dying when they weren't because they believed they were, and therefore, the fear of death was real, although there was no threat of dying. I've heard of instances in which people have chased an oasis in the desert because they saw a mirage and believed it was real.

Sometimes Satan is permitted to show us mirages of death, and they are as real unto us as we think them to be, as Paul was placed in a situation in which he was certain he would be martyred for his faith, although God delivered him from what seemed to be certain death. Though nothing is wrong with us, if we believe something is wrong with us, we act as though something is wrong with us, and the fear of something being wrong with us becomes a reality in our lives, although nothing is actually wrong with us. Some people have been terrorized by sicknesses when they weren't sick at all. Yet, we wonder why.

Why would God allow Satan to show us a mirage that causes us to think we are dying? We must be inoculated. We must be exposed to death without dying. Though we're not going to die, we think we are going to die, as did Paul. This horrific fire teaches us to trust God for the resurrection. Therefore, death is no longer fearful because we have accepted it as coming and have completely trusted God to resurrect us. Yes, we have embraced the resurrection and the life to come to the extent that we are no longer afraid of death. The fear of death has been overcome through facing death. Through facing death, we were forced to trust in Christ for the resurrection, and once full faith and confidence are in God to raise us from the dead and glorify us in His Paradise, then we are no longer afraid of death, though we had resided ourselves unto it. This is what it means to be freed from the fire, by the fire, while in the fire.

The fire never quit raging when Paul was freed from the fear of death. It still looked like he would be martyred, but he was free from it because he had come to the place where he was no longer afraid of death, for he had placed full faith in God for the resurrection. God comforted Paul before the threat of death was removed. This means it was overcome in the fire, not out of it. If we come out of the fire before the victory over the fire is won. It is likely we won't overcome it unless we are again placed back into the fire for the same thing, which could also be considered as the process of forging, where we must go in and out of the fire until faith is forged in us.

Sometimes, we must go in and out of the same fire because we are too frail to stay in the fire long enough to accomplish the entire work, or the forging process requires it. Yet, we are still in the tongs, and it is determined that we must again be placed back into the fire until the forging process is done. Though we may have been brought out of the fire for a while, we are determined to return to the fire until the forging process is completed. Therefore, we aren't really taken out of the fire because we are still in the tongs, and it has already been determined that we will be placed back into the fire, for the process hasn't been completed. Though we have been taken out, we are not yet completely freed from our bonds; therefore, another trip into the fire is certain. So, a little is forged here and a little there over multiple instances in the fire. Yet, whether all at once or over multiple times in the fire, we must be set free from our bonds in the fire, by the fire. The victory over the fire must come in the fire before we will ever be freed by the fire and come out of the fire. If Paul comes out of the fire, which is the threat of martyrdom, before he has come to this place of faith in God for the resurrection, then it is likely he will never come to that place of faith in God for the resurrection, unless he is placed back into the same fire again. Therefore, it is necessary that we remain in the fire until we are set free by the fire. The tribulation you face will no longer be a tribulation unto you once you have stopped fighting it, have come to a greater revelation of God, and have committed it unto Christ through faith, for we now view the promises of God to be greater than the fire, as we see Jesus walking in the midst of the fire with us. When we come to this place of resting in Christ, no longer trusting in ourselves to resist the fire, we will be set free by the fire, for the fire has now burned the fleshly cord that bound us.

Paul had resided himself unto death. He had come to the place where he just knew he would die, but in this dark time, the resurrection began to shine so brightly in his life that he was no longer worried about what death could take from him because he knew God had promised him the resurrection. Therefore, the fire burned this bond out of Paul's life, and he was free from death and the fear of it, even before he was set free from those who threatened his life. When Paul came out of this fire, he had not only lost something but gained something as well. He lost the bond that bound him (fear of martyrdom) and received the comfort of God (he trusted completely in the resurrection, as the resurrection meant more unto him than it ever had before).

Again, Paul knew about the resurrection and preached the resurrection before he was placed in this fire, but he had never trusted in the resurrection as he did while in the fire. This brings us back to Spurgeon's statement: "In prosperity, God is heard, and that is a blessing, but in adversity, God is seen, and that is a greater blessing."

The three Hebrew men heard God's word outside of the fire, which is why they refused to bow unto the idol, but while in the fire, they saw Jesus walking in the midst of it with them. The fire often reveals things to us, but things are often revealed to us outside of the fire. The resurrection was revealed to Paul before he found himself in the fire, but in the fire, he learned to trust in the resurrection completely. Let me say it like this, God willing. Many times, revelation comes unto us outside of the fire, but inside of the fire, we learn to completely trust in the revelation that was given unto us outside of the fire, and then your bonds will be burned from you, as you see Jesus walking in the midst of the fire with you.

So, we must stay in the fire until we are set free by the fire; then, we will be able to come out of the fire freed from the fleshly bonds that bound us before we went into the fire. The fire burns our bonds, for we must stay in the fire until we are no longer afraid of it. We must stay in the fire until God has blessed us to conquer it by faith; then, we are freed in the fire, by the fire, and will soon walk out of the fiery furnace. We must stay in the fire until we understand that we can live in the fire. The fire doesn't have to be put out for us to live, for the Lord will bless us to make it despite the fire. The fire doesn't have to be quenched for Paul to have peace and comfort from God, though it seems certain that Paul will be martyred. The certainty of martyrdom doesn't have to be removed for him to be comforted by God, for there, in the fires of certain martyrdom, Paul overcame martyrdom, although martyrdom seemed certain. Though Paul felt it was certain that he would be killed for his faith, he knew he would live in the resurrection. God had brought Paul to such a place of comfort in the resurrection that the fires of death no longer had any power over him. Paul knew he could live in this fire because of the resurrection. Therefore, Paul was set free from the fear and pain of death before walking out of the fire. The fear of pain and death had to become so real and certain unto Paul that he wholly trusted it unto God, and therefore, the fire set him free from the fleshly bond that bound him. Paul didn't have comfort because he thought God would deliver him from being martyred but had comfort knowing God would resurrect him after death. Paul got a greater view of Christ in this fire. The resurrection had to become as real and as certain as the martyrdom and pain did, and when it did, Paul was free, even before he walked out of the furnace.

The Saint must stay in the fire until the fire burns their bonds. Then you have become free, whether in the fire or out of the fire, for you are sure that you can survive the fire because you have seen Jesus walking in it with you. Yes, you have been brought unto a place of faith in the promises of God, which are provided unto us through the finished work of Christ. Therefore, the purpose of the fire is to get a greater revelation of God, a greater revelation of ourselves, forge faith in our lives, and be set free from certain things that bind us, having had our handcuffs and shackles dissolved by the fire.

Now, back to Shadrach, Meshach, and Abednego. Why were they cast into the fiery furnace to begin with? Was it because they had done something wrong? Was it because God was angry with them? Was it because they had sinned against God? No, no, no, it was none of these things. They were cast into this fire because of their faith in God, no other reason.

1 Peter 1:7. *"That the trial of your faith, being much more precious than of gold that perisheth, though it be tried with fire, might be found unto praise and honour and glory at the appearing of Jesus Christ:"*

Shadrach, Meshach, and Abednego's faith in God caused them to refuse to bow down to the idol, and because of their faith, they were cast into the fiery furnace. We must also go through fiery trials because of our faith. They were cast into the fiery furnace because of their faith, and as sure as we have faith, we are determined for the fire, which purifies our faith and grows us spiritually.

(Notice, God blesses Peter to say that the trial of our faith is likened unto the purification of gold. When one finds gold, chances are, the gold isn't pure. Gold usually has impurities in it called dross. These are materials in the gold, which aren't gold, nor are they as valuable as gold. Therefore, the dross must be separated from the gold so that the gold would be purer, which would cause it to be more valuable. This process is called refining.

When refined, gold is melted, which grants the finer [the person refining it] the ability to separate the dross from the gold and make it purer.

The same is true with our faith, which Peter says is more valuable than gold. Our faith is purified in the fires of tribulation, as more of our flesh is burned in the fire. This grants us greater ability in our calling as we learn to trust more in God and less in ourselves.)

There are many fires the believer must be cast into, but we should understand that the fires of tribulation aren't a sign of God's wrath upon us but have come into our lives because of our faith. God doesn't allow us to live our Christian lives without tribulation, for He loves us too much for that. God has a great purpose for our lives. Therefore, He doesn't allow us to be exempted from the fires. These fires grow us, give us greater revelations of God, cause us to trust more in God's word, cause us to desire heaven more than earth, and free us from our bonds. Our faith determines that we will be cast into the fiery furnace, and God allows it so that our faith may come forth unto praise, honor, and glory at the appearance of Jesus Christ. As sure as we are determined for the fire because of our faith, God has also determined that we will see Jesus in the fire and have our bonds dissolved by the fire as well.

Earlier, I stated that I wasn't trying to use the fire's temperature to determine what Shadrach, Meshach, and Abednego were bound with when cast into the fiery furnace, but now I will use it in theory.

Why so hot? Why must the fiery furnace be heated seven times hotter? We know that Nebuchadnezzar did it because he was furious with them, for the furnace didn't have to be any hotter than normal to kill them, but we must also look for the spiritual meaning.

Let's ask two questions. What were they bound with, and why was the furnace there? The scripture doesn't directly tell us the answer to these two questions, but we may have some hints as to why the furnace was there. They had just completed the golden idol that Nebuchadnezzar commanded them to build. This was a huge idol, and it was made of gold. So, this gold would have had to be purified and shaped, which would have required a furnace. Therefore, it is probable that this furnace was there to purify and shape the gold.

Let's try to deal with the other question now. What were Shadrach, Meshach, and Abednego bound with? Nebuchadnezzar's response after looking into the fiery furnace is worth mentioning. He asked if they bound these three Hebrew men before throwing them into the fiery furnace. When the people told him they were bound before they were cast into the furnace, Nebuchadnezzar said he saw them, and they were free and walking about. This may show that he bound them with chains because he still expected them to be bound. If they were bound with ropes, I wouldn't think he would have been as surprised as he was to see that their bonds were burned. Nebuchadnezzar was very surprised to see them freed from their bonds, and I don't think he would have been that surprised if they were bound with ropes, for ropes would have burned easily in the furnace.

Nebuchadnezzar may not have considered how hot the fire was; therefore, he may have felt they should still be bound, although they were amid the flames. He may not have considered that by heating the furnace up seven times hotter than they usually heated it, the fire was now hot enough to melt chains.

However, the Bible doesn't say what they were bound with, and I cannot prove what they were bound with. Yet, in relation to the chapter of this book, I'd like to put this theory forward, which may explain the spiritual meaning behind why the furnace was heated up seven times hotter than it was normally heated. For the sake of this point, let's say that these three Hebrew men were bound with chains. We have already put forth some evidence as to why the fiery furnace was there (in the plain of Shinar), which was probably used to purify and shape the gold used in the building of the idol. If the purpose of the furnace were to heat the gold, then they would have normally kept the fire at a certain temperature, which would be the temperature necessary to melt the gold they were using to build the idol. Now, gold is softer than chains. Therefore, it would melt at a lower temperature. Yet, if these three Hebrew men were bound with chains, it would take a greater temperature to melt them than it would gold, and we can see that they were freed from their bonds while in the fire. Therefore, the spiritual reason behind the furnace being heated up seven times hotter than it was normally heated could be that God intended to melt the chains the three Hebrew men were bound with. The furnace would have normally been heated to the temperature used to melt gold, but the temperature needed to melt gold isn't hot enough to melt chains. Therefore, it must be heated up hotter than they normally would heat it for the furnace to reach the temperature required to melt chains.

This is why the fires of tribulation must sometimes be so hot in our lives, for the bonds God desires to have us freed from have a very high melting point; therefore, the furnace must be heated up seven times hotter. We fall down bound in the fiery furnace, but before we come out, we are set free from our bonds and walking amid the fire, as our faith is totally and completely in the promises of God, for we see Jesus walking in the fire with us. The circumstances of the furnace no longer cast us down, nor are we bound by the fleshly cord God intended to have burned out of our life, for we have received the strength of the promises of God and walk in them by faith. The fire no longer has power over us, seeing that faith in the promises of God has given us victory over the fire. Yet, we don't come out of the fire the same way we went in, for the fleshly cord that bound us is burned out of our lives, and a greater revelation of Christ is forged in us. We are no longer bound and fallen in the fiery furnace, for the fleshly cord that weakened us has been burned out of our lives, and now, we are strong enough to walk in the midst of the fire. The fleshly cord that held us down has now been burned by the fire. The very thing that bound us and caused us to fall unto the floor of the furnace has been burned out of our lives by the fire, and now, we have the ability to rise up and walk with a greater revelation of Jesus in our lives. The fire has now burned the fleshly cord that kept us in bondage, and we are free to walk by faith in the promises of God. This fleshly cord is now dissolved and won't be able to hold us down any longer, for the fire has burned it out of our lives. We now walk uprightly by faith, for we have been set free in the fire. We have victory over the fire in the fire. Yes, we have been freed in the fire by the fire. Yet, the furnace had to be heated seven times hotter than normal because the fleshly cord that bound us was very strong. It had a very high melting point. Therefore, the furnace was heated seven times hotter, for God wanted this strong fleshly cord to be dissolved so that we may be freed from it.

It is faith and faith alone that frees us from the fleshly cord that binds us, and it is faith and faith alone that allows us to receive a greater revelation of Jesus, not the fire, but often, the fire forces us to trust completely in the finished work of Christ. The fire is not the thing that grants us a greater revelation of the Lord or releases us from our bonds. It is faith!

Yet, it is the fire that forces us to lean harder on the promises of God. Therefore, we are set free in the fire by the fire. The fleshly cord that binds us may require a hot fire because it is not easily overcome. It is something that requires a certain amount of faith that would never be realized in our lives without the fire forcing us to do so. It takes a very hot fire to bring us to the place where we completely trust in Christ to remove the fleshly bonds that bind us. Therefore, the furnace must be heated seven times hotter than normal.

The fire is simply the vehicle that brings us to the place of faith required to see more of Christ and be freed from our bonds. These things come by faith, but it is the fire that forces us to trust in Christ's finished work. The fire brings us to a place where we know we can't trust in ourselves but must trust in the promises of God which come to us through faith in the finished work of Christ. The fire causes us to lean harder on the promises of God. Therefore, we get a greater revelation of God and are set free in the fire by the fire.

In our Christian lives, we will see many revelations and victories come to us amidst the fiery furnace. Therefore, those who will be great in theology must also be great in suffering.

# CHAPTER 12
# THE WORD OF GOD IS TRIED, AND THE WORD OF GOD TRIES US

Psalms 18:30. *"As for God, his way is perfect: the word of the LORD is tried: he is a buckler to all those that trust in him."*

Psalms 105:17-19. *"He sent a man before them, even Joseph, who was sold for a servant: Whose feet they hurt with fetters: he was laid in iron: Until the time that his word came: the word of the LORD tried him."*

As God blesses us to consider these verses, we see that the word of God is tried, and the word of God also tries us. In these verses, we see two individuals. We see that the word of God tried Joseph and that the word of God was tried in David's life.

Let's start with Joseph. Joseph's father was Jacob. God changed Jacob's name to Israel, which means, a prince who has power with God. Jacob had twelve sons, which would become the twelve tribes of Israel. God had promised that the descendants of Israel would become a great nation, dwell in the Promise Land (Israel), that He would be their God, and that the Messiah would come forth from them, etc. God had also told Abraham (Jacob's grandfather) many years prior that his descendants would be in bondage and that He would deliver them and bring them into the Promise Land.

Joseph was Jacob's most trustworthy son. Joseph told Jacob about a few of his brothers' false dealings with his father, and I'm sure his brothers figured out how Jacob learned about their evil report. Yet, it seems that Jacob had determined to set Joseph up as his successor. Jacob honored Joseph by making him a coat of many colors. Jacob set Joseph in a position that would have made his brothers accountable to him in some respects. This caused his brothers to become jealous of him. It alienated Joseph from his brothers.

Our text shows that Joseph was sent to Egypt before his family. Why? God had determined that the Israelites would be moved to Egypt for 215 years. The circumstances that would come to pass, which would cause the Israelites to move to Egypt, would be a seven-year famine. Therefore, God sent Joseph to Egypt before them so there would be food for the famine and to take care of the Israelites when they arrived.

So, how did Joseph end up in Egypt? To start, God gave Joseph two dreams. He dreamed that he and his brothers were gathering wheat into sheaves. Then, all his brother's sheaves bowed down before his sheave. The other dream was that the sun, moon, and eleven stars bowed down before him.

Joseph's brothers interpreted these dreams to mean they would bow down before him. They felt that Joseph saw himself as being their ruler. They didn't see these dreams as God-given but viewed them as Joseph's pride and desires. This caused great anger to be added to their jealousy. They despised Joseph. Yet, Jacob adored him.

While Joseph's brothers were away with the flocks one day, Jacob sent Joseph to check on them. When his brothers saw Joseph coming, they were enraged, saying to one another, *"Behold, this dreamer cometh. Come now therefore, and let us slay him, and cast him into some pit, and we will say, Some evil beast hath devoured him: and we shall see what will become of his dreams"* (Genesis 37:19-20). However, Reuben, the oldest brother, delivered him out of their hands, saying, *"Shed no blood, but cast him into this pit that is in the wilderness, and lay no hand upon him; that he might rid him out of their hands, to deliver him to his father again"* (Genesis 37:22). So, when Joseph came unto them, they stripped him of his coat of many colors and cast him into a pit that had no water in it. When they set down to eat, they beheld some Ishmeelite traders from Gilead with camels bearing spices, balm, and myrrh to take to Egypt. Then Judah, the fourth oldest brother, said, let's sell him to these traders and not shed his blood, for he is our brother. So, they sold him for twenty pieces of silver, and the merchantmen brought him to Egypt.

When Reuben returns, he finds out what has happened and rips his clothes, for Rueben intended to deliver Joseph back to his father. Then, the brothers killed a goat and dipped Joseph's coat in it. They took Joseph's coat back to Jacob, covered in goat's blood, telling him we found this, asking him if this was Joseph's coat. Jacob immediately knew it was Joseph's coat and concluded that he had been torn to pieces by a wild animal. Then Jacob ripped his clothes, put on sackcloth, and mourned greatly over Joseph for many days, refusing to be comforted, saying, *"I will go down into the grave unto my son mourning"* (Genesis 37:35).

In Egypt, Joseph was sold as a slave to a prominent man named Potiphar. Potiphar was an officer of the Pharaoh and captain of his guard, which would have caused him to spend much time away from home. Yet, the Lord was with Joseph and prospered everything he touched. Potiphar noticed that the Lord prospered everything Joseph set his hands to. Therefore, Potiphar promoted Joseph to be the overseer of his house and all that he had. Because of this, God blessed Potiphar's house and all he had for Joseph's sake. Potiphar placed everything he had into Joseph's hands to the point that he didn't even know what he had except for the food he ate.

The Bible teaches us that Joseph was a nice-looking man, and Potiphar's wife set her eyes upon him. Potiphar's wife enticed Joseph to sleep with her, but Joseph refused, saying,

Genesis 39:8-9. *"Behold, my master wotteth not what is with me in the house, and he hath committed all that he hath to my hand; There is none greater in this house than I; neither hath he kept back any thing from me but thee, because thou art his wife: how then can I do this great wickedness, and sin against God?"*

Yet, day after day, she continued to entice Joseph to sleep with her, but he continually refused. Then, a day came when Joseph went into the house to perform the duties his position required, and no one else was in the house with him. While there, Potiphar's wife grabbed him by his garment, saying, *"Lie with me"* (Genesis 39:12), but he ran out of the house, leaving his garment in her hand. When she saw that Joseph had left his garment in her hand and ran out of the house, she called for the men of the house, telling them that Joseph tried to rape her, and when she cried out with a loud voice, he fled, leaving his garment in her hands. So, she laid up Joseph's garment and waited for Potiphar to return home. When he returned, she told her husband that Joseph tried to rape her, using his garment as evidence to confirm her lie. When Potiphar heard this, he was furious and imprisoned Joseph, where the king's prisoners were kept.

Yet, God was still with Joseph through all of this. God continued to prosper Joseph, although he was locked away in a dungeon. There are no limits for God. The prison walls and bars couldn't stop God's blessings upon Joseph. The Saint of God will never find themselves in a place where the Lord is not there with them, for David said, *"If I ascend up into heaven, thou art there: if I make my bed in hell, behold, thou art there."* (Psalms 139:8). Though Joseph was in prison, God's mercy was there with him and blessed him to find favor with the warden.

The warden must have noticed the favor of God upon Joseph as Potiphar did, because he placed the entire prison under his hand, making him the overseer of it, and God caused everything Joseph did to prosper.

While Joseph was in prison, Pharaoh's chief butler and chief baker had offended him. Therefore, Pharaoh placed them in the same prison Joseph was overseeing. After a while, the chief butler and the chief baker both dreamed a dream during the same night that troubled them. When Joseph came to them in the morning, he noticed something was bothering them. So, he asked them, why do you look so sad today? They said we have dreamed a dream, and there is no interpreter to interpret it. Joseph said, *"Do not interpretations belong to God?"* (Genesis 40:8). Then Joseph asked them to tell him about their dreams.

The chief butler told him his dream, saying,

Genesis 40:9-11. *"In my dream, behold, a vine was before me; And in the vine were three branches: and it was as though it budded, and her blossoms shot forth; and the clusters thereof brought forth ripe grapes: And Pharaoh's cup was in my hand: and I took the grapes, and pressed them into Pharaoh's cup, and I gave the cup into Pharaoh's hand."*

When Joseph heard the chief butler's dream, he said,

Genesis 40:12-15. *"This is the interpretation of it: The three branches are three days: Yet within three days shall Pharaoh lift up thine head, and restore thee unto thy place: and thou shalt deliver Pharaoh's cup into his hand, after the former manner when thou wast his butler. But think on me when it shall be well with thee, and shew kindness, I pray thee, unto me, and make mention of me unto Pharaoh, and bring me out of this house: For indeed I was stolen away out of the land of the Hebrews: and here also have I done nothing that they should put me into the dungeon."*

When the chief baker heard this, he also desired Joseph to interpret his dream.

Genesis 40:16-17. *"When the chief baker saw that the interpretation was good, he said unto Joseph, I also was in my dream, and, behold, I had three white baskets on my head: And in the uppermost basket there was of all manner of bakemeats for Pharaoh; and the birds did eat them out of the basket upon my head."*

When Joseph heard the chief baker's dream, he said,

Genesis 40:18-19. *"And Joseph answered and said, This is the interpretation thereof: The three baskets are three days: Yet within three days shall Pharaoh lift up thy head from off thee, and shall hang thee on a tree; and the birds shall eat thy flesh from off thee."*

Three days after these dreams were interpreted, it was Pharaoh's birthday, and he made a great feast for all his servants. On that very day, three days after Joseph interpreted the chief butler and chief baker's dreams, the interpretations came to pass exactly as God blessed Joseph to interpret them. The chief butler was released from prison and restored to his office as Pharaoh's cupbearer, and the chief baker was hanged on the same day. Yet, the chief butler didn't remember Joseph as he had requested, but he forgot about him and didn't speak to Pharaoh on his behalf.

Two years had passed since God blessed Joseph to interpret the chief butler and chief baker's dreams. Then Pharaoh dreams two dreams, which were,

Genesis 41:1-7. *"And it came to pass at the end of two full years, that Pharaoh dreamed: and, behold, he stood by the river. And, behold, there came up out of the river seven well favoured kine and fatfleshed; and they fed in a meadow. And, behold, seven other kine came up after them out of the river, ill favoured and leanfleshed; and stood by the other kine upon the brink of the river. And the ill favoured and lean fleshed kine did eat up the seven well favoured and fat kine. So Pharaoh awoke.*

*And he slept and dreamed the second time: and, behold, seven ears of corn came up upon one stalk, rank and good. And, behold seven thin ears and blasted with the east wind sprung up after them. And the seven thin ears devoured the seven rank and full ears. And Pharaoh awoke, and, behold, it was a dream."*

When Pharaoh awoke in the morning after these dreams, his spirit troubled him. Although he didn't know what these dreams meant, he understood that there was something extraordinary about them. Therefore, he sent for Egypt's magicians and wise men, wanting them to interpret these two dreams. After he told them the dreams, they couldn't interpret them. At that moment, the chief butler remembered Joseph.

Genesis 41:9-13. *"Then spake the chief butler unto Pharaoh, saying, I do remember my faults this day: Pharaoh was wroth with his servants, and put me in ward in the captain of the guard's house, both me and the chief baker: And we dreamed a dream in one night, I and he; we dreamed each man according to the interpretation of his dream. And there was there with us a young man, an Hebrew, servant to the captain of the guard; and we told him, and he interpreted to us our dreams; to each man according to his dream, he did interpret. And it came to pass, as he interpreted to us, so it was; me he restored unto mine office, and him he hanged."*

When Pharaoh heard this, he sent for Joseph and his servants went and retrieved him, quickly bringing him out of the dungeon. After shaving himself and changing his clothes, Joseph was brought before Pharaoh. Pharaoh speaks to Joseph, saying, *"I have dreamed a dream, and there is none that can interpret it: and I have heard say of thee, that thou canst understand a dream to interpret it"* (Genesis 41:15). Joseph answered Pharaoh, saying, *"It is not in me: God shall give Pharaoh an answer of peace"* (Genesis 41:16).

What Joseph was saying is that he can't interpret dreams by his own abilities; only God can do that, but he believes that God will bless him to interpret the dreams, and by doing so, the Lord will give Pharaoh a peaceful interpretation. Pharaoh was extremely troubled by these dreams, but Joseph was confident that God would bless him to interpret them, and this interpretation would bring peace to Pharaoh.

So, Pharaoh tells Joseph the two dreams concerning the seven fat-fleshed kine (cows) and the seven lean-fleshed kine. He tells him that the seven lean-fleshed kine ate up the seven fat-fleshed kine. Yet, it wasn't noticeable after eating them because they were still as lean-fleshed and ill-favored as they were before they ate them. Then he tells him the dream of the seven good and rank ears of corn that came up on one stalk, and the seven thin ears of corn blasted with the east wind which sprang up after them. He tells him that the seven thin ears of corn devoured the seven rank ears of corn.

After hearing the two dreams, God blesses Joseph to interpret them, saying,

Genesis 41:25-36. *"And Joseph said unto Pharaoh, The dream of Pharaoh is one: God hath shewed Pharaoh what he is about to do. The seven good kine are seven years; and the seven good ears are seven years: the dream is one. And the seven thin and ill favoured kine that came up after them are seven years; and the seven empty ears blasted with the east wind shall be seven years of famine. This is the thing which I have spoken unto Pharaoh: What God is about to do he sheweth unto Pharaoh. Behold, there come seven years of great plenty throughout all the land of Egypt: And there shall arise after them seven years of famine; and all the plenty shall be forgotten in the land of Egypt; and the famine shall consume the land; And the plenty shall not be known in the land by reason of that famine following; for it shall be very grievous. And for that the dream was doubled unto Pharaoh twice; it is because the thing is established by God, and God will shortly bring it to pass. Now therefore let Pharaoh look out a man discreet and wise and set him over the land of Egypt. Let Pharaoh do this, and let him appoint officers over the land, and take up the fifth part of the land of Egypt in the seven plenteous years. And let them gather all the food of those good years that come, and lay up corn under the hand of Pharaoh, and let them keep food in the cities. And that food shall be for store to the land against the seven years of famine, which shall be in the land of Egypt; that the land perish not through the famine."*

When Pharaoh heard this, the interpretation was good in his eyes and in the eyes of all his servants. After the interpretation, we read,

Genesis 41:38-45. *"And Pharaoh said unto his servants, Can we find such a one as this is, a man in whom the Spirit of God is? And Pharaoh said unto Joseph, Forasmuch as God hath shewed thee all this, there is none so discreet and wise as thou art: Thou shalt be over my house, and according unto thy word shall all my people be ruled: only in the throne will I be greater than thou. And Pharaoh said unto Joseph, See, I have set thee over all the land of Egypt. And Pharaoh took off his ring from his hand, and put it upon Joseph's hand, and arrayed him in vestures of fine linen, and put a gold chain about his neck; And he made him to ride in the second chariot which he had; and they cried before him, Bow the knee: and he made him ruler over all the land of Egypt. And Pharaoh said unto Joseph, I am Pharaoh, and without thee shall no man lift up his hand or foot in all the land of Egypt. And Pharaoh called Joseph's name Zaphnathpaaneah; and he gave him to wife Asenath, the daughter of Potipherah priest of On. And Joseph went out over all the land of Egypt."*

Joseph became an exceedingly great and important man in Egypt. The Bible says Joseph was the governor, ruling over all the land, meaning he literally ruled all of Egypt (Genesis 41:41). Other than the Pharaoh, no one throughout Egypt held a higher rank than Joseph. Egypt was the most glorious, powerful, influential, and wealthiest nation on the face of the earth at that time, and God set Joseph over every bit of it.

Joseph also managed Egypt's food supply for 14 years, meaning he managed the food supply for the entire world during the 7 years of famine. People came from far and wide, literally everywhere, to buy food from the Egyptian storehouses he oversaw, for the Bible says that the famine was over all the face of the earth (Genesis 41:56). God blessed Joseph to supervise this incredible food supply flawlessly, gathering, storing, and distributing it throughout Egypt and the known world at that time.

The world's wealth would have flowed through Egypt during the years of the famine, undoubtedly increasing its wealth exponentially. During the famine, many people came to Egypt to buy food, for Egypt had plenty to spare because of Joseph's wise instructions, which were the precise directions he received directly from God.

Joseph's family, living in Canaan (Israel, The Promise Land), were very distressed during this time because of the famine. Yet, they had heard that there was food in Egypt. Therefore, Jacob (Joseph's father) would send his sons to Egypt to buy food during this time. When they first came, Joseph recognized them, but they didn't recognize him. They came and bowed before him, and when they did, Joseph remembered the dreams of his youth, which proclaimed that this would happen (his brothers would bow before him).

After some time and certain circumstances, Joseph eventually revealed himself to them, letting them know he was their brother. He told them not to be angry with themselves for selling him into slavery; though they meant it for evil, God meant it for good so that their family (the family of Abraham) and many others could be kept alive during the famine. Joseph had his brothers return to Canaan to bring his entire family to Egypt so he could take care of them. The children of Israel would remain in Egypt for the next 215 years until God sent Moses and Aaron to deliver them from Egyptian bondage and bring them to the Promised Land.

Now, let's look at David for a moment, God willing. When David was born, Saul was the king of Israel. Saul became king of Israel 10 years before David was born. God had called and anointed Saul for this position. God worked mighty things in Saul's life. Saul was a great warrior, and under his reign, God blessed him to unite the twelve tribes of Israel, and they began to come out from under the oppression of the other peoples, tribes, nations, and kingdoms that dwelt in the Promise Land.

Yet, Saul became very prideful, and because of this, God told him through the prophet Samuel that his kingdom wouldn't continue, telling him that He would raise up another king who had a heart after the Lord's own heart and that He had torn the kingdom from him and had given it unto another who was better than him.

For the rest of Saul's life, he would do everything in his power to establish his kingdom, although God had torn it away from him. For the rest of his life, he would try to work things out so that his son could reign after he died, having the future kings of Israel come from his descendants, although the Lord had said it wouldn't happen because of his disobedience. He wanted the throne of Israel to be called the throne of Saul, although God had rejected him and his house and given the kingdom to another.

After God told Saul He had torn the kingdom away from him, He sent Samuel to Jesse's house to anoint one of his sons to be the next king of Israel. When Samuel arrived, Jesse gathered his sons and caused them to pass before Samuel. When Eliab passed before him, Samuel thought he was surely the one God had chosen to be king because he looked like a king, but God spoke to Samuel and told him not to look at their outward appearance, for God looks upon the heart. So, all seven of Jesse's sons were gathered before Samuel and passed before him, and God hadn't instructed him to anoint any of them to be the next king of Israel. Then Samuel asked Jesse, is this all your sons? Jesse said the youngest is not here because he is keeping the sheep. Samuel told Jesse to send and fetch his youngest son, for he wouldn't sit down until he came. So, Jesse fetched his youngest son, David.

The Bible describes David as being ruddy (probably meaning he had red hair), of a beautiful countenance (possibly meaning that he had pretty eyes), and that he was good to look to (probably meaning that he was a good-looking fellow).

When David arrived, the Lord spoke to Samuel and said, *"Arise, anoint him: for this is he"* (1 Samuel 16:12). Then Samuel took his horn of oil and anointed him in the midst of his brethren (family), and the Spirit of the Lord came upon David from that day forward.

After David was anointed king of Israel, Samuel left, and David went back to tending the flocks. While tending the sheep, a lion and a bear took a lamb out of the flock. David killed both of them in what seems to have been in a supernatural manner, for the Bible says this about the encounter with these two ferocious animals, *"And David said unto Saul, Thy servant kept his father's sheep, and there came a lion and a bear, and took a lamb out of the flock: and I went out after him, and delivered it out of his mouth: and when he arose against me, I caught him by his beard, and smote him, and slew him"* (1 Samuel 17:34-35).

After David's anointing, Saul began to be troubled by an evil spirit. Saul's counselors told him they should seek out a cunning player of music to play before him, which would cause this evil spirit to retreat from him. Someone recommended David. Evidently, they knew that he was very skillful on the harp. So, they brought David to Saul, and when the evil spirit troubled him, David would play the harp, and the evil spirit would leave. This seems to have continued for some time, and Saul thought so highly of David that he made him his armor-bearer.

Sometime later, war broke out between Israel and the Philistines. Sometime before this war, David had left Saul's presence and returned home to tend his father's sheep. The Philistines gathered their armies in a place called Shochoh, located in Judah, which was part of the Promised Land, which God had given to the children of Israel. So, King Saul gathered his troops and led all the military-aged men to fight against the Philistines, and three of David's older brothers joined the Israelite army.

During this battle between Israel and the Philistines, Goliath, the giant, went down into the valley, which separated these two armies and challenged Israel. The challenge was for the army of Israel to pick out a champion to come down and fight with Goliath. If the Israelite champion won, then the Philistines would unconditionally surrender to the Israelites, and if Goliath won, then the Israelites would have to surrender to the Philistines unconditionally. Goliath also cried out while challenging them, saying, *"I defy the armies of Israel this day"* (1 Samuel 17:10), meaning that he defied the armies of the living God.

The Bible says that Goliath's height was six cubits and a span. This would mean that Goliath was a nine-foot, nine-inch giant (if a cubit is 18 inches and a span is nine inches, which most scholars think it to be, although other scholars think a cubit is greater than 18 inches). The Bible says that Goliath was armed with much armor, had a helmet of brass upon his head, wore a coat of mail, had greaves (shin plates) of brass upon his legs, a target of brass between his shoulders (a round shield-like plate covering his chest and abdomen), a unique sword, a huge spear, and had an armor bearer who went before him carrying a shield.

The children of Israel were terrified of Goliath and wouldn't accept his challenge. Yet, for forty days, morning and evening, Goliath would walk down into the valley and bellow out this challenge, and every time he bellowed out from the valley below, Israel would tremble with fear.

During this time, David was home tending the flocks because he was too young to join the army (According to the Law of Moses, one must be at least 20 years old to fight in the army). David's three eldest brothers were fighting with the army, but David was too young.

Well, one day, while the Israelites and Philistines were still at war, Jesse, David's father, told him to take some food to his brothers and others in the army of Israel, and David did.

When David arrived at the site, he left the food with a person and went down and shouted for the battle. While there, he heard Goliath bellow out from the valley, defying the armies of Israel and offering his challenge. The men around him asked him, *"Have ye seen this man that is come up? surely to defy Israel is he come up: and it shall be, that the man who killeth him, the king will enrich him with great riches, and will give him his daughter, and make his father's house free in Israel"* (1 Samuel 17:25). When David heard this, he asked the men around him, *"What shall be done to the man that killeth this Philistine, and taketh away the reproach from Israel? for who is this uncircumcised Philistine, that he should defy the armies of the living God"* (1 Samuel 17:26)? In other words, what reward will the king give to the man that accepts this Philistine's challenge and defeats him? David was informed of the reward, which would be that the king would make the person who kills Goliath extremely rich, give him his daughter to be his wife (making that person part of the royal family, son-in-law to the king), and that person wouldn't have to pay any more taxes for the rest of his life.

When the people saw how David acted and spoke, they knew he was courageous enough to accept Goliath's challenge. His brother tried dissuading him, but David wouldn't listen. Sure, his older brother was looking out for him, trying to protect him. Yet, David said, *"What have I now done? Is there not a cause"* (1 Samuel 17:29)? In other words, David understood that his father had sent him to the army of Israel to deliver food, but God had sent him to slay a giant.

When the people rehearsed David's words to Saul, Saul called for him, telling him, you are too young to fight this giant, for this giant is not only big and strong but also very well trained in the art of war.

Then David answered King Saul like this,

1 Samuel 17:34-36. *"And David said unto Saul, Thy servant kept his father's sheep, and there came a lion, and a bear, and took a lamb out of the flock: And I went out after him, and smote him, and delivered it out of his mouth: and when he arose against me, I caught him by his beard, and smote him,*

*and slew him. Thy servant slew both the lion and the bear: and this uncircumcised Philistine shall be as one of them, seeing he hath defied the armies of the living God."*

After the conversation, Saul agreed to let David go into the valley and fight with Goliath, but Saul wanted to arm him first. Therefore, Saul gave David his armor, which would have been the best in the whole army of Israel. After David suited up, he told Saul he couldn't take his armor because he had never tested it. Therefore, David refused to go armed against Goliath.

It is also noteworthy to notice that David called Goliath an uncircumcised Philistine. What does circumcision or uncircumcision have to do with anything concerning this face-off? The Israelites were circumcised, which meant they had a covenant with God, and inside of this covenant, God gave the land that the Philistines were contesting to the Israelites. Therefore, David is saying that this guy has no covenant right to this land. God gave this land to His covenant people. Therefore, I will defeat this giant. Although I'm a youth with no experience in war, and the giant is stronger than me, I will win the challenge because God's covenant is stronger than the giant. God's covenant can't be defeated! Therefore, David went down into the valley to fight the giant by faith in God's covenant with Israel.

So, David took his staff in his hand, chose five smooth stones out of the brook, placed them in his shepherd's bag (traveling pouch), took his sling in his hand, and walked down into the valley to meet Goliath. When Goliath saw David, he said,

1 Samuel 17:42-44. *"And when the Philistine looked about, and saw David, he disdained him: for he was but a youth, and ruddy, and of a fair countenance. And the Philistine said unto David, Am I a dog, that thou comest to me with staves? And the Philistine cursed David by his gods. And the Philistine said to David, Come to me, and I will give thy flesh unto the fowls of the air, and to the beasts of the field."*

To which David replied,

1 Samuel 17:45-47. *"Then said David to the Philistine, Thou comest to me with a sword, and with a spear, and with a shield: but I come to thee in the name of the LORD of hosts, the God of the armies of Israel, whom thou hast defied. This day will the LORD deliver thee into mine hand; and I will smite thee, and take thine head from thee; and I will give the carcasses of the host of the Philistines this day unto the fowls of the air, and to the wild beasts of the earth; that all the earth may know that there is a God in Israel. And all this assembly shall know that the LORD saveth not with sword and spear: for the battle is the LORD'S, and he will give you into our hands."*

After this, the Philistine arose and approached David, and David hastened and ran towards the army to meet the Philistine.

I think David's boldness and courage during this time is worth noting. The Philistine was confident he would win the battle; David was no match for him physically or militarily, for Goliath was a giant and extremely trained in the art of war. Yet, we see that David is also extremely confident, for he speaks as though he has already won the challenge before it takes place.

Yet, we should notice the faith both fighters had. The Philistine trusted in his great strength and military training. The Philistine trusted in himself, saying that he would feed David's corpse to the birds. Yet, David proclaimed that God would deliver the giant into his hands. David was very confident in God, saying that God would not only bless him to behead the giant, but would also feed the flesh of the Philistine army to the birds of the air and wild beasts of the field.

The time had come for the duel between these two champions to take place. David ran towards the giant, placed his hand into his bag, took out one of the stones, slung it, and hit Goliath so hard that the stone literally sunk into the giant's forehead. The giant fell to the ground, and David took Goliath's sword out of the sheath and cut off the giant's head.

When the Philistine army saw this, they ran for their lives. When the army of Israel saw this, they arose, shouted, pursued the fleeing Philistines, slew many of them, and then returned and spoiled their tents. After this, Saul enlisted David in his military, making him a general in the army.

After the slaying of Goliath, David led the army of Israel and played music for Saul when the evil spirit troubled him. Although David was a great blessing to the kingdom of Israel, Saul became increasingly jealous of him. Jealous because the women sang songs that ascribed greater exploits to David than to Saul. Saul also perceived that David was the one Samuel spoke of as the next king of Israel. Therefore, he sought to lay traps for him and kill him.

Saul offered David his daughter (Michal) to be his wife, hoping that he could use her as a snare for David. Yet, David was very modest and had no dowry for a royal bride, nor did he view it as a light thing to be the king's son-in-law. So, Saul saw this as an opportunity to have David slain. Saul had his men tell David that the king desired no bounty for his daughter's hand in marriage but desired a hundred foreskins of dead Philistine soldiers to be the dowry for this royal bride. Saul thought David would be killed trying to obtain these foreskins in battle. Yet, God blessed David to fight valiantly, and he brought back two hundred foreskins to Saul instead of the one hundred he requested. Then Saul gave David his daughter to be his wife.

Saul's jealousy towards David increased, and he continually tried to find a way to kill him. Saul knew that David was the one Samuel spoke about, who would take his place as king. Therefore, Saul spoke to Jonathan (his son and next in line to be king according to succession) and all his servants, saying they should kill David, but Jonathan told David about his father's plans. Jonathan told David to hide himself until he could talk to his father. After Jonathan spoke to his father about David, Saul swore before the Lord that he wouldn't have him killed.

Afterwards, the evil Spirit troubled Saul, and David played music for him. While David was playing before the king, Saul took hold of his javelin and threw it at David, intending to kill him. Yet, the Lord blessed David, and he dodged the javelin and fled from Saul. Then Saul sent some men to watch David's house, planning to slay him in the morning, but David's wife, Saul's daughter, heard of it and told David, and he escaped through a window and went and hid himself.

After this, David lived as a fugitive while Saul and his army continually sought to kill him. Yet, God sent David six hundred men to be his army. For years, Saul sought David with a mighty army, and David was so distressed by it that he once told Jonathan that there was only a step between him and death (1 Samuel 20:3).

So, Saul continually pursued David, trying to kill him while David hid in caves and anywhere he could. David even had two chances to kill Saul but didn't, for he said Saul is the Lord's anointed. David goes on to tell his men that he knows he will be king, but he will not kill Saul, for no person can touch the anointed of God and be guiltless. David goes on to say, concerning Saul, *"As the LORD liveth, the LORD shall smite him; or his day shall come to die; or he shall descend into battle, and perish"* (1 Samuel 26:10). In other words, David is saying, I will not try to establish my own kingdom, for the Lord is the One Who has chosen me to be king. Therefore, God will work it out in His own way.

David knew that Saul must be moved out of the way for him to become king. Yet, he knew it wasn't his responsibility to remove Saul from the throne. Therefore, he says God will do it in some form or fashion. Although David didn't know how God would do it, he mentions three ways it might happen (The Lord will smite him, his day shall come to die, or he will die in battle [1 Samuel 26:10]).

We can learn a lot from this. God chose, anointed, and ordained David to be king. Yet David didn't try to make himself king, even when it was in his power to kill Saul twice. David understood that God was the One Who ordained him to be king, which means it was God's responsibility to make him king and to do whatever needed to be done to set David on the throne.

This is also true with our callings as Christians. We don't have to help God out. God will move the pieces of the chessboard by His own power, His own wisdom, and in His own time. One may say, do we not have responsibilities as well? Do we do nothing to bring this call to pass? Our responsibility is as simple as David's. We are to trust in God's promises.

David trusted that God would place him on the throne. David knew if he set himself on the throne by his own power and wisdom, someone could dethrone him with their power and wisdom, but if God put him upon the throne, he could never be moved. He could never be moved because he would be set there by God, and for one to dethrone him, one would have to overcome God's power and wisdom to do so.

Therefore, we shouldn't try to establish our own kingdom, seeing that the things we build can corrode or be torn down by others. Yet, if God builds it, then corrosion nor any power of the earth can overtake it. What the Lord does, He does forever; nothing can be added to it, nor taken from it (Ecclesiastes 3:14).

There were many more trying times for David. Naturally, according to the circumstances he faced, it seemed that he would also be slain on other occasions, as he fought battles and was pursued by Saul day and night. David eventually fled Israel, the Promise Land, the place God promised David would rule, and went to live in the land of the Philistines because he was afraid that Saul would eventually kill him. During that time, things got so hard for David and those with him that his men spoke of stoning him. Yet, while they were speaking of stoning David, at that very moment, Saul was either descending into battle where he would be killed or was already lying dead on the battlefield. However, they didn't know it. They were ready to give up on the dream, God's promise, the Kingdom of David, which will one day be Christ's throne, as He sits on the throne of His father David, ruling the entire earth in righteousness for 1,000 years. It had gotten so dark that they had almost or completely lost view of God's promise concerning David. Yet, amid this darkness, the Bible says that David encouraged himself in the Lord his God (1 Samuel 30:6).

My brothers and sisters in Christ, it may be dark in your lives as you read this. Still, I encourage you to do as David did in his dark times and encourage yourselves in the Lord. Here, we see it was in David's darkest time that God worked the greatest work in his life. In only a few short days, God's promise to David would come to fruition, although it seemed so far away.

After the death of Saul, southern Israel (Judah) anointed David to be their king, and afterwards, God made sure that David was king of the entire nation of Israel, just as He promised him over a decade earlier.

Now that God has blessed me to speak somewhat about Joseph and David let's get back to the title of this chapter. The title of this chapter is, the word of God is tried, and the word of God tries us. David spoke of these things in the Psalms when he said the word of the Lord is tried, and Joseph was tried by the word. Now that we have briefly summarized David and Joseph's lives, let's try to expound on the verses we used for the text of this chapter, God willing.

Let's look at the journey that brought Joseph to this place of great authority. It all started over a decade earlier. It all started with two dreams from God. Joseph dreamed of his brother's sheaves bowing before his. He also dreamed of the sun, moon, and eleven stars bowing before him. So, God had called Joseph to a position of great authority years before it came to pass. God had promised Joseph that he would be a man of great power years before sitting in the governor's chair, ruling over the land of Egypt as the second most powerful man on the planet. Yet, it didn't happen immediately, quickly, or even soon. It happened many years later.

David's journey isn't the same as Joseph's, but still similar in many ways. After Samuel anointed David, the Lord blessed him to do amazing things. However, this also set him on a collision course with Saul. This caused David to live like a vagabond, being destitute, persecuted, rejected, reproached, and one step away from death. David suffered many things between being anointed king and sitting on the throne of Israel.

Joseph also suffered many things between the time of the dreams and sitting in the governor's chair, ruling over all of Egypt as the world's second most powerful man.

Many times, certain callings are revealed to the children of God days, months, and even years before they come to pass. David was anointed king of Israel over a decade before he set on the throne. God promised Abraham he would have a son 25 years before Isaac was born. Joseph was promised a position of great authority over a decade before it came to pass. Why? The word of God tries us. We must be steadfast in faith, continuing to believe in the promise while being prepared for it in many cases.

So, why does God give us the promise ahead of time? Why doesn't He wait until it is time for the promise to come to pass and then give it to us? God willing, I'd like to mention two reasons.

First, God's promise is the hope we need to sustain us until it comes to pass. It is the hope we need while the word of God tries us. While we are being tried by the word (the trying that prepares us for the promise, our calling), we need hope to get through the trials. Hope comes from God's word (Psalms 119:81,114). The promise God gives to us is the ray of sunshine that shines deep in our hearts. It is a ray of sunshine, which no fetter can bind, a ray of sunshine, which the lies of Potiphar's wife can't quench, a ray of sunshine that can light up the deepest darkest dungeon of Egypt, a ray of sunshine that lets us know the word is trying us that we may be prepared for the fulfillment of it.

God had called Joseph to be an enormous man of power, but the trying of the word prepared him for it. He was tried repeatedly until the word came to pass, and then the trials ceased when he set in the governor's chair, ruling Egypt for some 80 years to come.

Secondly, the word of God must be tried in our sight (Psalms 18:30). Although we view the word of the Lord as pure, we often don't or can't see how pure it really is.

Therefore, it is tried in our sight so that we can see it as purer than when we first viewed it.

When we are being tried by the word of the Lord, which is preparing us for its fulfillment, the word of God is also being tried. The word of God is being refined and becoming purer in our sight as we, too, are being refined. Every fire we go through, we see the word of God to be purer than before. Why? It continues to be sufficient for everything we face on our way to the governor's chair. We see that the word of the Lord is not only able to deliver us from the pit but also from Potiphar's wife, and not only able to deliver us from Potiphar's wife but from the prison as well. We see the word of God will not only deliver us from the paw of the lion and the bear but also deliver Goliath into our hands, and not only Goliath, but it can also deliver us from Saul, the Philistines, and everything else that stands between us and the throne of Israel.

Every fire we must pass through as the word of God tries us causes us to see the word of God to be purer than before. Why? We see that it is also sufficient for the next trial we face. We repeatedly see something new in this promise as the word of God is tried in our lives. Every test we face, we see that the word of God is sufficient for the challenge. We see it to be purer and purer after every fire. The word of God is not only sufficient for the pit, the lion, and the bear but also for the prison, Goliath, and all the enemies of the promise we carry in our hearts.

At first, we hold the word of God in our hands, but trial after trial breaks us more and more, and we see the word of God become purer and purer. At first, we hold the promise in our hands, but through every trial, it comes closer to our hearts. Finally, these trials become the branding iron that brands the promise upon our hearts.

We thought the pit would kill us, we thought the prison would finish us, but we see that the promise is sufficient. More of ourselves has fallen away, burned up by the fiery trial, but the promise remains intact. We get to the point where we see how impossible it is for the word of God to come to pass in our lives by human hands or wisdom, and therefore, we learn to trust solely in it. We eventually come to the place where all we can see is the promise, for it is our only hope. It has been tried in our lives repeatedly, which causes us to cling to it, knowing that somehow or someway, it will bring us to the governor's chair when it seems impossible for this ever to happen.

The word of God, like gold, is tried in our lives, and as gold, after every refining, becomes more precious unto us. We finally are brought to the point where it becomes the main treasure of our hearts and the only thing we will lean on. It has become our meat and drink. It strengthens us, delivers us, and causes us to know that this prison isn't strong enough to lock it up. It becomes more valuable unto us, for we now see that it, and it alone, can bring us out of the pit, out of the prison, and set us in the palace. We no longer value any fleshly thing to be the means by which we will sit in the governor's chair, for we know that only the promises of God can accomplish it. They become the most valuable thing in our lives, for every fire has caused the word of the Lord to be purified in our sight. Now, after the pit and Potiphar's, we sit in the prison, and the only thing we treasure is the promises of God. The pit, Potiphar's, and the prison have caused us to stop treasuring all the other things we held so fondly to, for the word of God has been purified in our lives and has become our greatest treasure.

God's word is magnificent! His promises are great! They are unfailing! Sometimes, we may feel that the word of God is too good to be true. We may feel that His promises are too great to expect. Yet, when His word is tried, it will come to pass. When His word is tested, it will accomplish every promise. When we test God's word by trusting in it, we will see that it always passes with flying colors, for God will perform every word we trust Him to fulfill.

In David's distress, the word of God was tried. As David's enemies compassed him about, the word of God was tested. When David tried the word of God, we see that God became a buckler unto Him, and he was preserved from the hands of his powerful enemies who sought his demise. David trusted in the word of the Lord (he was called to be king), and God wrought miraculous things in his life, as the entire chapter of Psalms 18 and many other scriptures proclaim.

The word of God is tried by faith. We test the word of God by trusting in it. When we do, we will see that the word of God is true, although it promises the miraculous. The word of God will never fail, for God is a buckler unto them that trust in Him.

The word of God is tested when it makes promises to us. God promised David that he would be king of Israel. This seemed impossible, and Saul's kingdom tried to kill him because of this promise. Yet, through all this, God delivered David, and he set upon the throne of Israel just as God's word said he would.

There will always be resistance to God's word, but God's word will truly come to pass, for God will personally watch over His word and ensure that none of His promises fall to the ground.

The word of God is tried (refined). The refining process removes the dross from the gold so that it may become purer, which causes it to become more valuable. Yet, we see that the word of God is purified. Why would the word of God need to be purified? Isn't it perfect already? Isn't it pure to begin with? Sure, it is, but it must be purified in us. It must be seen as purified in our own eyes. It must be purified in our sight. It is not that the word of God must become purer because it is already perfect, but that it must become purer in our sight. David said that God's word was so pure that it was as silver tried in the furnace, purified seven times (Psalms 12:6). Here, we see that the word of God is so pure that it can't become any purer. We can also see how David viewed the word of God, for he viewed it as completely pure.

God gave David the promise of being king of Israel, although it seemed impossible for this promise to come to pass. Yet, through every trial David went through, the word of God became purer unto him. Through these trials, David would be blessed to see the word in purer form. David would see more of this promise every time he was placed in the fires of tribulation. The word of God was already pure, but the more fires God blessed David to walk through, the purer the word of God became in his sight. The truer David saw it to be. The more fires God blessed David to walk through, the more precious the word of God would have become to him. Every time God's promise delivered David, he saw it purer than before. David would see that it was pure enough to deliver him from sure destruction and that it could be established in his life.

Every time the word of God is tested in our lives, we will find it sufficient for the fire we walk through. Every fire causes the promises to be revealed to us in greater detail. We see its power, faithfulness, and love as it becomes even more precious unto us. Though the fires get hotter, we see the word of God purer every time. We come to the place where we understand that nothing can stop the word of God in our lives. Therefore, we trust it to be our buckler (breastplate of protection). We no longer trust in ourselves or anything else but trust in the promises of God, knowing He will be our shield and exceeding great reward. David knows Saul can't kill him because the word of God has been tested, and David sees it to be purer after every trial than before. David knows that Saul would die before the promises of God would fall to the ground and perish.

It's one thing to have the promises of God, but it is entirely another to see the promises of God refined in our lives. It is one thing for Joseph to know that God had promised him the governor's chair, but it is quite another to see the word of God deliver him from the pit, Potiphar's, and the prison. The word of God becomes purer in our sight after every fire, for we continually learn to trust in it more. Yes, the word of God delivered David from the lion and the bear, and then he saw it to be pure enough to deliver Goliath into his hands. The promises of God were already pure enough to deliver Goliath into David's hands, but he may not have seen it to be that pure until it blessed him to kill the lion and the bear.

The slaying of the lion and the bear prepared David for his battle with Goliath. The slaying of the lion and the bear encouraged David when he heard Goliath bellow out from the valley. David had seen the promise of God do valiantly in his life. He had seen the word of God tried. The word of God had already started becoming refined in David's life before he ever stepped on the battlefield to face Goliath.

God's promises to David were great enough to give him victory over everything he would face for them to come to pass, but after every fire, David would see them to be purer than before. The fire of the lion and bear caused David to see the word of God as pure enough to defeat Goliath. Then he saw it to be pure enough to deliver him from Saul repeatedly, and then he saw it to be pure enough to set him on the throne. The word of God is tried as we go through the fire, but after every fire, we see the word of God to be purer than before.

Think of this for a moment. What promise did Joseph have from God? He had two dreams when he was young. This is all he had, and although he may have believed that they could give him the position of authority they spoke of, did he really understand that these two dreams could deliver him from the pit, Potiphar's, and the prison as well? Did he really know that they would not only set him in a position of authority but in the position of authority that would govern the entire world? Sure, he must have believed they could give him a position of authority, but when he was tried, he saw that the word of God was also tried. He would see that these two dreams could deliver him from the pit and transport him to Egypt, and he would also see that these two dreams could deliver him from prison.

The point I'm driving at is that Joseph wasn't given any more promises, only the two dreams, but as he was tried, they were tried, and Joseph saw them to be purer every time they were. Joseph saw the dreams as a means to an authoritative position at first, I'm sure, but I don't think he saw them as a means of deliverance from the pit, Potiphar's, and the prison at that time. Yet, the word would become purer in his sight, for he saw it deliver him repeatedly. The same promise he had from his youth became his source for everything he faced. I'm sure he didn't see the dreams as such, to begin with, but the word of God was purified in his sight, for he saw more and more of it as he faced trials repeatedly. In other words, there were more in these two dreams than Joseph first realized, but as he was tried, he saw that the word of God could not only set him in the governor's chair but deliver him from everything in his path while he ascending to it. No matter what Joseph faced on his way to the seat of authority, the promises of God contained in those two dreams were enough to get him through every obstacle he faced on his way to it.

The same was true with David. What promise did he have from the time Samuel anointed him to the day he set on the throne of Israel? He had this one promise, which said he was the Lord's anointed and would sit on the throne of Israel. Yet, when he faced the lion and bear, Goliath, all of Saul's attacks, battles with enemies, etc., he found that that one promise was sufficient for everything he faced. That one promise crushed the impossibility of David becoming king. Every time David was tried, the word of God was tried in David's sight, and he saw it to be purer after every trial.

David and Joseph leaned on the promises of God, and they never failed them. Over time, they had to lean harder and harder on these promises, but they found that these promises were sufficient for everything they faced. Yes, through their trials and tribulations, they had to lean on the promises more and more, for the word of God was tried and always passed with flying colors.

David saw that God's promises never failed him and always came to pass. David saw this repeatedly and said this about the word of God: "*The words of the Lord are pure words: as silver tried in a furnace of earth, purified seven times*" (Psalms 12:6).

Twenty-two years ago, God called me to preach. The first response to God's call upon my life was that I couldn't do that. How can I preach? I'm not qualified to preach. Yet, God insisted. Though I was full of fear, I accepted the call. I would have to trust that the Lord would enable me to do what He had called me to. Yet, little did I know how unqualified I was. Little did I know the peaks and valleys this calling would lead me to and through. I was ignorant of the fiery trials that would be sent my way, preparing me for this call or the bliss I would feel when God used me in ways that were clearly beyond my own ability. So, I nervously and fearfully accepted God's call, knowing I would have to trust God to fulfill it as I pleaded with Him to enable me to do what He had called me to do.

I can't tell you how many times I felt like I couldn't preach, had blown my calling, was unqualified, or had disqualified myself. I can't tell you how many times I felt like I couldn't understand the Bible well enough to preach it or how often I have said to myself that no person is qualified to handle the word of God. I can't tell you how many times I have thought, how can I counsel others? They have problems and come to me, desiring, expecting, or hoping I can give them spiritual solutions. They have family problems, marital problems, financial problems, questions about important decisions, or sorrows upon sorrows. How can I do that?

I can't tell you how often I felt I couldn't preach. Yet, that one simple promise God gave me when He called me was enough to sustain me through it all. When I felt like I couldn't preach, I'd say to myself, God has called me to preach. Therefore, I will stand behind the pulpit, open my mouth, and trust God to fill it. I want you to know that God always has.

When I felt like I couldn't understand the Bible, I'd say to myself, God has called me to preach His word. Therefore, I will read the Bible and trust God to give me the understanding necessary to preach His word.

When I felt like no one (especially me) was qualified to handle the word of God, I'd say to myself, God uses people, and I am one of the people He has called to preach His word. Therefore, I will carry the word of God to others and trust God to enable me to handle His Divine Word.

When I felt unqualified, I'd say to myself, God enables those whom He calls, and He has called me to preach. Therefore, I will continue to walk in this calling, trusting in God to be my qualifier.

When I felt like I disqualified myself, I'd say to myself, God has called me to preach, and His calling upon my life is bigger than my mistakes, shortcomings, failures, and sins. Therefore, I will get back up and trust Christ to wash my defiled feet, for God has called them to carry the gospel of peace and bring glad tidings of good things (Romans 10:15).

During these times when I felt like I had disqualified myself, God would often direct me to Aaron, the first high priest of Israel. While Moses was on Mount Sinai receiving the Ten Commandments, God also instructed him in many other matters. One of those instructions was that God had called Aaron to be the high priest of Israel. Yet, while God was telling Moses that Aaron would be the high priest of Israel, Aaron was at the foot of the mountain building a golden idol. Aaron's sin, as great as it was, didn't annul his calling, for God knew his frame and remembered that he was dust (Psalms 103:14) before he ever called him, and my sin, as great as it is, didn't annul God's call upon my life either, for God knows my frame, and remembers that I am dust as well.

God would also direct me to the verse, which says, *"For the gifts and callings of God are without repentance"* (Romans 11:29). Sure, this verse is about Israel. Israel had sinned every sin that could be sinned. Yet, God's call on their life has never changed. God will still use them as He called them to be used. Although I have failed repeatedly and sinned greatly, God has a calling upon my life. Yes, God knows my frame. God is also omniscient (all-knowing). He knew Israel would fail, and He knew I would fail. However, He called me anyway. Therefore, I trust that God will continue using me as He promised to do with Israel. God didn't change His mind (repent) concerning Israel's calling, and I don't believe He has changed His mind concerning mine. So, when I felt like I had destroyed my calling, I would lean upon that one simple promise, for God had called me to preach.

When people came to me for counseling, having problems that were very hard and confusing, God would bless me to trust in that one simple promise, for God had called me to this. I'd whisper a prayer to the Lord, asking for wisdom, or say to myself, God has called me to this, and therefore, it is His responsibility to enable me to perform it. So, God would bless me to trust Him for the answer, and I can't tell you how often the perfect answer came. How often God blessed me with the spiritual answer they needed is almost unbelievable. The answers would amaze me. To think that such a proper and wise answer could come out of my mouth would sometimes astonish me. Yet, I knew that this answer didn't come from my brain. God gave it to me because that was part of my calling, and He wanted those people to know the spiritual answer to their dilemma.

Through all this, God blessed me to lean upon this simple promise, which I have always found sufficient. When God called me to preach, I didn't know how amazing or sufficient this promise was. I have often thought that I needed something else from God or this ministry would fail, but I have found that this promise has always been sufficient, for God said to me 22 years ago, "I have called you to preach My word."

There have been times when I thought the ministry God gave me had been destroyed. I felt like I blew my calling or thought sickness had consumed it. I have also felt like I would never get to where I was going. Yet, in every dark time of ministry, I have found that that one simple promise granted me the ability to continue. God has blessed me to lean upon that one simple promise over and over again, and I have always found that it was sufficient for everything I needed in ministry.

Though the fires got hotter or the task got greater, that one simple promise sustained me, enabled me, and qualified me. Every time I leaned on that promise, that promise never failed me. Through all of this, I have seen the word of God tried and found it remarkably sufficient. Over the last 22 years, I have seen that this one promise from God was sufficient for everything I needed or faced in ministry.

Yes, we are tried by the word that we may be prepared for the calling, and the word of God is tried so that we may understand how pure and sufficient it is. It is all we need to fulfill the calling upon our lives. Trial after trial and test after test stand in the path of our calling, but it is only to try the word as the word is trying us. The word of God will overcome them all. The impossible will be made possible by it. During these times, we are forced to trust in the promise, and when we do, we see that it is sufficient and view it as purer than before the last test. The word is tried, which causes it to become purer in our sight. The more we see its pureness and sufficiency, the more we learn to lean on it, for it will never disappoint us.

I can't tell you how many obstacles this promise has overcome in this ministry, nor can I say how many times this promise has enabled this ministry. Yet, I will say this: the promise from God has crushed the impossibility of this uneducated country boy becoming a preacher. It is all to the glory of God because I know I couldn't overcome the obstacles that came because of this call, nor could I enable myself to perform this task. Yet, God has watched over His promise, which has never failed, and yes, I, too, with the sweet Psalmist of Israel, say, *"The words of the Lord are pure words: as silver tried in a furnace of earth, purified seven times"* (Psalms 12:6).

As gold becomes more valuable after every time in the furnace, the word of God becomes more valuable unto us after every trial. It becomes more precious to us. The things we once held so dearly are no longer the most valuable things in our lives, for the word of God has been tried in our lives, and we now see it to be the true treasure that it is. After every trial, the word of God becomes more precious to us, and eventually, it becomes our greatest treasure. It is more valuable to us than anything else because we understand that it is the means by which we are preserved, delivered, victorious, comforted, provided for, enabled, and strengthened. It is also our source of rejoicing. The word of God has become our joy and our song, for the fires have tried it in our lives, and we increasingly see it as the treasure it is. The word of God has become our dearest treasure in this life, for it has been tried, and we now see it to be precious. Our strength can't secure the throne, our wisdom can't secure the throne, our loved ones can't secure the throne, but the word of God can and will. Therefore, it becomes so precious to us. It has become the very beating of our hearts because we understand it holds our life in God's faithfulness.

# CHAPTER 13
# SIFTED LIKE WHEAT

Luke 22:31-32. *"And the Lord said, Simon, Simon, behold, Satan hath desired to have you, that he may sift you as wheat: But I have prayed for thee, that thy faith fail not: and when thou art converted, strengthen thy brethren."*

As God blesses us to look at these verses, we will see similarities to the circumstances, which came about before Job was tried.

Let's start by noticing who speaks to whom in these two verses. Jesus is talking to Simon, and Simon is Peter. So, Jesus is speaking to Peter.

The context in which these verses are mentioned is also important. Jesus and His disciples are partaking in what is commonly referred to as the Last Supper. Jesus has already washed their feet and ministered communion unto them. Then the Lord says that someone is sitting at the table with Him who would betray Him. This caught the disciples off guard and stunned them to say the least. They began to enquire who would do such a thing. Jesus said, *"He it is, to whom I shall give a sop, when I have dipped it. And when he had dipped the sop, he gave it to Judas Iscariot, the son of Simon"* (John 13:26). After Judas received the sop, Satan entered him, and Jesus said unto him, *"That thou doest, do quickly"* (John 13:27). Judas immediately left after Jesus said this and received a band of men from the chief priest that he may betray Jesus.

We won't go into detail on Judas betraying Jesus, but this is the context of the two verses I mentioned at the beginning of this book's chapter. Immediately after these verses, Peter says unto the Lord, *"I am ready to go with thee, both into prison and to death"* (Luke 22:33), but the Lord tells Peter, *"That this night, before the cock crow, thou shalt deny me thrice."* (Matthew 26:34).

In these two verses, we see Jesus talking to Peter and telling him that Satan desires to have him so that he may sift him as wheat. This sounds similar to God's two conversations with Satan concerning Job (Job 1:8-12; 2:3-6).

Notice that Satan desired to sift Peter like wheat. This means Satan may have made a request to the Lord, asking Him to allow him to sift Peter like wheat. We already discussed this concerning Job earlier in the book. Still, here, we can see something similar, and possibly exactly like the conversation between God and Satan concerning Job.

Satan can't sift Peter like wheat anytime he wants, or he would have already done it, for it is evident that Satan had this desire before this conversation between Jesus and Peter took place, but he hasn't fulfilled it yet. Why? Because he can't! And why can't he? Doesn't he have the power to sift Peter as wheat? Yes, he does, but he doesn't have the authority.

Though Satan desired to sift Peter like wheat, he probably ran into the same problem he had with Job. Satan has considered Peter. He probably examined Peter. He probably scoped Peter out like a hunter does his prey. Yet, he probably saw the hedge of God around Peter like he did Job. Satan didn't have the authority or power to sift Peter like wheat. He didn't have the authority, seeing God hadn't permitted him, and he didn't have the power to break through the hedge God had around Peter. Yes, Satan is more powerful than Peter, but he isn't more powerful than the hedge God has placed around him. Although the scriptures don't say that God had a hedge around Peter, it is evident that He did, or Satan would have already sifted him like wheat. Therefore, Satan must ask for God's permission to sift Peter like wheat because he can't break through God's hedge around him.

Again, notice the word *"desired."* Satan's desire is known unto the Lord. When looking at Strong's definition of this word (*"desired"*), Satan probably communicated this desire unto the Lord because the definition indicates the word's meaning to be: to demand (for trial) or to ask someone to give someone up to the authority of another. Yet, Satan hadn't sifted Peter like wheat when this conversation occurred between Jesus and Peter. Why? Satan can't sift Peter like wheat unless he has permission to do so, and we also know that God will set the bounds of this sifting if He does grant Satan this permission. So, it seems that Satan has asked the Lord for permission to sift Peter like wheat.

Will the Lord permit Satan to do so? The second verse of our text indicates that the Lord will allow Satan to sift Peter like wheat, for Jesus tells Peter, *"I have prayed for thee, that thy faith fail not: and when thou art converted, strengthen thy brethren."* This shows that the Lord has or will permit Satan to sift Peter like wheat. Yet, Jesus wants Peter to know something before the sifting takes place. Notice that Jesus tells Peter that He has prayed for him that his faith wouldn't fail, tells him he will be converted, and then tells him what to do after his conversion (*"strengthen thy brethren"*).

When we look at the word *"converted,"* we often think about the experience a person has when they trust in Christ and are saved. When a person is saved through faith in Christ, we often say they have been converted, but I don't believe this is what Jesus uses this word for. The Greek word translated *"converted"* is epistrefw, which, according to the Strong's Concordance, means to revert (literally, figuratively, or morally):--come (go) again, convert, (re-)turn (about, again). So, Jesus is saying, strengthen your brethren when you come again or return. To come again or to return would mean that you have already been there before. It would mean you have been there, gone away, and now you have returned. So, at the time of this conversation between Peter and Jesus, Peter is at a certain place. During the sifting by Satan, Peter will leave that place, and after the sifting is over, Peter will return. Therefore, before Satan sifts Peter, Jesus wants him to know that He has prayed that his faith wouldn't fail, that he will return, and what he will do or is to do after he returns.

Also, notice that the words turn (about again) are also used in the definition of *"converted."* This is what repentance means. Repentance means to do an about-face. To turn 180 degrees from the direction you're going. It is to turn about.

Let's take a moment to try and understand what the sifting of Peter like wheat was. The very next verse, after Jesus tells Peter he will be sifted like wheat and that he will also be converted, is spoken by Peter, which says, *"And he said unto him, Lord, I am ready to go with thee, both into prison and to death"* (Luke 22:33). This may indicate that Peter understood what this sifting would be. When we look at Matthew we receive more information.

Matthew 26:31-35. *"Then saith Jesus unto them, All ye shall be offended because of me this night: for it is written, I will smite the shepherd, and the sheep of the flock shall be scattered abroad. But after I am risen again, I will go before you into Galilee. Peter answered and said unto him, Though all men shall be offended because of thee, yet will I never be offended. Jesus said unto him, Verily I say unto thee, That this night, before the cock crow, thou shalt deny me thrice. Peter said unto him, Though I should die with thee, yet will I not deny thee. Likewise also said all the disciples."*

Again, this may indicate that Peter understood what this sifting would be. Satan would try and cause Peter to deny the Lord in his sieve, which is similar to what Satan told God Job would do if he were allowed to touch him and his possessions. Satan told the Lord that Job would curse Him to His face if he were allowed to touch him and his stuff. So, Satan would try to cause Peter to deny the Lord by sifting him like wheat, but Peter says this will never happen, for he said he was willing to go to prison and even die for Jesus.

Peter is saying that he would go to prison or die before he would deny Jesus. Peter has a lot of confidence that he will never deny the Lord, but we will soon see that he will. Peter has a lot of confidence in himself, believing he will never deny the Lord, but we will soon see that his confidence in himself will let him down.

(God has already blessed us to state earlier in this book that Peter was willing to die for the Lord and proved it by single-handedly fighting the temple guards in the Garden of Gethsemane, but we also know that Peter denied the Lord three times that very night. Peter was willing to die for Christ in a sword fight, but not on a cross.)

It is probable that Peter had some idea of what this sifting would be and what Satan's intentions were. Satan would sift Peter, trying to get him to deny Jesus, but Peter said, this will never happen, for I'm ready to go to prison or even die before I deny the Lord. In other words, Peter is saying that there is nothing Satan can bring upon me that would cause me to deny the Lord. I'm willing to go to prison and even die before I deny Jesus.

Again, we can see that Peter is extremely confident that he will never deny Jesus, and this confidence is probably in himself. Peter knew how much he loved Jesus, and he felt that he was strong enough to face anything Satan could throw at him.

So often, we are the same. We have this same confidence in ourselves and feel that nothing can cause us to stray away from the Lord or His ways, and although this confidence comes from our love for Jesus and a holy zeal for Him, if our confidence is in ourselves, we are badly mistaken. We don't possess the power to resist Satan on our own, and we don't possess the power to hold on to Christ, for He must hold on to us. Our own power is insufficient, and the mighty Peter would soon learn this.

Though Peter was strong, courageous, bold, and a man we may refer to as a man's man, he would soon see that this wasn't enough.

It would also be a great blessing for Peter to see this, for the sieve of Satan would be a great blessing unto to him, although he probably didn't think it was while being sifted.

After Peter said he would never deny the Lord, Jesus speaks to him in the next verse, *"And he said, I tell thee, Peter, the cock shall not crow this day, before that thou shalt thrice deny that thou knowest me"* (Luke 22:34). So, Jesus tells Peter that Peter would deny ever knowing Him on this very night. Peter didn't think he would deny the Lord, but Jesus told him he would do so that night. That night, the soldiers came to Gethsemane to take Jesus, and Peter took hold of a sword and fought with them.

Peter may have felt that this proved he would go to prison and die for the Lord. Yes, he was willing to do so in a sword fight but not willing to bear the shame and pain of a cross to do so. Jesus told Peter to put down his sword, healed Malchus' ear, which Peter had cut off in the sword fight, and was taken captive by the temple guards. The temple guards took Jesus to the house of the high priest, and there they held a mock trial before the Sanhedrin (the Supreme Court of Israel).

Peter and another disciple followed Jesus to the high priest's house, and while Peter was warming himself by the fire, he was approached three different times. Peter was accused of being a disciple of Jesus all three times, and all three times, Peter denied knowing Him. Then the rooster crowed, and Jesus looked at Peter. Their eyes probably met only momentarily, but it would have seemed like an eternity for Peter. I'd say he couldn't get the sound of the rooster or the look on Jesus' face out of his mind. It must have tortured him day and night.

I don't think Jesus looked upon Peter angrily or disgustfully, for I feel it was probably a look of compassion, knowing what Peter would now have to endure. That short glance of Jesus into the eyes of Peter immediately after the rooster crowed must have crushed him. Peter had looked into the eyes of the One he loved so dearly, into the eyes of the One Who loved him immeasurably, knowing that he and Jesus both knew what he had done. Yet, this wasn't all of it. At this very time, Jesus was being mocked and judged wickedly by others who declared He wasn't the Messiah. Yet, Peter had denied Him after knowing He was the Messiah. The very lips of Peter, which had previously said unto Jesus, *"Thou art the Christ, the Son of the living God"* (Matthew 16:16), are the very lips that denied Him three times during the beginning of His Passion. Oh, how Peter would have known this, and oh, how he would have hated himself for doing it. The guilt would have been heavier than the sand upon the seashore and as immeasurable as the universe.

Try to imagine this crushing weight of guilt and condemnation for a moment. A crushing weight of guilt such as this drove Judas to hang himself, for he felt it was better to die and try to be rid of it than to live with it. Yet, there may have also been more to it, for Satan is a master at taking our failures and magnifying them before us. Satan wants them ever-present in our thoughts, written in large, bold letters, before our eyes.

Peter may have thought something like this. During the hardest time in Jesus' life, I forsook Him. I should have been there by His side, but I only added to His grief. When He needed me the most, I forsook Him. How could I ever think that I was His disciple? I acted like all the others who were condemning Him. What a coward I am!

This would have been the thing Peter despised most. The thing he hated most. Yet, when he looked into the mirror, he would have seen this very thing staring back at him.

It is also apparent that Peter had come against a decisively mightier foe than himself. Peter was outnumbered in the Garden earlier that night by the temple guards. However, he still seemed to have a fighting chance and was holding his own. On the other hand, at Caiaphas' house (the house of the high priest), there was not only an angry mob but also the temple guards and the authority of the Sanhedrin. Peter would have quickly seen that he didn't have a fighting chance at Caiaphas' house, and if he were going to confess Christ, he would have to embrace the cross.

I've said this many times, but I feel compelled to repeat it. The sieve of Satan, or the tribulation we face, is always greater than we are, and that is by design. It must be, for God allows Satan to sift us so that we may see our own strength. God wants us to see that our own strength isn't sufficient, which will cause us to look for a greater power than ourselves as we learn to trust in the finished work of Christ instead of trusting in our own abilities and strength. There, in the sieve of Satan, we receive a greater revelation of ourselves and a greater revelation of God.

Let's also consider the sound of the rooster. When it crowed, it got Peter's attention, but immediately after it crowed, Jesus looked at Peter, which would have caused the reality of what he had done to begin to sink in. The sound of the rooster was the thunder of conviction in Peter's soul, and looking into Jesus' eyes confirmed what he had done. When Jesus looked at Peter, Peter would have seen that he had done exactly what Jesus said he would do, which was precisely what Peter said would never happen. When Jesus looked at Peter immediately after the rooster crowed, it would have shown Peter that the rooster's crow was no coincidence.

Sometimes, when a rooster crows, it gets our attention, and we immediately look towards the sound. When the rooster crowed, Peter's eyes met the eyes of Jesus. Did the sound of this rooster cause Peter to look in the direction of Jesus? I don't know, but I do know Peter heard the rooster crow, and immediately after hearing the rooster crow, he looked into the eyes of the Lord, which were looking back at him. Peter knew what the sound of this rooster meant, for it was the sound of conviction, yet when he looked into the face of Jesus, the weight of the situation would have sunk in. The rooster's crow was the sound of conviction in Peter's life, and looking into Jesus' face was the evidence of the sin he had committed. When conviction crows, it causes us to look in a certain direction, revealing how we have sinned. It wouldn't have taken long after this for the guilt and shame to have seemingly become unbearable unto Peter. The rooster's sound must have pierced Peter's heart like a cold blade.

Oh, how Peter's faith would have been broken into pieces when he stared into Jesus's face. His faith broke into pieces, but not his true faith, only his faith in himself. Sure, he may have thought all faith was broken out of his life, but only faith in himself was broken. There's no doubt that Peter would eventually see this, for Peter, the man's man, wasn't strong enough to hold on to Jesus, but he would soon see that Jesus was strong enough to hold on to him.

(Many times, as Christians, our faith is in ourselves. What do I mean by that? Sometimes, we trust in our own abilities to serve the Lord or secure our salvation. We look to our own willpower, zeal, oratory skills, mind, wisdom, education, knowledge, finances, position, influence, strength, power, courage, righteousness, &, etc., instead of looking unto the finished work of Christ to empower us to walk in righteousness, fulfill God's calling upon our lives, and to have our names written in the Lamb's Book of Life. Sometimes, we feel that we must rely upon ourselves to secure our salvation instead of trusting solely in Christ's finished work to secure our souls. Sometimes, we feel we must accomplish the call of God upon our lives by our abilities instead of trusting Christ's finished work for it.

Though our desire to serve the Lord is correct, we often look to the wrong place for the ability to do so. We often look to our own abilities to serve the Lord instead of faith in the finished work of Christ. Faith in self is never sufficient for salvation, sanctification, blessing, answered prayers, to fulfill God's calling on our lives, &, etc.; only faith in the finished work of Christ is.)

Sometimes, when faith in ourselves is broken, we feel like all our faith is broken, but that isn't so, for this only shows us how much we have been trusting in ourselves. We often can't see how much we trust in ourselves until our faith in ourselves is broken. When this happens, we think we have lost all faith, but we have only lost faith in ourselves. Yet, this shows us that we have been trusting too much in ourselves because we feel we have lost all faith when faith in ourselves is broken. This shows that we have a lot of faith in ourselves because when faith in ourselves is broken, we feel like we have none left. This shows us that much or most of our faith is in ourselves, or we wouldn't feel like all faith is gone when only the faith in ourselves has been broken and, often, we can't see that we have this much faith in ourselves until we are sifted.

Then, it eventually becomes apparent because when faith in ourselves is broken, we feel like all faith is broken. This shows that we had way too much faith in ourselves because if most of our faith were in the finished work of Christ, then when faith in ourselves is broken, we wouldn't feel like all faith is gone. If most of our faith were in the finished work of Christ, then we wouldn't feel as though we had lost all faith when only faith in ourselves is broken.

The amount of faith that we place in ourselves is incredible! Sometimes, seeing how much faith I have placed in myself amazes me. Although we may not always know it, when our faith is sifted, causing faith in ourselves to be broken, we soon realize how much we have been trusting in ourselves instead of the finished work of Christ. When faith in self is broken, and we feel as though we have no faith left, it is evident that most of our faith is in ourselves instead of the finished work of Christ.

Peter must have felt like all his faith was broken and discarded, but only faith in himself was broken, for the godly faith remained. Yes, the faith Peter had in himself was broken, but the faith Peter had in the revelation God gave him, which he proclaimed when he said unto Jesus, *"Thou art the Christ, the Son of the living God"* (Matthew 16:16), never broke. The sieve of Satan would have helped Peter realize the amount of faith he had in himself and prompted him to search for the true faith within him. This, in turn, would have caused him to grow in godly faith and become a source of strength for his fellow believers (strengthener of the brethren).

Let's look at ourselves as a clay pot for a moment. Let's say this clay pot holds a hundred pints of faith. Let's say that 95 pints of faith is faith in ourselves, and 5 pints is faith in the finished work of Christ. When we are sifted, the 95 pints will be broken, separated from the 5 pints, and discarded. Therefore, 95% of our faith has disappeared. Now, we feel like all our faith is gone, but it isn't, for there remains the 5% of godly faith we had to begin with. Only the ungodly faith in ourselves has been broken out of our lives. Now, we are left with the 5% of godly faith we began with, but that 5% is more valuable than the 95% that was broken out of our lives. All that is left is the 5% of godly faith in Christ. Once we recognize what has happened, we will begin to look unto the 5% we have, which will accomplish more in our lives than the other 95% we lost. Then, we begin to lean on the 5%, and though it seems small, we will see that it is all we need. Now, all the faith we have left is in the finished work of Christ, and though it is as small as a mustard seed, mountains will be moved by it (Matthew 17:20).

(This is true in our lives and their many different categories. Sometimes, we may have godly faith in one area of our life, but in another, we may have faith in ourselves. For example, we may trust in Christ's finished work for salvation but trust in ourselves for sanctification. This means we have submitted the salvation of our souls to Christ's care but have placed the sanctification of our lives in our own hands. Therefore, we may be sifted in our sanctification so that faith in ourselves would be broken, causing all that remains in this category to be faith in the finished work of Christ or, at the very least, less faith in ourselves in this area of our lives.

Though these chastisements and tribulations are very hot and intense, they will never break true faith in Christ, for they only break faith in ourselves. Though Satan's sieve may seem to have destroyed every fragment of faith in your life, it hasn't, for his sieve doesn't have the power to do that, regardless of how violently it shakes us. Faith in oneself can shatter, but true faith in the finished work of Christ is unbreakable. Satan's sieve breaks ungodly faith, while true faith is purified by trials and tribulations. [1 Peter 1:7].)

Though 95% of faith has been broken out of our lives, and only 5% remains, this 5% is more precious than the other 95% that was broken out of our lives. This 5% is all we need because it is entirely placed in the finished work of Christ. Currently, all that remains is 5%, and the proper environment now exists for this 5% to grow into 7%, 10%, 20%, & etc. Yes, it is like the mustard seed, which is the smallest of all seeds, but when it is grown, it is the greatest among the herbs, becoming a tree that the birds of the air lodge in (Mark 4:31-32). Our godly faith now has room to grow. With the ungodly faith removed from the clay pot, there is room for the godly faith to expand. May God bless our faith so that it may grow enormously. May the same thing said of Stephen be said of us, for the scriptures say, "*And Stephen, full of faith and power, did great wonders and miracles before the people.*" (Acts 6:8).

This is the faith we need to walk spiritually before the Lord; the other 95% we lost couldn't, for it was evident that Peter couldn't stand up against Satan in his own strength, although he was a very strong and courageous man.

The sieve only separates the chaff from the wheat. The chaff is discarded, and the wheat remains. Faith in ourselves will hinder our walk before the Lord because our own abilities aren't strong enough to walk in His ways. Therefore, the Lord allows our faith to be sifted so that faith in self would be broken out of our lives. Saints can only serve the Lord properly and powerfully through faith in Christ's finished work. Hence, our faith is sifted because the more that faith in self is broken out of our lives, the more we will trust in the finished work of Christ, which is the only means of eternal salvation, sanctification, blessing, &, etc.

Sifting is necessary because it is unlikely that we would ever remove faith in ourselves from ourselves. Sifting is necessary because it is unlikely that we will stop trusting in ourselves. We are so inclined to look to our own abilities to live our Christian lives, but faith in self will never be what is needful to walk out the godly calling upon our lives. Therefore, God allows us to be sifted so that faith in the finished work of Christ and faith in self or any other faith other than faith in Christ's finished work would be separated and the ungodly faith discarded. We are sifted so that the wheat and chaff of our faith would be separated. The wheat is gathered into the barn, and the chaff is discarded and burned.

When Jesus looked at Peter after the rooster crowed, Peter's strength may have left him, and a great weakness may have fallen upon him. Sorrow must have laden him with such a heavy weight that it seemed to crush his soul. Peter ran away with tears streaming down his face. He could bear this no longer. He had to get away from this crowd. I'm not sure Peter even knew where he was running to, but I feel like he was looking for a secluded place. A place where no one else would be, for his grief was so great and his sin so damning, he must have sought a vacant place to try to pray, understand, and weep for what he had done. He must have run with all his might, and his vision may have been blurred as his tears fell as torrential rain. He may have run to a place of seclusion and then collapsed as soon as he found it. Oh, how he wept, for the scriptures say he wept bitterly (Luke 22:62). I'd say he wept so hard that he felt physical pain. Peter would have lain in a pool of his own tears while guilt lay heavy upon his soul.

The guilt must have pressed so heavily upon Peter that it seemed like he would drown in a pool of his own tears. Peter may have felt like the cursed serpent as the guilt pressed him deeper and deeper into the dust. Oh, how he must have eaten the dust of the earth, which would have been mingled with his own tears, for his guilt was too heavy to bear. Oh, how he must have felt like the accursed serpent, like a reprobate, and like an abominable thing, for his sin was ever before his face. How heavy was this burden of guilt and shame that lay squarely upon the shoulders of Peter? We may never know. Yet, we know it was too heavy for the mighty Peter to bear, for it would have driven his face into the dust and dug a trench with his nose. Peter may have wished to die so that he could get out of the pain he was feeling. Guilt may have weighed upon him as heavily as it did Judas. Peter may have understood the Psalm of David, which says, *"I am weary with my groaning; all the night make I my bed to swim; I water my couch with my tears"* (Psalms 6:6). I don't know, nor can I describe Peter's feelings that night, but the scriptures say, "*Peter went out, and wept bitterly"* (Luke 22:62).

Satan was sifting Peter, and it had become evident that he wasn't strong enough to bear it. Before the sifting started, Peter felt he was strong enough, saying unto Jesus, I will go to prison or die before I deny You, but when placed in Satan's sieve, he quickly found out his strength was insufficient. Again, this was by design. Peter was trusting in his own strength to confess Christ; therefore, the sieve of Satan showed him that his own strength wasn't sufficient. This would eventually cause Peter to cast away faith in himself and trust entirely in Christ.

This was important for Peter's calling, for he was called to be a strengthener of the brethren, but his own strength wasn't sufficient to do so. He would have to stop trusting in his own strength and trust in Christ's power instead. Therefore, the sieve of Satan was necessary because this would cause Peter to see how insufficient he was, which would cause him to cast away faith in himself and eventually trust in Christ for His strength. This is the only way Peter can be a strengthener of the brethren, and this is why God allowed Satan to sift him. Peter's faith would be sifted, as all faith he had placed in himself would have to be separated from him and discarded.

Sifting is a process in which the chaff (outer shell) is separated from the wheat. The chaff and wheat must be separated. The wheat and the chaff are connected, and it takes some effort to separate them. If one sought to do this by using their hands alone, doing one harvest would take an enormous amount of time. This is why the sieve is used.

Why is it important to separate the wheat and chaff? There are a few differences between wheat and chaff. Wheat is edible, but the chaff isn't. Wheat is valuable, while the chaff is useless. (Wheat is also heavier than the chaff, which is also important, allowing it to be separated from the chaff during the sieving or winnowing process.) The chaff is the outer shell of the wheat. The wheat and chaff must be separated, and a person would spend way too much time separating it by hand than it would profit them; therefore, the sieve is used for this process. It would probably be impossible for a person to separate the chaff from the wheat without this sieving process, for it would probably take an incredible amount of time to pick through it by hand.

The chaff is separated from the wheat in several ways, but our text speaks of using a sieve. The wheat in its natural form is placed into the sieve and shaken violently for some time. This breaks the wheat's outer shell (chaff), separates it, and discards the chaff. The wheat in its natural form must be broken before the chaff can be separated from the wheat. The breaking unbinds the wheat from the chaff, and then the continual sieving eventually separates the chaff from the wheat, and the chaff is discarded. The wheat is valuable, strengthening, and life-giving, but the chaff is useless, though it is bound unto the wheat, and therefore, the two must be separated in the sieve.

Why would God allow Satan to sift Peter like wheat? There were some things in Peter's life that God wanted removed. There was something in Peter's life that had to be separated from him. What was this? It was Peter's faith in himself. Peter's faith in himself had to be separated from the true faith in Christ. Both lie within him, but now they must be separated because one is godly, and the other is ungodly. God wants the ungodly faith to be removed from Peter's life; therefore, the godly faith and ungodly faith must be separated. They must be separated so the true faith in Peter isn't thrown out with his ungodly faith. They must be separated so that the ungodly faith wouldn't remain with the godly faith in him. Peter has two kinds of faith; God wants one discarded and the other kept. In other words, they must be separated so the baby isn't thrown out with the bathwater. In other words, they must be separated so the chaff doesn't occupy space in Peter's barn.

Faith in ourselves and Christ are often connected so closely together in our lives that it is impossible for us to separate one from the other, seeing we don't have the ability. In our lives, godly faith and faith in self can be mingled together in such a manner that we can't separate the two with our own hands. They are often so connected in our lives that we can't see their differences. Yet, it is the sieve that identifies the one from the other. After the sifting, they can be identified because the sieve has separated them. We can now discern one from the other.

We mistakenly think fighting the temple guards in the Garden of Gethsemane with our own strength is the proper way to serve the Lord. We erroneously believe that doing our best to keep ungodly people from crucifying Christ is the proper way to walk righteously. Yet, Jesus tells Peter to put down his sword.

Remember when Jesus asked the disciples, who do you say I am? Peter said, *"Thou art the Christ the Son of the living God"* (Matthew 16:16). Jesus said, flesh and blood didn't reveal this to you, but My Father, which is in heaven. Shortly afterward, Jesus said He would be crucified. Then Peter said, *"Be it far from Thee, Lord: this shall not be unto Thee"* (Matthew 16:22). Then Jesus said unto Peter, *"Get thee behind Me, Satan: thou art an offence unto Me: for thou savourest not the things that be of God, but those that be of man"* (Matthew 16:23).

So often, we are as confused about the difference between godly faith and ungodly faith as Peter was about the will of God. We incorrectly think we must do something for Jesus when it is Jesus Who must do something for us. Such thinking causes us to try to serve the Lord without the cross of Christ when we must have the cross of Christ to serve the Lord properly. This shows us how unidentifiable ungodly faith can be in our sight, for Peter truly thought this was a godly way to act.

Godly faith embraces Christ on the cross. Godly faith embraces the crucifixion of our flesh. Godly faith embraces the cross of Christ as the means for eternal salvation, sanctification, and every part of God's grace that will be worked in our lives. Ungodly faith does neither. Ungodly faith magnifies one's own abilities as the proper way to live for God. Ungodly faith is to trust in ourselves to walk out

God's calling on our lives. Ungodly faith runs from the cross because it doesn't want to see our flesh crucified or weakened. Ungodly faith leans upon an arm of flesh instead of the cross of Christ. Ungodly faith is the hard shell of pride that incases the wheat. Therefore, ungodly faith has the strength of the flesh, while godly faith has the power of God.

This is why we must be sifted. The sieve separates godly faith from ungodly faith when we can't. The sieve identifies which is which in our sight when we can't tell the difference between the two. The sieve separates the two when we can't. We must discard one of them, but how can we, seeing we can't tell the difference between them? This is why the sieve must be used. After the sifting, we can now see where we have leaned on the chaff instead of the wheat, and now we cast the chaff aside and view it to be as useless as it really is. Therefore, it is necessary for the sieve to come into our lives because it gives us the ability to identify between godly faith and ungodly faith. After the sieve has identified the difference between the two for us, we now have the ability to discard the chaff and store the wheat in our barn. The sieve has identified the ungodly faith in ourselves that we have ignorantly trusted in, but now we can see it, which allows us to discard it from our lives. The sieve has also identified the godly faith in our lives that we have ignorantly ignored, allowing us to store it in an appropriate place. In other words, the sieve has identified the difference between the chaff and wheat so that we can discard the refuse and cling to the weightier matters of faith. In other words, the sieve allows us to identify godly and ungodly faith in our lives. This grants us the ability to discard faith in ourselves and cling to faith in Christ's finished work. This is why God allowed Satan to sift Peter.

How does the sieve identify these two different faiths to us? How does the sieve display them in such a way that we can identify them? God allows faith in ourselves to be broken, which allows us to see which is godly and which isn't.

How is the ungodly faith broken? It fails when demonic forces oppose it. It fails when trying to fulfill our godly calling. It fails when it tries to live a sanctified life. It fails when battling against the sinful nature (spirit of disobedience). It can't perform the godly works of the Holy Spirit, nor can it defeat or stand against the demonic forces of Satan. So, it fails in the spiritual realm. It fails to produce the power necessary to prosper in spiritual things. It can't walk in the Spirit, and it can't withstand the spiritual forces of Satan. It is like chaff. The chaff doesn't produce strength in our bodies; only the wheat can. Therefore, ungodly faith will not produce the power of the Holy Spirit in our lives; only godly faith can. So, ungodly faith is broken in the spiritual realm. It can't stand up to Satan or confess Christ amid the mob at Caiaphas' palace, nor can it be a strengthener of the brethren.

Ungodly faith in self is broken in the spiritual realm. Its power source is the flesh (our own fleshly abilities); therefore, it can't prosper spiritually. This ungodly faith is faith in the flesh, which means that it can only produce carnal things, and spiritual things are stronger than carnal things. Ungodly faith in self will always be broken in the spiritual realm. In the sieve, ungodly faith in ourselves is broken, and any faith other than faith in the finished work of Christ is broken, and we can clearly see that it is broken when it fails. Yet, godly faith is unbreakable. It remains when everything around us is smoldering in ashes or is as shattered as the pottery on Job's estate. This is why God allowed Satan to sift Peter.

Yes, I understand that sometimes we seem to succeed by the means of the flesh. Sometimes, we seem to succeed in our calling by trusting in our own abilities. This causes us to become delusional. This causes us great confusion, although we don't understand that we are bewildered. Why? Because we aren't experiencing any immediate consequences from having the wrong object of faith. This causes us to continue to lean on the flesh as the means by which we live righteously and walk out our calling. Though the word of God plainly states this to be improper, we can't see it; though the Holy Spirit is teaching us differently, we can't hear it, for pride has become a blindfold covering our eyes and earplugs stopping our ears. Therefore, the sieve must come into our lives because if this is left unchecked, we will never turn from it. We can't identify the difference between godly faith and ungodly faith, and our seeming successes embolden us to continue to walk in the flesh. Therefore, the sieve must come into our lives. Yes, something bigger than we are. Something big enough to shatter our ungodly faith into pieces.

Peter had spent a lifetime succeeding through the means of the flesh, but now he has come to Christ. He has been delivered out of the power of darkness and translated into the Kingdom of God's Dear Son (Colossians 1:13). He is no longer in a worldly system; he is in a spiritual one, and he will have to learn the appropriate way to walk in this Celestial Kingdom. Therefore, the sieve comes into his life. Something bigger than he is, something greater than he is, something that can crush his own abilities into dust so that he can see the difference between godly faith and ungodly faith. Therefore, God allows Satan to sift Peter.

Peter's faith (faith in self and godly faith) was being sifted. Often we can't see the difference between the two, for we are usually self-righteous, although we think we aren't. Peter doesn't have the ability to separate these two faiths and possibly doesn't even know that he has two different faiths (faith in self and godly faith) within him. Therefore, Peter must be sifted. This process wouldn't be easy, for Peter would have to be crushed in the sieve. His faith will be sifted so that faith in self would be separated from faith in Christ. That faith in self may be discarded from Peter's life while faith in Christ remains.

On the night Jesus was betrayed, Peter was confident that he wouldn't deny the Lord, even if it came down to imprisonment or death. Though Peter had good intentions, Peter's faith was in himself. Peter felt like he had the ability to face this night. Peter felt like he had the strength to face this night. Peter relied on himself to face this night, but Peter soon saw that he didn't have the ability to face it with his own strength, zeal, and courage. Peter's faith was sifted, as faith in himself was separated from godly faith. This was something Peter couldn't or wouldn't do, yet God would see that they were separated, and this process would be performed in the sieve of Satan. Peter was shaken violently in Satan's sieve, but God allowed it so that faith in self would be removed from his life, while the true faith (*"Thou art the Christ, the Son of the living God"*) remained.

Sometimes, we wonder why God allows Satan to sift us and how God knows it will work out for our good and His glory. First and foremost, I must say that God is God, Who's ways are perfect and past finding out.

Yet, from my limited knowledge and understanding, there are some things God has revealed to me about this. God sees our faith. God understands where our faith is resting. God knows if we are trusting in the finished work of Christ, in ourselves, or in something or someone else. God also knows Satan better than Satan knows himself. God knows how Satan will react to any given situation.

Yet, from my limited understanding, I can see that our faith is sifted to remove any other faith besides faith in the finished work of Christ, and I can also see how powerful Satan is and how much he desires to kill, steal, and destroy. Therefore, when God allows Satan to sift us, Satan uses every fiery dart God permits him to use, and it will always be greater in power than the person or thing our ungodly faith rests in. This causes us to see that the thing or person our ungodly faith rests in isn't sufficient for the task at hand, and therefore, we learn to trust in the finished work of Christ for it, for the finished work of Christ is stronger, mightier, and more powerful than Satan, as God said unto the old serpent in the Garden of Eden, *"And I will put enmity between thee and the woman, and between thy seed and her seed; it shall bruise thy head, and thou shall bruise his heel"* (Genesis 3:15).

Peter was sifted in Satan's sieve, and although his guilt and shame may have seemed unbearable, a few words Jesus spoke to him that night may have given him the strength to go on.

Jesus told Peter, *"I have prayed for thee, that thy faith fail not, and when thou art converted, strengthen thy brethren"* (Luke 22:32).

These words may have seemed to have been drowned in the ocean of Peter's tears. Still, they were there and may have been the only thing that kept Peter going, for the Psalmist says it like this, *"I had fainted, unless I had believed to see the goodness of the Lord in the land of the living"* (Psalms 27:13).

Though Peter was far from being comforted, he must have remembered these words, although only for short moments. I'm sure his failure would have been the loudest voice he heard during these times, which Peter needed to hear. However, I'm convinced that the words of Jesus weren't completely lost upon him, for it is no coincidence that Jesus told Peter these words before he was sifted, and it is no coincidence that Jesus spoke these words to Peter when He told him that he would be sifted.

Jesus intentionally gave Peter these words to help him while he was being sifted. I'm sure these words would have become more precious to Peter in the sieve of Satan than when Jesus first spoke them unto him.

Somehow, someway, Peter must have remembered these words, and they must have been part of God's grace, which granted Peter the ability to bear the sifting of Satan.

Guilt, shame, and condemnation must have gripped Peter like a vice. A huge vice, which Peter may have thought would crush him into oblivion, yet the words of Jesus must have been a glimmer of hope, which would have kept him from being completely swallowed up by darkness, although it may have been hard for Peter to see any hope at all.

This sin may have seemed to strip purpose completely out of Peter's life, for Peter's entire life was wrapped up in Christ. Can you imagine how this must have felt? One of the hardest things for a person to feel is that all purpose is stripped from their life. To feel you have no reason to live on this earth. To feel as though you have no reason to get out of bed in the morning. This is a hard place to find oneself in, for many people have committed suicide or simply die because they feel they have no purpose in life.

I've heard about people who were very healthy and strong, although advanced in years. They were still working, productive, and loved what they were doing, but they were forced to retire because of age and died shortly afterward.

Having a purpose in life is very valuable and necessary, and feeling like you don't have a purpose is extremely difficult to deal with. The feeling of having no purpose is horrible, and sometimes, Saints come to this place when they sin against God. They may feel that they have sinned so badly that God will never use them again, as they feel they have disqualified themselves from the call of God upon their lives. They may feel like they can never look for God's goodness anymore. They may feel that they can never look unto their Mighty Fortress for protection any longer, as they feel like the children of Israel when they first came unto the Promise Land and saw the giants and walled cities and cried out, God brought us here to destroy us because He hates us (Deuteronomy 1:27). They were saying, God brought us here to have us killed because our sins have caused Him to hate us.

Oh, how hopeless we feel in times like this, as we allow our sins to build an imaginary wall between God and ourselves. No, the wall isn't real. God forgives us and still has a purpose for our lives. However, we feel as though the wall is real and that we can never look to God for any good in the land of the living, only judgment for our sins, for we regard iniquity in our hearts although God has forgiven us.

(We must remember that God forgives. The blood of Christ cleanses us, even if we've been eating a steady dose of hog slop and wallowing in the mire with the Prodigal Son. We must trust in the finished work of Christ for this forgiveness. We must look to Christ's finished work for forgiveness and restoration. We must look unto the finished work of Christ for a good conscience towards God, even when we have denied Christ with Peter, wallowed in the mire with the Prodigal Son, fulfilled our lusts and harmed others with David, or murmured against God and built idols with the children of Israel. In such situations as these, we should call out unto the Lord like Samson after he laid his head in Delilah's lap, saying, remember me, O Lord, and strengthen me [Judges 16:28]! We must look unto Christ and His finished work, for this is the only cure for sin. Yes, it is more than sufficient!)

Feelings like this can cause the grapes to wither on the vine. These feelings can cause us to wither away, although there is no physical reason for it. This is a horrible feeling, but I'd like to comfort you with these words, *"For the gifts and calling of God are without repentance"* (Romans 11:29).

God knew all our faults and failures before He called us. God didn't say, whoops, when Adam and Eve ate the forbidden fruit. God knew they would, for the scriptures say that Christ was crucified from the foundation of the world (Revelation 13:8). God knew he would create man, and He also knew man would fall, but it is evident that God had already planned for this, in that Christ was slain from the foundation of the world.

1 Peter 1:18-20. *"Forasmuch as ye know that ye were not redeemed with corruptible things, as silver and gold, from your vain conversation received by tradition from your fathers; But with the precious blood of Christ, as of a lamb without blemish and without spot: Who verily was foreordained before the foundation of the world, but was manifest in these last times for you."*

God knew we would fail before He ever called us, as He knew Adam would fail before He created him, for it is evident that God had already made plans to send Christ to die for the sins of the world before creating Adam. God can see around the corner. Yes, God knows we will not live a sinless, perfected life, but He reminds us that He doesn't throw away clay, for He remolds it into something pleasing unto Himself (Jeremiah 18:1-6). God doesn't change His mind about His calling upon our lives when we sin, for His gifts and callings are without repentance. It is a horrible and hopeless feeling to think that we have no purpose in our lives, but as we will see with Peter, though he may have felt all purpose was gone from his life, it wasn't, for God's grace and calling upon our lives is bigger than our sins.

Though Peter may have felt like his life no longer had a purpose, the words of Jesus, which said, *"When thou art converted, strengthen thy brethren,"* must have given Peter enough hope to continue to endure the sieve of Satan. I have prayed for you, said Jesus unto Peter that very night. I have prayed that your faith wouldn't fail. I'm sure Peter may have thought his faith was gone, but Jesus had prayed that it wouldn't fail.

Has Jesus ever prayed a prayer that God the Father didn't answer? We may think of the prayer in the Garden of Gethsemane, when Jesus prayed, *"Saying, Father, if thou be willing, remove this cup from me: nevertheless not my will, but thine, be done"* (Luke 22:42). Jesus prayed for the cup to be removed, but only if it was the will of the Father to remove it. Therefore, it wasn't an unanswered prayer of Jesus when He drank the cup, but actually an answered prayer, for it was God's will for Jesus to be made a sin offering for humanity, and Jesus prayed for the Father's will to be done.

Though Peter was tormented on the torture racks of shame, guilt, condemnation, and failure, the words of Jesus, which said, I have prayed for you, must have kept Him from fainting. Although it may have seemed impossible for Peter to see the light at the end of the tunnel, these words must have given him some hope; even if it only seemed like a small flicker of a candle, it would have been enough to sustain him through this torturous and dark time. Peter knew Jesus prayed for him, and he also knew that Jesus said he would be converted and strengthen the brethren. Although it seemed like the sieve of Satan was going to do Peter in, he must have known that the same Jesus Who told him the rooster would crow after you've denied Me three times is the same Jesus Who told him I've prayed for you that your faith fail not, and after you're converted, strengthen your brethren.

Saints of God, I know when we find ourselves weeping bitter tears, it's hard to see a way out of this pit of guilt, condemnation, and shame, but our God doesn't throw away clay. He remolds it into something pleasing unto Himself. Remember, all things work together for good to those who love God and to those who are the called according to His purpose (Romans 8:28). Our sins may have gone over our heads, and we may feel as though we have denied Christ, but God's grace is bigger than our sins. The very scriptures teach us this truth, for they say, *"Where sin abounded, grace did much more abound"* (Romans 5:20).

Though we find ourselves in the sieve of Satan, his cruel sieve can't separate these words from us, though we may not be paying much attention unto them at the moment because our sin speaks so loudly at the present. Yet, they are there, and when we think we can't take another step because of the weight of guilt, condemnation, and shame, they will rise up within us and give us enough strength to bear the burden. Eventually, other words of God (*"and Peter"* [Mark 16:7]) may come and knit themselves together with them and cause us to throw off the burden completely.

Although Peter found himself in this horrible place, Jesus gave him something to take into the sieve with him. Jesus gave Peter a few words from His very own lips. Jesus let Peter know he would go into the sieve; He (Jesus) had prayed for him, his faith wouldn't fail, he would be converted, and when he came out, he would be a strengthener of the brethren. The words Jesus gave Peter were given to him before he was sifted, for the Lord ensures we don't go into the sieve empty-handed.

A much-quoted verse of the Bible has to do with this very topic. This verse says, *"For I know the thoughts I think towards you, saith the Lord, thoughts of peace, and not of evil, to give you an expected end."* (Jeremiah 29:11).

The Lord spoke this verse to the Jews who had been brought into Babylonian captivity. After these Jews were carried away captive by the Babylonians, God had Jeremiah to let them know that their captivity wouldn't last forever, saying they would come forth from their captivity after seventy years (Jeremiah 29:10). They were experiencing a very trying time. Yet, God didn't want them to experience this empty-handed. Therefore, God sent them some words from his very lips to accompany them in their captivity. Words that would give them hope when they seemed to be in a hopeless situation. A glimmer of light in a dark place. A promise from God in their trying circumstances. Yes, they, too, were given a promise that they would be converted, for they would return to the Promise Land after 70 years. They were to continue in their faith, continue the line of Abraham and David, have children, for the Jews would once again return to their homeland. God gave them a promise while in captivity so that they would have hope, something to believe in, and wouldn't feel like they had no purpose in life.

Before Adam and Eve were expelled from the Garden of Eden, God didn't allow them to be driven out before giving them a promise that the Messiah would come and crush the head of the serpent who was instrumental in causing them to eat of the Tree of the Knowledge of Good and Evil (Genesis 3:15). Though their way back into the Paradise of God seemed hopeless after they fell, God didn't send them out of the Garden of Eden without giving them a promise of a coming Redeemer Who would undo all the work of the serpent in their lives and on the earth. Therefore, they had something to give them hope of a future in God's presence again, although they were banished from Eden. So many times, we read about promises God gives to His people before they are chastened or tried.

Why does God do this? These promises are given to us beforehand to strengthen us during the chastisement or tribulation. Think of Joseph for a moment. God gave Joseph dreams of him becoming a great man of authority before he was betrayed by his brothers, thrown in a pit, sold as a slave, falsely accused of attempted rape, and thrown into prison. Why did God give him the dreams ahead of time? Joseph needed these dreams to be a ray of hope in the darkness he would experience between the times of the dreams and their fulfillment.

The same is true with all Saints. There are so many promises in the Bible that will sustain us through tribulation or chastisement. For example, when we are chastened, we are told that God only chastens His children, that God loves us, and that the chastening will work a peaceable fruit in our lives, and then the scriptures say, lift up the hands that hang down and the feeble knees (Hebrews 12:5-12). In other words, knowing that God only chastens His children, loves those He chastens, and will work a peaceable fruit in our lives through the chastening should strengthen us during the chastisement.

We are also told that we should rejoice in tribulation, knowing that tribulation works patience in our lives, and when the work of patience has completed her work, then we will be perfect and entire, lacking nothing (James 1:2-4).

There are so many more promises than these, but the point is that God doesn't send us into the sieve of Satan empty-handed. He gives us promises to carry into the sieve with us, promises that are mightier than the sieve. Though the sieve is mightier than we are, the promises of God are mightier than the sieve. The sieve can't break them, for they are mightier than the sieve, and they will not only strengthen us but eventually crush the sieve that is crushing us.

God sends these promises into the sieve with us, and as the sieve shakes us violently, the promises damage the sieve. Sure, the sieve is breaking us, but God's promises are breaking the sieve at the same time.

Let's try to say it like this. We are made of soft material; the sieve is made of material that is harder than we are, but the promises of God are made of the hardest existing material. Therefore, while the sieve shakes us violently, we, being softer than the sieve, are broken by it. Yet, the promises of God are with us, and while the sieve is violently shaking us, the promises of God are breaking the sieve because they are harder than it is. Therefore, with every movement, we are broken more by the sieve, but the sieve is broken more by the promises of God. Eventually, the promises of God crush the sieve after the chaff in our lives is removed. Eventually, the promises of God break the sieve before the sieve can do more unto us than God has permitted. The promises of God break the sieve out of our lives, and once we have come to the place where we trust them completely, the sieve will be broken.

Let me try to say it like this, God willing. Let's say you have some clay. Let's say you placed a very hard rock inside the clay while it was wet and soft. Then, you give the clay time to dry and harden. Let's say you place the clay into a drinking glass and cover the opening with your hand. Let's say you began to shake the drinking glass violently. The clay would eventually begin to break into pieces, but the more the clay was broken, the more the rock inside would be exposed. The shaking would continually break the clay into smaller and smaller pieces, but when it did, there would be nothing to protect the glass from the rock inside. After the drinking glass has broken the clay by violently shaking it, the rock would break the glass through the same movement.

The clay is the Saints of God, the drinking glass is the sieve of Satan, and the rock is the promises of God. So, the sieve breaks us, but after we are broken, the promises of God break the sieve. The sieve is meant to break us, but after we are broken, the promises of God will destroy the sieve before the sieve completely destroys us. Therefore, the sieve of Satan is its own worst enemy. Sure, it desires to break us through violent shaking, but at the same time, it is destroyed by the promises of God through this same action.

The sieve will not be permanent in our lives! It is only allowed so much liberty! After the chaff is removed and God's promises are revealed, the sieve will be broken by those very promises.

God has placed special promises and callings inside us, but they can't be seen because they are inside the clay. Therefore, God allows Satan to sift us so that the parts of the clay that conceal these promises may be broken and removed. After they are removed, the promises of God become manifest unto us and in our lives. Then the rock breaks the glass, and we are freed from it. God only allows the sieve to reveal the promises of God in our lives, no more and no less, but after the promises are revealed in our lives, the promises break the sieve. Remember, Jesus said, in the world, you will have tribulation, but be of good cheer; I have overcome the world (John 16:33). These promises sustain us during the sieving process and will be established in our lives after the sieving process is completed. These promises sustain us, break the sieve that is breaking us, and will be established in our lives after the chaff has been removed from us. We are sent into the sieve because of the promises of God, sustained in the sieve by the promises of God, delivered from the sieve by the promises of God, and the promises of God will be established in our lives after the chaff has been removed from us. God has a calling upon our lives.

God has promised Peter that he would be a strengthener of the brethren. It is because of this call and God's promise upon Peter's life that he is sent into the sieve. God will establish this promise and calling in Peter's life, but He wants the chaff removed from him before He does. Therefore, the sieve comes into Peter's life to remove it. While in the sieve, the promises of God sustained Peter and continually damaged the sieve. Once the chaff is removed from Peter's life, the promises of God will have completely crushed the sieve that is crushing Peter. Then, God's promises will be established in Peter's life.

Let's, for a moment, mention Joseph again. God gave him dreams, which meant he would become a man of great authority, and although Joseph may not have understood much more than that, these dreams were promises that meant he would sit in the governor's chair, reigning over all of Egypt. However, after the dreams, Joseph didn't immediately sit in the governor's chair, for he would be betrayed by his brothers, thrown into a pit, sold as a slave, falsely accused of attempted rape, and cast into prison beforehand. These things came into his life because of these dreams. Yet, the day would come when Joseph would be delivered from prison and placed in the palace. It was the promises that invited the sieve into his life, but it was also the promises that preserved his life throughout. It was the promises that gave Joseph hope in the sieve. It was the promises that invited the sieve, and it was also the promises that unlocked the prison and set him in the palace. Therefore, the promises invited the sieve into his life, gave him the hope he needed to endure it, unlocked the prison doors (broke the sieve), and set him in the governor's chair.

Saints of God should always remember that God permits us to be sifted so that His promises may be revealed in our lives. This is the purpose of the sieve, and this is why God allowed Satan to sift Peter.

God had called Peter to be a strengthener of the brethren, but this wasn't manifest in Peter's life. Therefore, God permitted Satan to sift Peter like wheat so that His promise would be revealed. Peter went into the sieve with a promise concealed but came out with the promise revealed. Peter was the clay, the rock was the strengthener of the brethren God called Peter to be, and the sieve was the drinking glass. The sieve was allowed to sift Peter until the rock was revealed, and once the rock was revealed in his life, the drinking glass was broken by the rock. Again, God only permits Satan to sift us so that His concealed promises in our lives may be revealed, and once they are revealed, the promises of God break the sieve.

This is the purpose of the sieve. The sieve removes the chaff that conceals the promises of God in our lives so that they would be revealed. The promises of God will not allow the sieve to destroy Peter because once the chaff that conceals the promise in his life is removed, then the strengthener of the brethren will be revealed, and the sieve will be destroyed.

Christians have the promises of God wrapped up in them, but sometimes, they are concealed by the chaff in us. Therefore, God allows Satan to sift us so that the chaff would be removed, revealing the promises. Once the concealed promises are revealed, they will destroy the sieve because the purpose of God has been accomplished in our lives. Again, God permits Satan to sift us so that the concealed promises in our lives may be revealed.

God called Peter to be a strengthener of the brethren, but this wasn't being displayed in his life. Therefore, God permitted Satan to sift him so that God's call would become manifest in his life. This is the purpose of God allowing the sieve to come into Peter's life, and this is also the purpose of allowing it to come into our lives.

Let's take a moment to notice the words Jesus spoke unto Peter before his sifting. Notice the word *"I"*. Jesus said, *"I have prayed for thee, that thy faith fail not"* (Luke 22:32). These words indicate what would be sifted in Peter's life. It would be his faith that would be sifted. Peter's faith would have consisted of faith in Christ (walking in the Spirit) and faith in himself (walking in the flesh). We also can see that Jesus told Peter he would come out of this sieve and have a calling of God upon his life. Yet, the word *"I"* would insinuate that Jesus has done something for Peter, something that Peter couldn't do for himself.

Peter's faith was sifted, and his weakness was exposed. Though Peter was a man's man, yes, a very brave, accomplished, bold, and strong man, he wasn't sufficient for the sieve of Satan. Peter's faith would be sifted, and this was done by exposing his weakness. Though Peter may have relied on his own strength and courage throughout his life, here, in the sieve of Satan, he would find that it wasn't enough. Peter's weakness was exposed so that he would learn that he couldn't trust in himself. This part of Peter's faith was the chaff that the sieve would separate from him while faith in Christ would remain. Peter's weakness would be exposed so that he would have the ability to see it, showing him that his faith in himself was misguided. This would also cause him to understand that faith in Christ was the only faith he should have. The hard shell of pride (faith in self) would have to be removed from Peter, as humility (faith in Christ) remained.

Peter was trusting in his own abilities to confess Christ. When we trust in our own abilities to live for God, we will fail. We will fail in areas we never deemed possibly, as did Peter. Yet, when we fail and fall into the pit of sin, often, we try to claw our way out by the same method that caused us to fall to begin with. We try to climb our way out by using our own strength and abilities. Often, we try to atone for our sins by living righteously. When we do this, we erroneously think we can fix what we broke. We mistakenly think we can fix the sin we committed through righteous actions. We may say, I will pray, study, attend church, give, or witness more, etc. Although these things are good, they can't atone for the sin we committed. Although these things should be in the lives of Christians, they can't atone for sin, and all the while we seek atonement through works (as commendable as they may be), we will never accomplish our goal. Yet, if we remember that Jesus has prayed for us, we can come out. We can be confident that we are forgiven and restored because Jesus sets on the right hand of God, making intercession for us. We can't deal with sin by ourselves, for sin is only dealt with through the blood of Christ.

Therefore, we shouldn't seek to make atonement for our souls through works but look unto Jesus, Who is the sacrifice for our sins. If we try to deal with sin in another manner other than through faith in the finished work of Christ, guilt, shame, and condemnation will remain. Yet, the Holy Scriptures say, *"if we confess our sins, He is faithful and just to forgive us of our sins, and to cleanse us from all unrighteousness"* (1 John 1:9). We are kept in favor with God through the continual intercession of Christ on our behalf. Yet, until we trust in His High Priestly Ministry, we will continue to be weakened by our sins, as guilt, shame, and condemnation become our constant companions.

Jesus spoke to Peter before he went into the sieve and told him that He had done something for him. Jesus had told him He had prayed for him. There was something Jesus had done for Peter, and there is something Jesus has done for us. So often, we, with Peter, place too much faith in ourselves; therefore, it is necessary for our faith to be sifted. When we are sifted, it is made apparent that we don't have the strength to stand up to Satan, which causes us to remember that Jesus has already done something for us. Jesus has been crucified, buried, and raised from the grave so that we may be forgiven and empowered.

In Satan's sieve, our weakness is exposed as our faith is sifted. Our weakness is exposed, so we will understand that our faith is misguided. Our weakness is exposed, so we will see that we aren't sufficient to stand up against Satan. This causes us to forsake faith in ourselves and forces us to place faith in what Christ has already done for us. There, in Satan's sieve, our faith is sifted, as the hard shell of pride (faith in self) is broken in our lives and separated from us. Now, we trust less in ourselves and more in the finished work of Christ.

So often, this is done in different stages, as there are many aspects of our lives. Sometimes, we haven't committed one aspect of our lives unto the Lord, while we may have committed another unto Him. In other words, there are many different categories of our lives, such as eternal salvation, sanctification, finances, relationships, blessings, & etc. Although our relationships are not currently being sifted, our finances may be. We must learn to trust in Christ's finished work for everything. We must learn to trust in Christ's finished work for our eternal salvation, sanctification, finances, relationships, blessings, & etc. Yet, when we are sifted in a certain area, we stay there until the hard shell of pride is broken and separated, and humility is the only thing that remains. We are sifted until we have forsaken faith in ourselves in this matter, having completely trusted it to the finished work of Christ. We usually aren't sifted in every category at once because it may be more than we can endure, and therefore, we may be sifted one category at a time. Sort of like the refining process for silver, as God blessed David to say, *"The words of the Lord are pure words: as silver tried in the furnace of earth, purified seven times"* (Psalms 12:6). The refining process of silver requires many different trips into the fire, as some dross is removed on the first trip, and some more dross is removed on the second trip, and so on until the silver is recognized as pure after the seventh trip. All the dross isn't burned out of our life at once. Sometimes, one category of our lives is sifted, and then another, as some dross is removed each time the silver is placed into the fire. One category after another may be sifted, and sometimes the same category multiple times because it may be more than we can stand to have the entire category sifted at once, for the goal is to cause us to commit everything unto the Lord, for God has predestinated (planned, predetermined) us to be conformed into the image of Christ (Romans 8:29). Yes, we continually go in and out of the fire until we say unto our Lord, into Thy hand, I commit my spirit (Psalms 31:5; Luke 23:46).

There are also times in our Christian life when we can't see how much faith we place in ourselves or in our own righteousness until we are sifted. Then, the chaff is revealed in the sieve as it is separated from the wheat. Yes, chaff we couldn't see before, and chaff we couldn't separate on our own, for it is the job of the sieve to separate the chaff from the wheat. The chaff and wheat are separated in the sieve, and we find out what is more valuable in our lives. Faith in any other thing or person than Christ's finished work is broken, discarded, and considered useless. However, faith in the finished work of

Christ is cherished and valuable, for it is gathered into the barn to be properly kept.

The chaff is useless, although we may have cherished it in times past and tended it as we tended the wheat. When the chaff is separated from the wheat, it is discarded or burned because it isn't profitable. There is no life or strength in it, but the wheat is gathered into the barn because we know that it provides life and strength. We know we can feed upon it, which will sustain our lives and strengthen us. There is much chaff in our faith that we don't even know about, but the sieve is designed to separate it from faith in the finished work of Christ, so we no longer tend to it or look unto it for life and strength. Wheat represents the weightier matter of faith, and in it abides the life and strength we need. Peter's faith would be sifted, as faith in himself would be separated from faith in Christ.

Though the sieve was harsh enough to destroy Peter, it wasn't great enough to destroy his faith. Though Peter must have felt like his faith had been broken, it is evident that it never failed. Peter had faith in Jesus, which would be tested, but it would never fail, for Jesus had prayed that it wouldn't. Peter's faith was broken in the sieve of Satan, but not his godly faith. The faith Peter had in himself to serve and confess Jesus was broken, but not faith in Christ. This was part of God's purpose of allowing Peter to be sifted, if not the entire purpose. His faith would be tried, and the chaff would be separated. Peter's faith in himself would be broken, and then it would be discarded, but his godly faith would remain. Peter would learn that he lacked the strength to hold on to Jesus. Yet, he also learned that Jesus was strong enough to hold on to him.

This is what the sieve of Satan does. It is greater than we are by design. Our strength isn't sufficient to handle the sieve, but Christ's strength is. In the sieve of Satan, we learn we aren't strong enough, which causes us to look for a greater power source. We find this greater power source in the finished work of Christ, and therefore, the sieve of Satan causes us to forsake faith in ourselves and trust solely in Jesus. When this happens, the godly work the Lord sees fit to produce in our lives is accomplished in the sieve, and now we come forth forsaking all faith in ourselves, only trusting in the finished work of Christ.

Peter came out of this sieve as a strengthener of the brethren because he no longer relied upon his own strength but only on Christ's. Now, he has strength to spare, and now, he has strength to share, for the strength of the Lord is always more than enough. The sieve of Satan has broken the faith he had in himself, as he has failed, but it has caused him to place faith in the finished work of Christ, which will never fail and always remains.

Sometimes, Saints are sifted to the point that they feel like they have lost their faith, but we only think we have, for I'm convinced that Jesus has also prayed for us. In these times, let's look unto Jesus, for He is the author and finisher of our faith. Jesus is not only the author of our faith but the finisher of it, for as sure as Jesus authors our faith, He will also finish it. Yes, dear Saints of God, Jesus is the finisher of it, for Philippians 1:6 says, *"Being confident of this very thing, that he which hath begun a good work in you will perform it until the day of Jesus Christ."*

Sometimes, we may feel that the sieve of Satan will separate all faith from us, but it will not, for the Lord only allows us to go into the sieve that the chaff may be separated from us, not the wheat. The Lord will not allow one grain of wheat to fall unto the ground (Amos 9:9). Though Peter was sifted, as his faith came under assault, we know Jesus prayed for him before he ever went into the sieve, and we also know Peter's faith didn't fail. It is evident that Peter's faith didn't fail, for after God blessed him to come out of this sieve, we see that Peter's faith was greater than when he went into it. Peter's faith in himself failed, but his faith in Christ didn't. Peter went into the sieve, trusting too much in himself, but he came out trusting only in Christ. His faith in himself failed, for he denied Jesus, but this caused him to trust more in Christ, Who never fails.

After Peter's sifting, we see that he preached to the Jews during Pentecost and to the people in the temple. Yes, he preached Jesus to the very ones who had Jesus crucified, and we also learn from Christian history that when it came time for Peter to be martyred, he desired that they crucify him upside-down, for he said, I'm not worthy to be crucified like my Lord.

Let's look at the two promises Jesus gave Peter before he went into the sieve of Satan. Two promises which would come to pass after Peter came out of Satan's sieve. These two promises were that Peter would be converted and that he would strengthen his brethren.

We have already looked at the Greek word translated converted and its definition. The word converted means turned again, come again, or to return. So, to come again or return would mean that you were at a certain place, left, and have come back to the place you left. So, where was Peter, when did he leave, and when did he return? When Jesus was telling Peter that Satan desired to sift him as wheat, Peter was confessing Jesus as the Christ; when Satan sifted Peter, Peter denied Christ, but when Peter was converted, he returned to confessing Christ. Peter confessed Jesus as the Christ, but the night Jesus was betrayed, he denied even knowing the Lord. Peter's own faith wasn't sufficient to keep him in the place he was (confessing Christ). Therefore, Peter failed, denying Christ, but Peter would return. Yes, Peter did return, for he left in his own power but returned in the power of the Lord. He left trusting in himself but returned trusting in Christ.

There are times in our Christian walk when the sieve of Satan will come into our lives. We, too, will find ourselves there, for in the sieve of Satan, God allows faith in ourselves to be separated from us so that we would trust more in Christ.

Peter's faith was sifted, and faith in himself was crushed and discarded. Now, his faith consisted more of faith in Christ than in himself. Remember, Peter said he would never deny the Lord, even if it meant imprisonment or death, but deny the Lord he did, for he wasn't strong enough to confess Him in the sieve of Satan. Peter's faith in himself was broken, crushed, and eventually separated from him that he would trust in Christ instead. Now that Peter's faith in himself is separated from him, and he relies upon Christ's strength instead of his own, he is now a strengthener of the brethren. Peter was sifted, and Peter failed because his strength wasn't enough. Yet, the promised conversion would come just as Jesus said it would.

As sure as the sifting came, the conversion would come, and as sure as the rooster crowed, Peter would return.

Three days after the crucifixion, Christ rose from the grave. The women came unto the tomb early that morning and saw that the stone in its mouth had been rolled away. They entered the tomb and saw an angel who told them that Jesus had risen from the dead. Then, the angel gave them these instructions, which said, *"But go your way, tell his disciples and Peter that he goeth before you into Galilee: there shall ye see him, as he said unto you"* (Mark 16:7). The women came and told the disciples that Jesus had risen from the dead, which stunned them to say the least, and then the women would have given the disciples the angel's instructions, which told them to go to Galilee to meet Jesus.

Let's think about Peter during this amazing conversation. Peter had denied Christ only three days earlier. Had he gotten over this? I'm sure he hadn't. I'm sure he was still experiencing a lot of guilt and shame. I'm sure his denial of Christ was still fresh in his mind, but let's notice the instructions the angel gave unto the women at the tomb, which said, *"But go your way, tell his disciples and Peter that he goeth before you into Galilee: there shall ye see him, as he said unto you"* (Mark 16:7). Jesus had risen, and as He had told them before His crucifixion, He would go before them into Galilee. The angel told the women to tell the disciples *"and Peter"* that they were to come and meet the risen Christ at Galilee.

Notice, in these instructions, only one disciple is called by name. The angel told the women to tell Jesus' disciples *"and Peter."* Why not, and John, or, and James? Why, *"and Peter"*?

Peter was the one who denied Jesus on the night He was betrayed. Peter was the one who wept bitterly because he denied Christ. Peter was the one who felt guilty for denying the Lord. Peter may have been struggling and possibly feeling unworthy of being called a disciple of Christ. Yet, in these heavenly instructions, which the women carried back unto the disciples, the Lord let Peter know He wanted him to come and see Him in Galilee. Those two words would have let Peter know that the Lord wanted him to come and meet Him as well. These two words would have let Peter know that the Lord still saw him as a disciple. Jesus knew Peter needed to hear these two words, and the Lord ensured that he did.

These two words would give Peter confidence to believe God would restore him after his epic failure. Remember, it only took one word (*"Come"*) for Peter to have the faith to walk on the water (Matthew 14:29), but here we see that Jesus gave him two words (*"and Peter"*). It is often harder for us to believe the Lord will restore us after we have sinned than to walk on water before we have failed. Yet, Jesus wants Peter to know His grace has restored him, and I believe He also wants us to know the same. Though we sin and fail Christ in epic proportions, our Lord will restore us, for the gifts and callings of God are without repentance (Romans 11:29).

Though the Prodigal Son was prodigal, he was still a son, and though the failing Saints are failing, they are still Saints. Though the Prodigal Son left his father's house and wasted his inheritance in the far country, living riotously, his sonship restored him to his position in the father's house (Luke 15:11-32). The actions of the Prodigal Son could never restore him, for he told the father that he was no longer worthy to be called his son, begging him to make him one of his hired servants. Yet, the father could never see him as a servant because he was his son.

The same is true with the Saints of God. Sometimes, we fail, but the Father restores us because we are his children. Sure, we often think we must work our way back into the Father's good graces, but we, too, are like the Prodigal Son. We have nothing to offer.

The Prodigal Son wasted everything the father had given him in the far country. There was no possible way that he could restore these things. He was so destitute that he took a job feeding the swine, longing to eat the slop he fed to the hogs. We can do nothing to restore ourselves, but we should learn a lesson from the Prodigal Son. He ran back to the father. He relied on his father's mercy to raise him out of the hog slop he was wallowing in in the far country. He hoped the father's mercy would allow him to return home and be a servant.

I'm sure the Prodigal Son probably felt like he would be asking a lot of his father, seeing he sinned so greatly against him. He hoped the father's mercies would be great enough to allow him to return to his house as a servant. Yet, he would be pleasantly surprised, for he found that the mercies of the father were greater than he imagined. The Prodigal Son hoped that the father's mercies would grant him the office of a servant in his house, but the mercies of the father were far greater than he anticipated. The mercies of the father did raise him out of the hog slop as the Prodigal Son had hoped. Yet, the mercies of the father raised him higher than the Prodigal Son ever dreamed. The mercies of the father raised him above his request. The mercies of the father raised the Prodigal Son above that of a servant in his house, for the father restored him as a son. Why? The love and mercies of the father were greater than the sins of the Prodigal Son!

In the Bible, we are told that God's mercies are new every morning and endure forever (Lamentations 3:22-23; Psalms 107:1). Yes, we must lean hard on God's mercy, for there, and there alone, we are restored. We are not only received in the Father's house, but our authority and duties are restored as well.

When the Prodigal Son returned to the father's house desiring to be one of his servants, the father placed a ring on his finger. The ring probably bore the family crest, which would have identified him not only as a son but also as one who had the authority to conduct business on the father's estate, in the father's house, and in the father's name.

Remember, God not only forgives but also restores. We are restored because we are His children, restored because of the Father's mercy. Though we have greatly failed the Father, we should return to Him speedily because of His mercy. He will receive us, for we are His children, not His servants.

If our relationship with God were solely based on that of a servant and a master, then returning after failures would be impossible. This is because the relationship between a master and a servant is entirely based on service, and we haven't always conducted ourselves appropriately, nor can we repay, fix, undo, or amend our failures. We, like the Prodigal Son, have nothing to offer. Yet, our relationship to God is that of children. Therefore, we can come back to the Father because of His mercy. If we are to leave the far country and return to the Father's house, we must rely completely on His mercy. This is the only hope we have. Yet, it is greater than hope, for God's mercies are guaranteed. God's mercies are the incentive we have to run back to Him after we have failed, and knowing of God's infinite mercies grants us the faith to come home, for we are sure He will treat us like sons, although we don't even deserve to be called His servants.

Let's get back to Peter after the resurrection of Christ, God willing. The angels had sent the women back to instruct the disciples *"and Peter"* to go to Galilee to meet up with Jesus. Though Peter probably felt he was no longer worthy of being called a disciple of the Lord, Jesus sent these two words (*"and Peter"*) to let him know that he was still His disciple. Though Peter, the disciple of Christ, had failed, he is still a disciple of Christ! Jesus wanted Peter to know His grace had restored him. Jesus wanted Peter to know that he was still His disciple.

Peter would come and meet the risen Jesus at Galilee, and fifty days after the resurrection, he would preach Christ mightily on the day of Pentecost. Peter would never deny Jesus again, for he would spend the rest of his life confessing Him as the Christ and the only way of salvation. Peter would never again allow the fear and shame of the cross to keep him from confessing Jesus, for according to Christian history, he was crucified upside-down for preaching the gospel because he said he wasn't worthy to be crucified like his Lord. Peter was converted! Peter once again confessed Christ and had become a strengthener of the brethren.

Now, after coming out of the sieve of Satan, Peter was a strengthener of the brethren, but we must also understand that Satan wasn't going to fold up his tent and quit trying to tempt and hinder Peter. Satan would still seek to resist him on every hand. I don't know all the ways Satan would have sought to tempt and hinder Peter, but we do know that Peter's relationship with the Gentiles was one of the ways, although we won't speak of that. Let's look at something Satan tries to tempt and hinder us with instead. Let's look at the crowing rooster.

Mark 14:30. *"And Jesus saith unto him, Verily I say unto thee, That this day, even in this night, before the cock crow twice, thou shalt deny me thrice."*

Jesus told Peter the night before the crucifixion that he would deny Him three times. Peter insisted that he wouldn't. Yet, Jesus told him that he would do so that very night, saying, *"Before the cock crow twice, you will deny Me thrice."* That very night, Peter denied the Lord three times, and immediately after the third time, the rooster crowed.

I've often wondered how Peter would have felt when he heard a rooster crow throughout the rest of his life. I'd say he heard roosters crow many times after he denied Christ and was converted. I've often wondered how the rooster's crow affected Peter after that night when he denied knowing the Lord. This may have caused him to feel guilty, shameful, and dirty every time he heard a rooster crow, and so it is with us as well.

So often, when we are strengthened in the Lord, Satan will ensure that we hear the rooster crow. Satan will make sure we are reminded of our past sins in some form or fashion. The purpose behind Satan desiring us to hear the rooster crow is that he wants to weaken us. He wants to take us back to the time we denied the Lord, to the times of our sins and epic failures. Satan doesn't want us to walk in the forgiveness of God but in condemnation before Him.

During these times, we often feel the strength drain out of us because we concentrate more on our sins than God's forgiveness. How many times would Satan have tried to weaken the mighty Peter through the sound of an eight-pound rooster? How many times would Satan have tried to cause Peter to stop in his tracks concerning his walk for the Lord by the crowing of a small rooster? Satan does the same thing to us, as he tries to cause us to live in the time of our sins instead of the freedom and joy of God's forgiveness. If he can cause us to feel condemned before God, he has weakened us in our heavenly calling. So often, we run well, but the sound of the little rooster hinders us. Our joy ceases in these times because we aren't walking in God's forgiveness, although we have been forgiven, for we are walking in condemnation before God, although we aren't condemned.

The rooster's crow is designed to cause us to feel unforgiven, unrestored, condemned, guilty, shameful, and dirty when we are forgiven, restored, cleansed, and justified. The rooster's crow is designed to bring this unforgiven, grief-stricken feeling to the forefront of our minds. It is designed to cause us to feel condemned, guilty, and dirty before God when we aren't. As stated earlier in this book, how we feel or think can become real to us, even though it isn't real.

If Peter is going to walk in the power of his calling, he will have to overcome the sound of the rooster, as will we. How can Peter get this sound out of his mind? How can he keep the crowing rooster from causing him to feel guilt, shame, and condemnation, which produces weakness? How can we?

Peter must remember the two words of the angel on the resurrection morning. Peter must remember, *"and Peter,"* for this will grant him the ability to overcome the crowing rooster. Peter must place faith in these words and never forget them, for they are the words that told Peter that Jesus confessed him as His disciple. In other words, Peter is forgiven and restored. These two words not only gave Peter the confidence to go and meet Jesus in Galilee but would also be the means by which he could overcome the rooster's crow. Peter is forgiven and restored by the Lord Himself and called to be a strengthener of the brethren. The same is true with all Saints.

We will all sin at some point or another, and Satan will try to convince us that this disqualifies us from the calling of God upon our lives, but we must remember that the gifts and callings of God are without repentance (Romans 11:29). Yes, we must remember we are forgiven, not condemned, for the scriptures say,

1 John 1:8-2:2. *"If we say that we have no sin, we deceive ourselves, and the truth is not in us. If we confess our sins, he is faithful and just to forgive us our sins and to cleanse us from all unrighteousness. If we say that we have not sinned, we make him a liar, and his word is not in us. My little children, these things write I unto you, that ye sin not. And if any man sin, we have an advocate with the Father, Jesus Christ the righteous:*

*And he is the propitiation for our sins: and not for ours only, but also for the sins of the whole world."*

We must remember that God forgives and restores us, for these verses are written unto the children of God. We must trust in the forgiveness of God if we are going to overcome the sound of the crowing rooster.

Let's look at a time when the Jews were greatly saddened by their previous sins.

Nehemiah 8:10. *"Then he said unto them, Go your way, eat the fat, and drink the sweet, and send portions unto them for whom nothing is prepared: for this day is holy unto our Lord: neither be ye sorry; for the joy of the LORD is your strength."*

Let's look at what happened before this verse was written. This will help us understand the context in which it is written, granting us a greater and clearer meaning of this verse.

Nebuchadnezzar carried the Jews away captive to Babylon because of their sins. They were captives in Babylon for seventy years. Yet, Cyrus, king of Persia, after conquering Babylon, gave them the liberty and means to rebuild the temple that Nebuchadnezzar had burned to the ground.

Nehemiah 8:10 was written around a century after Cyrus' decree, which allowed the Jews to rebuild the temple. Nehemiah had come to Jerusalem to rebuild the wall Nebuchadnezzar had broken down. During this time, the word of the Lord was read to all the Jews who had come to Jerusalem, and they saw how great their sins were, and therefore, they became very sad. They were in mourning because of previous sins committed by them and their ancestors. They felt sorrowful, guilty, shameful, and condemned because of all the sins they had committed against God. Yet, Nehemiah, the governor of Jerusalem, Ezra, the priest, and scribe, along with the Levites, came and spoke unto the people the words of Nehemiah 8:10. They, in essence, let the people know that they should be joyful on this day, for it is evident by the rebuilding of the temple and the wall that the Lord's favor was upon them. It was evident that they were forgiven and still had a call of God upon their lives, and therefore, they should rejoice because the joy of the Lord is their strength.

The joy of the Lord is our strength as well, and this joy comes from knowing we are forgiven, and by knowing we are forgiven, we also know we have a calling of God upon our lives. The Bible doesn't say that Christians will live a sinless, perfected life, but quite the opposite. The Bible teaches us that Christians will sin. Yet, the Bible also says that if we confess our sins, God is faithful and just to forgive us of our sins, for our righteous Jesus is our advocate, Who sets on the right hand of God, ever living to make intercession for us (1 John 1:8-2:2).

Remember, Saints will sin, but when we confess our sins unto the Lord, we are guaranteed forgiveness and cleansing from all unrighteousness. Although we are to confess our sins, it is evident that our sins are forgiven before we even ask, for Jesus is always on the right hand of the Father, making intercession for us (Romans 8:34), and the Bible says that our heavenly Father knows what we need before we even ask (Matthew 6:8). Yet, we should still acknowledge and confess our sins before the Father, for this carries weight in this life. When we confess our sins unto the Father, it takes away chastisement and the destructive power of sin in this life on earth, although we have already been forgiven in heaven. This causes our fellowship with God to be unbroken or restored. This lines us up with the windows of heaven so that the blessings of God in this life won't be withheld from us.

Yet, the crowing rooster often causes us to remember our sins. This causes us to feel like an unforgiven sinner. This weakens us, causing us to fall into sadness and despair. When we do this, we aren't counting God as faithful, nor are we counting Him to be just because we are still acting as if we are unforgiven concerning the sin or sins we have confessed unto the Father. This is not about our faithfulness and justness but God's faithfulness and justness. When we carry sin or the guilt and shame of it with us after it has been confessed to the Father, we are doubting God's faithfulness and justness. God says He is faithful and just to forgive us of our sins when we confess them unto Him (1 John 1:9). Therefore, we are forgiven and should feel like we are forgiven. Remember, this isn't about our faithfulness and justness but about God's. As sure as God is faithful and just, these confessed sins are forgiven, and we are cleansed from all unrighteousness.

Previous sins saddened the Jews and, therefore, weakened them because the joy of the Lord is our strength. Remember, Jesus told His disciples after they had returned from preaching the Kingdom, healing the sick, and casting out demons, rejoice not because demons are subjected unto you, but rejoice because your name is written in heaven (Luke 10:20). Saints experience joy unspeakable and full of glory when we remember that we are forgiven. This, in return, strengthens us, for the joy of the Lord is our strength.

Abraham Lincoln once said, "Right makes might" when speaking of the challenges of abolishing slavery. Knowing we are in right standing with God causes us to be strong, for the joy of the Lord is our strength.

So, the next time we hear the rooster crow, which reminds us of previous sins, we should remember that we are as forgiven and cleansed of these sins as God is faithful and just. Then, the crowing rooster will no longer be able to steal your joy, for you have overcome him through faith in the mercies and promises of God, which come unto us through the finished work of Christ. Our joy will remain full, although the rooster crows all night and day, for the Father is faithful and just to forgive us of our sins. The sound of the rooster will be drowned out by the sweet melody of forgiveness when we truly trust God's faithfulness and justness to forgive our confessed sins. Yes, they have been cast into the depths of the sea, never to be remembered anymore, and as far as the east is from the west (Micah 7:19; Hebrews 10:17; Psalms 103:12).

Therefore, this lets us know who the crowing rooster is after we have been forgiven and restored. God no longer remembers our sins, which means He isn't the One reminding us of them, which means the crowing rooster is Satan in this instance.

Sure, the crowing rooster was the thunderclap of conviction on the night Jesus was betrayed, but after Peter is converted, the crowing rooster is Satan. The crowing rooster on the night Peter denied Christ was conviction, but after he was turned back, the crowing rooster is false conviction. Yes, we must take some caution in the discernment of the rooster's crow, for it is conviction when we sin, but it is the devil trying to condemn us through false conviction when it reminds us of past sins in which the word of God assures us that we have been forgiven of. Satan, transforming himself into an angel of light, as he is so adept at doing, wants you to continue to think that the crowing rooster is conviction after you have confessed and forsaken your sins. Yet, it is not conviction after the sin is confessed and forsaken, for God has forgiven us of this sin, and this forgiveness is as sure as He is faithful and just. Therefore, we are strengthened because of the joy of the Lord, which comes through forgiveness, and we overcome the rooster's crow when we trust in God's forgiveness. Remember, confessed sin is as forgiven as the Father is faithful and just, and may God bless us to hear and say *"and Peter"* every time we hear the rooster crow afterward.

If we take the rooster's crow to heart after we have been forgiven and allow it to cause us to feel unforgiven and disqualified in our calling, then we have allowed this small, feathered fowl to weaken us. He will cause us guilt and shame when we should be rejoicing in the Lord. This will hinder our calling, but if we will remember *"and Peter,"* then the rooster's crow won't be able to affect us.

We must rest in God's forgiveness, or the rooster's sound will overcome us. We must rest in the wounds of Christ so that we will no longer be faithless but believe. When we are doubtful, let us concentrate on the wounds of Christ and do as Jesus told Thomas to do, as He said in John 20:27, *"Reach hither thy finger, and behold my hands; and reach hither thy hand, and thrust it into my side: and be not faithless, but believing."*

When we truly concentrate on the wounds of Christ, our faith will be strengthened. The wounds of Christ save us, forgive us, restore us, and grant us all the promises of God. This will cause us to no longer be faithless but believing, for Christ's wounds have produced the entirety of God's grace and mercy in our lives. When we rest in the wounds of Christ, we understand that we have the grace and mercy of God because of these wounds, which will cause us to no longer place faith in ourselves but in the finished work of Christ. This will produce the works of God in our lives and cause us to understand we are forgiven children of God, for the blood of Christ has become our confidence, not our failing performance or anything else. We must rest in the forgiveness of God through Christ, or the rooster's crow will cause us guilt and shame, weakening us. Yes, we must trust in the finished work of Christ and the faithfulness and justness of the Father for the forgiveness of sin if we will successfully overcome the condemning crow of the rooster.

After the resurrection of Christ, we see that Peter became a leader among the apostles. Peter was now a strengthener of the brethren. Peter had come unto a place where he could strengthen his fellow Christians, for he no longer trusted in his own strength but in the strength of Christ. Oh, the power which was revealed in Peter and the mighty preaching that came from his lips. The ministry the Lord gave Peter was supernatural, for he was blessed to heal the sick, raise the dead, and preach the everlasting gospel of Christ with the power of heaven.

Peter was now a strengthener of the brethren, but how did this come about in his life? This came about in the sieve of Satan. Remember, Jesus told Peter that Satan desires to have you that he may sift you like wheat, but also told him He had prayed for him that his faith wouldn't fail, and when he was converted, he was to strengthen the brethren. Peter wasn't a strengthener of the brethren before he went into the sieve of Satan. Yet, when he came out, he was! There was an amazing work that was worked into the life of Peter through this sifting, which is why the Lord allowed it.

Peter learned something about himself in Satan's sieve that he previously didn't know. He learned that he wasn't as strong as he thought he was. Peter thought he would never deny Jesus, but in Satan's sieve, he did. Peter saw more of himself in this sieve and learned how to trust the Lord more.

Peter had to learn to trust Christ after he denied Him. This shows that Peter would have seen more of God's grace than he had previously seen. Mercy and grace become more evident when we recognize our need for them rather than when we fail to understand that need. This realization would have caused Peter to lean less upon himself and more upon the Lord, which would have made his ministry more powerful.

When Peter's faith was sifted, faith in himself was broken so that he would learn to trust in Christ. When Peter trusted in Christ instead of himself, then the power of Christ was greatly manifest in his life, which would have empowered him to be a strengthener of the brethren. Peter's own strength wasn't sufficient to strengthen the brethren, but the strength of Christ was. Therefore, Peter's faith was sifted that faith in himself would be broken and discarded, but faith in Christ remained. Through faith in Christ's finished work, Peter now had enough strength for himself and others, becoming the brethren's great strengthener.

We can also see that Peter was set free from something as well. Peter was no longer afraid of the pain and shame of the cross, for he rejoiced that he was counted worthy to suffer shame for Christ's sake when the priests had him flogged for preaching Jesus to be the Christ (Acts 5:41). It was also his preaching that caused him to be crucified upside-down (according to Christian history). The fear of the cross would no longer hinder Peter in the ministry, for the fiery trial had melted the great chain of fear that bound him.

We see that the sieve of Satan was a miserable place for Peter to be. However, God worked magnificent things in his life through it. This experience would have been something Peter would have carried around with him. Something that would have profited him throughout the rest of his life.

We can also see what wonderful fruit God worked in Peter's life after that. Such plenteous and huge fruit would have outweighed the cluster of grapes the Israelite spies put on a pole and had two men carry out of the Promise Land (Numbers 13:23).

Though this sifting of Peter nearly killed him, bringing him to the greatest depths of misery, we can see that the Lord had a plan in all of this, for the Lord would have never allowed Satan to sift Peter if it wasn't going to work something greater in his life. The sieve of Satan plumbed the depths of bitterness, condemnation, and sorrow in Peter's soul. Yet, God would make Peter a strengthener of the brethren, and the Lord caused this to come about in Satan's sieve.

Peter was converted and became one of the greatest strengtheners of the brethren this world has ever seen. God had called Peter to be a strengthener of the brethren, and Peter came out of Satan's sieve better than he went in, for true faith wasn't separated from him, only the chaff in his life.

Peter was converted, just as Jesus said he would be. Peter did return, just as Jesus said he would, but he didn't return the same. Peter returned a stronger Christian than when he left. Peter came out of Satan's sieve greater in Spirit and weaker in the flesh than when he went in.

God had called Peter to a great calling and would ensure he was prepared for it. This preparation came about in the sieve of Satan. God had a great plan for Peter; therefore, He allowed Satan to sift him like wheat. Yet, when Peter came out of the sieve, he was increased in the earth, meaning Satan was weakened therein. Once again, to paraphrase Spurgeon, Satan has thrown a brick into the air, never considering that it would come down and hit him on his own head.

# CHAPTER 14
# GETHSEMANE

Matthew 26:36-46. *"Then cometh Jesus with them unto a place called Gethsemane, and saith unto the disciples, Sit ye here, while I go and pray yonder. And he took with him Peter and the two sons of Zebedee, and began to be sorrowful and very heavy. Then saith he unto them, My soul is exceeding sorrowful, even unto death: tarry ye here, and watch with me. And he went a little further, and fell on his face, and prayed, saying, O my Father, if it be possible, let this cup pass from me: nevertheless not as I will, but as thou wilt. And he cometh unto the disciples, and findeth them asleep, and saith unto Peter, What, could ye not watch with me one hour? Watch and pray that ye enter not into temptation: the spirit indeed is willing, but the flesh is weak. He went away again the second time and prayed, saying, O my Father, if this cup may not pass away from me, except I drink it, thy will be done. And he came and found them asleep again, for their eyes were heavy. And he left them and went away again and prayed the third time, saying the same words. Then cometh he to his disciples, and saith unto them, Sleep on now, and take your rest: behold, the hour is at hand, and the Son of man is betrayed into the hands of sinners. Rise, let us be going: behold, he is at hand that doth betray me."*

Luke 22:39-48. *"And he came out, and went, as he was wont, to the mount of Olives; and his disciples also followed him. And when he was at the place, he said unto them, Pray that ye enter not into temptation. And he was withdrawn from them about a stone's cast, and kneeled down, and prayed, Saying, Father, if thou be willing, remove this cup from me: nevertheless not my will, but thine, be done. And there appeared an angel unto him from heaven, strengthening him. And being in an agony he prayed more earnestly: and his sweat was as it were great drops of blood falling down to the ground. And when he rose up from prayer, and was come to his disciples, he found them sleeping for sorrow, And said unto them, Why sleep ye? rise and pray, lest ye enter into temptation. And while he yet spake, behold a multitude, and he that was called Judas, one of the twelve, went before them, and drew near unto Jesus to kiss him. But Jesus said unto him, Judas, betrayest thou the Son of man with a kiss?"*

Gethsemane is the place Jesus went to after eating the Passover with His disciples on the night Judas betrayed him. Gethsemane was a garden of olive trees, and the word Gethsemane means oil press. This is where the olives would be pressed to produce olive oil.

During the time of Jesus, this pressing wasn't done with modern machinery but by placing weight upon the olives with a device they had invented. This device consisted of a pole standing vertically and another pole sitting upon it horizontally. The horizontal pole would move up and down upon the vertical pole, somewhat like a teeter-totter, and the horizontal pole was somewhat long.

The olives would be placed in a container, and the press would be attached to the horizontal pole. The horizontal pole would be lowered until the press met the olives, and then a basket of rocks would be hung on the horizontal pole, producing the weight required to press the olives. The olives would be under this weight for some time (I think an entire day). Then, the basket of rocks hanging on the horizontal pole would be moved outward towards the end of the horizontal pole, which would create more pressure on the olives and extract more oil. The olives would be left under this weight for a certain amount of time, and then the rocks would be moved outwards again, creating more weight and causing more pressure to be placed upon the olives, which would extract more oil. I think this was done three times. Under this weight, the olives were pressed, and the oil would be extracted.

Gethsemane is where Jesus and His disciples came after eating the Passover, or what many refer to as the Last Supper, on the night He was betrayed. There, in the Garden of Gethsemane, Jesus was exceedingly sorrowful unto death, and He cast Himself on the ground and prayed three times. During these prayers, Jesus was under so much pressure that His sweat became as great drops of blood falling onto the ground.

The time was at hand in which Jesus would be betrayed, beaten, mocked, and crucified, and this is what Jesus was praying about. Jesus asked the Father if there was any way this could pass from Him, and if so, could the will of God still be accomplished? The answer was no, and Jesus accepted it and went towards the cross, although He could have called for twelve legions of angels to deliver Him from it at any time.

I will not attempt to comment on what Jesus was feeling at this time, for this pressure would have been greater than any person has ever felt, greater than we could ever imagine or hope to understand. However, Jesus was in agony, to the point that His sweat became as great drops of blood falling to the ground. Jesus was under so much pressure that His sweat began to pour as blood. Jesus was being pressed in the Garden of Olives.

With this being said, I'd like to take a moment to look at Saints who must also travel to the Garden of Gethsemane. Although we never feel the pressure Jesus felt that night, we are brought unto Gethsemane and pressed on certain occasions. A messenger of Satan, which is sent to buffet us, may press us, or we may be pressed by guilt and shame because we have sinned. Regardless of the circumstances, whether it is chastisement or tribulation, we must be pressed sometimes, and sometimes this pressing may be for a little while or many days. We are placed into the press for the same reasons the olives are placed into it, for the oil won't flow without the pressing.

God allows us to be pressed for a reason. More of the flesh must be crushed, and we must learn to trust God in a greater manner so that the oil will flow more abundantly in our lives. The outer hulls of the olives keep the oil from flowing, and our flesh hinders the flow of the Holy Spirit in our lives. Remember, the olives must go through multiple pressings, and we often do as well. Sometimes, the Holy Spirit may be flowing in our lives. However, God has placed so much more in us than is coming out. God wants the Holy Spirit to flow greater in our lives, and therefore, He allows us to be pressed that the flesh would become pulp and the Holy Spirit would flow more abundantly. Remember, the olives went through multiple pressings so that all the oil would be extracted.

Those pressing the olives know there is more oil in the olives than the first pressing produces; therefore, they press them repeatedly until they are confident that all the oil has come out of them. The same is true with us, for we may be pressed today and then must be pressed later. God will see that enough oil is extracted for the godly task at hand, and when God decides to increase our calling, He will see that some more oil is extracted.

When we are saved, God places the Holy Spirit within us and has a calling for our lives. We have everything we need to fulfill our callings within us, in the person of the Holy Spirit, but He doesn't always flow in our lives as God intends Him to because of the flesh. We either lack faith or revelation or have too much lust and pride for the Holy Spirit to flow as greatly as God intends. Therefore, we must be pressed at Gethsemane so the oil will flow greater in our lives. God doesn't allow us to be pressed without a purpose, nor do the pressers of olives press them without a purpose, for there is something inside that is very valuable, and for it to come out, the olives and the flesh must be crushed.

We have spoken earlier in this book concerning the working of the Holy Spirit in our lives. The Holy Spirit is strong enough to take over our lives at any moment, but He doesn't work like that. For the most part, or probably always, the Holy Spirit doesn't make us do something against our will, for the Bible says, *"the spirits of the prophets are subject to the prophets"* (1 Corinthians 14:32).

Jimmy Swaggart correctly says that the Holy Spirit works through a prescribed order, which is faith in Christ's finished work.

Anytime we trust in ourselves to do the works of the Lord, it is pride, and the Holy Spirit will not work in our lives through pride, for that is not God's prescribed order. If we walk in lust, the Holy Spirit won't flow in that part of our lives because that is not God's prescribed order. Therefore, when the work of the Holy Spirit in our lives is hindered by these things, God allows us to be pressed so that the flesh would be crushed, and the Holy Spirit would flow greater in our lives.

Remember, the purpose of the olive press is to cause the oil to flow, and the purpose for Saints being pressed is to cause the Holy Spirit to flow more abundantly in our lives. The entire purpose of the press is to cause the oil to flow, not to inflict pain upon the olives. Although the press is painful to us, we must remember the purpose of the press. The press is designed to cause the oil to flow, but to cause the oil to flow, the olives must be crushed. The flesh will hinder the work of the Holy Spirit in our lives; therefore, God allows us to be pressed so that the Holy Spirit will flow in a greater manner. It is extremely painful for us to have the flesh crushed, but we must understand it is necessary, for God has a great call upon the lives of all Saints, and He will see that we perform it.

No, we can't perform God's call upon our lives by our own abilities, which are fleshly. No, we can't perform it through any means of the flesh. The flesh can't perform the call of God upon our lives, but so often, we rely on our own fleshly abilities to do just that. So often, we walk in the flesh and think we are walking in the Spirit, which hinders the work of the Holy Spirit in our lives. Therefore, God allows us to be pressed so that the flesh will be crushed and the Holy Spirit will flow greater in our lives.

Remember what Paul said when he thought he was going to be martyred? Paul said he was pressed out of measure and above his strength, for he had the sentence of death in himself, but this hard time forced Paul to trust in God for the resurrection (2 Corinthians 1:8-9). Yes, this brought Paul to a place where he learned to trust God for the resurrection, which greatly added to his ministry. Notice these verses.

Galatians 2:20-21. *"I am crucified with Christ: nevertheless I live; yet not I, but Christ liveth in me: and the life which I now live in the flesh I live by the faith of the Son of God, who loved me and gave himself for me. I do not frustrate the grace of God: for if righteousness come by the law, then Christ is dead in vain."*

Paul is saying he is crucified with Christ, but he is still alive, yet it is not him that is living, but it is Christ living in him, and the life that he now lives, he lives by the faith of the Son of God, Who loved him and gave His life for him. This is a lot to unpack, but we will look at some of the things these verses teach us, God willing.

Paul is saying that all the things he has been blessed to do as a Christian have been done in three ways.

First, Paul is crucified with Christ. Now, we know Paul wasn't literally crucified at this time, nor was he ever literally crucified, for Christian history states that Paul was martyred by being beheaded. This shows the flesh of Paul being crucified. This shows his flesh to have been killed. Sure, it was painful unto Paul, but it was necessary if he was going to fulfill the call of God upon his life.

God spoke to Ananias concerning Paul, saying, *"For I will shew him how great things he must suffer for my name's sake"* (Acts 9:16). Although Paul was known to be a person of great zeal and willpower, he didn't have the ability in himself to perform the call of God upon his life. Such zeal and willpower served him well before he became a Christian, but it wouldn't be the vehicle in which God would have him live for Him. (Zeal is good if pointed in the right direction and wrought by faith.) These things had to be crucified in Paul's life so that he would learn to trust solely in the finished work of Christ to perform the call of God upon his life.

This brings us to our second point, which is that Paul said he was crucified, yet he lived, but it wasn't him that was living; it was Christ living in him. So, the life of Paul and all the great things he was blessed to do as an apostle of Jesus Christ wasn't done by him but by Christ living in him. The Holy Spirit did all these amazing and godly works in the life of Paul, and so it is also with every Saint, for the Holy Spirit must work godliness in us. It was the power of the Holy Spirit in Paul that did all these wonderful things, not Paul, not his willpower, not his brainpower, and not his zeal. The Holy Spirit performed all these wonderful things in Paul's life.

If we, as Christians, are going to do the works of God, it will be the Holy Spirit working them in our lives through faith in the finished work of Christ, or they won't be labeled as godly works in the Lord's eyes, but fleshly works, which may receive the praise of men, but never the praise of God.

Thirdly, Paul says he lived this amazing life *"by the faith of the Son of God,"* Who loved him and gave His life for him. Most translations translate *"the faith of the Son of God"* to mean faith in the Son of God, which I believe is the phrase's meaning. This shows us that Paul lived this wonderful life through faith in Christ. Therefore, it is evident that this is how we should also live our Christian lives. Christ's finished work must be the object of our faith. The finished work of Christ is the death, burial, and resurrection of Jesus, which Paul calls the gospel in 1 Corinthians 15:1-4. Here, we see Paul pointing us to the cross of Christ as he says that Christ loved him and gave Himself for him.

So, the three points of Paul living this amazing life were that he was crucified with Christ, Christ lived or worked in Him in the person of the Holy Spirit, and this was done through faith in the finished work of Christ.

It is needful for Saints to be crucified with Christ so that our flesh may die, and we would no longer trust in it to live for God. When this happens, we are forced to, or learn to trust in the finished work of Christ for Christian living, and then the Holy Spirit will move us into all godliness.

Let's look at the following verse (Galatians 2:21), *"I do not frustrate the grace of God: for if righteousness come by the law, then Christ is dead in vain."* Notice that Paul says he doesn't frustrate the grace of God in his life. In this verse, the Greek word translated *"frustrate"* means to set aside, i.e., disesteem, neutralize or violate, nullify (Strong's).

So, when Christians frustrate the grace of God, the grace of God isn't moving in their lives. The grace of God is neutralized in our lives when we frustrate it. So, this is saying that Paul doesn't neutralize the grace of God in his life, and then he tells us how the grace of God can be neutralized in the life of a Saint, as he says, *"for if righteousness come by the law, then Christ is dead in vain."* So, if Saints try to live for God by keeping the law, they will neutralize the grace of God in their lives.

The law is kept through the abilities of the flesh, such as our own willpower, zeal, education, &, etc. One's own fleshly abilities were used to try and keep the law. In other words, the way one tried to keep the law was by their own ability. We know from the Bible that no person has ever been able to obey the law in its entirety with both their hands and heart (desire, thought, and action) except Christ, for the Bible says, *"all have sinned, and come short of the glory of God"* (Romans 3:23).

This shows us that it is impossible for a person to keep the law. The reason is that humanity's fleshly abilities are inadequate to do so.

(It was by design that God gave Israel His holy law, which they couldn't keep because of the infirmity of their flesh, so that they, and we, may look unto Christ for salvation, sanctification, and blessing, and not unto our own hands. The law shows us we are sinners and are entirely inadequate to keep it, but Jesus came and kept the entire law with both heart and hands [desire, thought, and action] so that we could be made the righteousness of God through faith in Him.

The law was given unto the children of promise until Christ came. The children of promise didn't always know the will of God, and thus, they would sin ignorantly. Therefore, God gave them the law that they would know how God desired them to live, that they would know what righteousness was and what sin was.

People should never look to the law as a means by which one can obtain eternal life, for the law can't give life [Galatians 3:21]. It is simply a schoolmaster who leads them until Christ comes. No one can keep the law except Christ because our own abilities aren't sufficient for this task. The law condemns every person born of Adam, for all have sinned, and no one can be declared righteous by the law except Christ and those who trust in Him [Christians].

The law was also a restrainer of sin until Christ came, for there were many who desired to commit adultery during the dispensation of the law but wouldn't because they were afraid of the punishment the law would impose upon them, which was stoning.

God knew Israel couldn't keep the law. So, God gave provisions within the law for sin because He knew Israel couldn't keep it. God placed the priestly order and sacrificial system within it. This would have allowed Israel to stay in favor with God although they had sinned, for the law demands judgment. The judgment of their sins would be imposed upon the sacrificial animals. The priests or high priests would do the intercessory work required to keep them in favor with God. Although the blood of these animals couldn't take away their sins and these priests weren't perfect, God imputed their sins to the cross of Christ and their needed intercessory work to Christ's resurrection ministry on the right hand of God, which was to come because they placed faith in the sacrificial system and priestly order God gave them.

The law was also their sanctification and calling. Through them seeking to walk in the law, they would live a holier life, and by doing so, they would evangelize the nations.)

When Christians try to keep the law, we also try to keep it by our own abilities, which will strengthen sin in our lives. The

Bible says the strength of sin is the law (1 Corinthians 15:56), which we have already covered in this book.

When we try to live for God by relying on our own strength and abilities, even if we are not strictly following the Law of Moses, we are placing ourselves under the law, or law, in principle. This causes us to frustrate the grace of God because we are trusting in ourselves and not in the finished work of Christ, which produces godliness in our lives through the power and guidance of the Holy Spirit. When we try to live for God by the means of the flesh, we neutralize God's grace in our lives. This doesn't mean we have lost our salvation, but it does mean that the Holy Spirit will not move in our lives as He is intended to do or as mightily as He is intended to do. The Holy Spirit will not honor faith in ourselves, for He will only honor faith in the finished work of Christ. Therefore, the grace of God will be neutralized in the lives of Saints who aren't trusting in the finished work of Christ to perform godliness (godly works, godly desires, and love, etc.) in their lives.

Earlier, we discussed what it means to frustrate God's grace in our lives. To frustrate God's grace in our lives is to neutralize it.

Now, let's look at the word neutralize for a moment. If we try to live for God by any means other than faith in Christ's finished work, then we are trying to live for God by the law or law principles, which is to try to live for God by the means of the flesh (our own abilities). This will neutralize the grace of God in our lives. The grace of God consists of more than salvation, although if that were all that the grace of God is, we couldn't praise God enough for it. The grace of God is eternal salvation, sanctification, and blessing, for every answered prayer, every revelation of God, every godly work, love, and peace, etc., is part of God's grace, and when we aren't trusting in the finished work of Christ for eternal salvation, sanctification (godly living), and blessing, etc., then we frustrate grace. No, this doesn't mean we have lost our salvation, but it does mean that the power of the Holy Spirit will not flow in our lives as God intends for Him to or as greatly as God intends.

Let's think of a muscle car. Let's think of a beautiful car with a huge motor. This car has enormous power but will go nowhere if we put it in neutral. We can press the gas pedal to the floor, but the car still won't move. Why? It's in neutral. Though the engine has tremendous power, the car will not move because it is in neutral. The rear end isn't connected to the motor's power because the car is in neutral. If we want the motor's power to be transferred to the rear end (wheels), we must put the car into drive. This is not decided by the motor but by the driver. When the car is placed into drive, all the motor's power is transferred to the car, and now the car can move because of the motor's power. It is not the motor's responsibility to place the car into drive; it is the driver's responsibility.

Saints have an enormous power source placed within them, called the Holy Spirit. He is in us and will always remain, but sometimes, we don't see His power in our lives. Why? We have frustrated grace. We have neutralized the grace of God in our lives by not trusting in the finished work of Christ, which causes the Holy Spirit to move us into all godliness. The power source is there, but we are in neutral; therefore, the Holy Spirit isn't moving us.

If we want the power of God to move in our lives, we must start trusting Christ's finished work for godliness. This places the car into drive, which transfers the power of the motor to the car, or in our case, the power of the Holy Spirit to us. So often, we aren't trusting in the finished work of Christ for godliness because we are trusting in our own fleshly abilities for it, which neutralizes the grace of God in our lives. Therefore, it may be necessary for our flesh to be crucified so that we learn to no longer trust in it. Yes, we may have to be brought into the Garden of Gethsemane and pressed until our flesh becomes pulp so that the Holy Spirit would flow greater in our lives.

The flesh is a great enemy of all Saints, for it hinders the work of God in our lives. Therefore, although painful, we must be brought unto Gethsemane to crush the flesh so that the Spirit may flow greater in our lives.

We often fight against the press at Gethsemane, for we hold tightly unto the flesh and don't want to see it crushed, or we don't want to suffer the pain, anguish, and agony of the cross. Yet, we are still placed into the press as we fight against it, and we remain there until we say unto the Lord, not my will, but Thy will be done.

There is something so special about the press at Gethsemane. It is so special to the Saints, for it is there that our will becomes God's will. At Gethsemane, we learn to forsake the flesh we love so dearly that we may embrace the will of God. Now, I'm not saying this is what Jesus had to forsake, for Jesus was 100% righteous and was going to be made sin on the cross, but we are fleshly and sinful, and there, under the pressure of the press, we learn to cherish God's will above the pain the killing of the flesh subjects us to.

We also learn to cherish God's will above our love for the flesh. Yes, at Gethsemane, the cry of victory is heard as we shout, Father, not my will, but Thy will be done!

Gethsemane is where our will is brought into submission unto God's will. It is the place where our will becomes God's will. When this happens, then we will be led to Calvary for the crucifixion of the flesh. So often, the crushing of our flesh isn't what we want or desire, but at Gethsemane, we learn to desire it, although it is hard on us.

When we look at Jesus praying in agony in the Garden of Gethsemane, we can learn some things about Gethsemane. Again, we must understand that Jesus didn't have to have His sinful flesh crushed because there was no sinful way in Him, for He wasn't sinful flesh but made in the likeness of sinful flesh, yet He would be crushed for our sins.

The sin of the world would be laid upon Jesus, and the wrath of God would be poured out upon Him. The Bible teaches us that it pleased the Lord to bruise Him (Isaiah 53:10). Why would it please the Lord to bruise Christ? Christ was made sin for us. Christ was made an offering for sin on our behalf. The wrath of God is always at odds with sin. In all reality, as I have heard it said by Paul Washer, God saved us from Himself, for it was the wrath of God that was poured out upon Christ for our sins, not His sins.

Jesus came into the Garden of Gethsemane on the night He was betrayed, and there, He prayed in such agony that His sweat became as great drops of blood falling to the ground.

Jesus was about to be crushed in a greater manner than any other person in the history of humanity, for He was made a sin offering for the sins of the world. In the Garden of Gethsemane, Jesus prayed for two things.

The first thing was for God's will to be done. This was the main thing Jesus prayed for in this Garden, for it was the most important thing to Him.

Secondly, Jesus prayed that if it were possible, this cup might pass from Him. The cup Jesus spoke of consisted of all He would have to go through for the world's sins. He would be made an offering for sin, mocked, ridiculed, shamed, beaten, and crucified. This was the cup that Jesus prayed would pass from Him, but we must remember how Jesus prayed. Jesus prayed unto the Father, asking Him if He was willing, then let this cup pass from Him, but nevertheless, not My will, but Thy will be done.

Through this prayer Jesus prayed at Gethsemane, we can see He wanted the cup removed from Him, but not at the expense of God's will. Therefore, the will of the Father was the most important thing to Jesus, and it is evident that it was more important to Him than having the cup removed, for He prayed, *"Not My will, but Thine, be done."*

There at Gethsemane, Jesus agonized in prayer and was under so much pressure that His sweat became as great drops of blood falling to the ground. Jesus knew what He was about to suffer for the world's sins, and yes, He prayed for this cup to be removed, but not at the expense of God's will.

I would have to say that this was the hardest prayer Jesus ever prayed, as He prayed, not My will, but Thy will be done, and so often, this is also the hardest prayer we pray. Where else do we see Jesus praying in such agony? His sweat became as great drops of blood falling to the ground as He said, not My will, but Thy will be done. Surely, this must have been the hardest prayer Jesus ever prayed, and it is for us as well.

Jesus prayed three times about this, but after the third time, He had come to a place where He was fully satisfied and at peace with drinking this cup. Through these three prayers, we can see Jesus in agony because He wants the cup to be removed, but more importantly, He wants the will of God to be done, and both can't happen. These prayers were agonizing because the will of God was the horrors of the cross, and Jesus wanted to escape them and still perform God's will at the same time. Jesus knows that the will of God is for Him to be crushed.

After these three agonizing prayers, we can see that Jesus has come to a place where God's will and His will completely line up. Jesus is no longer sorrowful unto death, as He was when He came into the Garden of Gethsemane, but He has fully embraced the cross as the Father's will and His will as well.

When Jesus came into this Garden, His will was for the cup to pass from Him if it didn't go against God's will, but after these three prayers, Jesus knows it isn't possible for the cup to be removed from Him and the will of the Father to be accomplished at the same time. Therefore, His will is now the same as God's, for Jesus has fully embraced the will of the Father. He no longer desires the cross to be removed from Him but that the cross would come unto Him.

Sure, the Bible says, Jesus endured the cross, despising the shame (Hebrews 12:2). Yet, it is evident that Jesus had fully submitted unto the will of the Father because He could have prayed at any time during His passion and the Father would have sent twelve legions of angels to deliver Him.

Jesus came into the Garden of Gethsemane with a question He wanted to ask the Father. The question was, could the cup pass from Him and the will of the Father still be done? In other words, is it possible, or can there be a gospel (The Father's will) and Jesus not go to the cross (Jesus' will)? If Jesus went straight to the cross and bypassed Gethsemane, would He still have been wrestling with that question while staring the cross in the face?

Hypothetically speaking, if Jesus wasn't fully committed to the will of God or didn't understand that His will and the Father's couldn't be done simultaneously, would He have called for those twelve legions of angels? Now, I'm not saying this is true, please don't misunderstand me, I've already stated that I wouldn't try to comment on what Jesus was feeling at this time, I'm just asking an exploratory question. We know that Jesus was always totally and completely committed to the will of the Father, even before Gethsemane. Yet, after Gethsemane, we see that Jesus was not only committed to the will of the Father but also understood that His will and the Father's will couldn't be performed simultaneously. However, I didn't put this hypothetical question forward to examine Jesus, for Pilate even said after examining Him, *"I find no fault in this man"* (Luke 23:4). I put this exploratory question forward to show why Gethsemane is so important to us. It prepares us ahead of time. It prepares us for the cross before the cross comes. It strengthens us beforehand. It allows us to embrace the cross ahead of time. It causes the oil to flow, granting us the heavenly strength to endure the cross. It causes us to experience and overcome the fear and shame of the cross beforehand. It causes us to embrace the Father's will before the cross ever comes into our lives. It keeps us from being double minded, undecided, or vacillating between two wills, because if we think there is a chance that the Father's will can be done without us bearing the cross, then we will be hesitant to embrace the cross, we will run from the cross, or call for twelve legions of angels if they are offered unto us.

It also seems from the text that Jesus is stronger after these three prayers than He was before He prayed them. Sure, the angel strengthened Him in the Garden as He prayed. However, Jesus seems to be at peace after these three prayers. He is no longer wrestling with the question He came into Gethsemane with when He was exceedingly sorrowful even unto death before He prayed. I believe this would have strengthened Him as well. Again, this was the hardest prayer Jesus ever prayed.

After these three prayers, Jesus is no longer sorrowful unto death, casting Himself on the ground and sweating blood, for His will and God's will are the same. Christ understands that His will and the Father's will can't be accomplished, for the cup can't pass from Christ, and God's Lamb be slain at the same time. His greatest desire is for the Father's will to be accomplished; therefore, Christ will willingly drink the cup of the wrath of God. Jesus never desired to go against God's will; the prayers He prayed were to see if it was possible for the cup to pass from Him and for the will of the Father to be accomplished simultaneously. After praying, Jesus knew that the cup couldn't pass from Him and the will of the Father be done. Christ has embraced the will of God and now travels towards the cross.

This is what Gethsemane does for us as well. We find ourselves in misery when our will collides with God's will. The misery will press us into submission, and after this pressing, we will no longer be under the press, for our will has become the will of the Father, although we travel down a road the flesh doesn't want to follow. We want to travel it because it is God's will, but we are hesitant to embrace the cross before the pressing. We want to do God's will but don't want the cross to come into our lives. Therefore, we try to find a way of not having our flesh crucified and still perform the will of God.

Before we go any further, I'd like to clarify something. Jesus always desired God's will, and it wasn't sinful for Jesus to ask the Father to remove the cup from Him, for Jesus came into the Garden placing the will of God above His own, and the will of God was His will. The Bible teaches us that Jesus didn't come into this world to do His own will but to do the will of the Father Who sent Him (John 6:38), and it also teaches us that Jesus delighted in the Father's will (Psalms 40:8; Hebrews 8:10). Jesus also said, *"My meat is to do the will of him that sent me, and to finish his work"* (John 4:34). It was never a question of whether Jesus wanted to see the will of God done, for this was Jesus' greatest desire and purpose for coming to the earth. This was the whole purpose of Jesus coming in the likeness of sinful flesh (Romans 8:3) and taking the seed of Abraham onto Himself (Hebrews 2:16-17). This was the whole purpose of God being made flesh. The three prayers at Gethsemane asked the Father if the cup could be removed and the Father's will still be accomplished.

We also see that Jesus didn't put His will above God's, for He Said, Not My will, but Thy will be done. This was never the question. The question was, could the cup be removed from Jesus and the will of the Father still be done? In the Garden, Jesus prayed three agonizing prayers concerning this, but during these prayers, He saw that it wasn't possible for both things to be done. Hence, Jesus chose to do the will of the Father over having the cup removed from Him.

I used the word chose because that's what Jesus did. Jesus could have opted out of going to the cross, for He said He could pray unto the Father, and He would send twelve legions of angels to deliver Him (Matthew 26:53). Therefore, Jesus chose to do the will of the Father over having the cup removed.

(The Bible also teaches that Jesus laid His life down freely, and if He laid His life down freely, then He had the power to take it up again; and this He had from the Father (John 10:17-18). It was not a command of the Father that Jesus lay down His life; it was Jesus' decision. It was totally and completely up to Jesus to decide whether He would go unto the cross or not. If Jesus asked, the Father would have sent twelve legions of angels to deliver Him. It wouldn't have been a sin for Jesus to call out for those twelve legions of angels, because the Father wouldn't have offered them if it would have been sinful. In other words, Jesus' will was not sinful. Therefore, Jesus wouldn't have sinned by not going unto the cross, but it would have spelled out the eternal doom of all humanity.)

After these three agonizing prayers, Jesus seems to have been strengthened and ready to face His betrayer. Jesus seems to be at peace with drinking the cup. Jesus had chosen the Father's will over having the cup removed and fully embraced the cross. There was no longer a question of whether the Father's will could be done and the cup removed at the same time, for Jesus had to drink the cup to fulfill the Father's will, and Jesus put the will of the Father above His own crushing. Again, this is the hardest prayer Jesus ever prayed.

Now, concerning Saints. We are often brought to Gethsemane because it is necessary for the flesh to be crushed. There, we see that it is the Father's will for it to be crucified. As God has blessed me to state previously in this book, Saints often don't want to have the flesh crushed. Sure, we pray that God would destroy the flesh in our lives, but we aren't willing to go to the cross to have it done. We despise the cross because we don't want to be crushed. It's hard for us to be crushed because it is hard to die a torturous and shameful death. Yet, we see the Father's will is for the flesh to be crushed, but we still run from the cross.

Here in Gethsemane, we also pray in agony, for we want the will of the Father but don't want to drink the cup, which will cause the will of God to come to pass in our lives. In Gethsemane, we are placed under tremendous pressure as we run from the cup, but we also see that it is the Father's will for us to drink it. We want the Father's will but don't want to drink the cup. Therefore, we are in agony because the Father's will is precious to us, but the cross is something we run from. In Gethsemane, we find ourselves praying our hardest prayers. We find ourselves under tremendous pressure, but we also find that God ministers unto us there.

Yes, the Father sent an angel to minister to Jesus in this very Garden, and God will also send His ministering spirits to us in Gethsemane. The pressure is real, but the angel is also real. Yet, amid this pressure cooker, we are strengthened there, and we cry out, not my will, but Thy will be done, dear Father. In Gethsemane, we see the will of God that we have so often delighted in and its importance. We learn that God has a great calling upon our lives, and if we are going to have the will of God performed in us, we must drink the cup. We know the cross will be hard, but we also see that the will of God in our lives is more important than the hardships we must suffer to have it performed in us. Yes, we pray, not my will, oh Father, but Thy will be done.

Yet, we are still in agony because we can see what is in the cup, but God will not let us leave Gethsemane until the angel comes and strengthens us for the cross we must bear. Sure, Gethsemane is a place where we are crushed. However, it is also a place where we are strengthened, for there the angel of the Lord comes down to us in our agony and strengthens us that we may endure the pressures of this Garden until we come to the place of complete submission unto the Father's will.

Notice the angel came to Jesus in the middle of these three prayers, not at the end. The agony Jesus was experiencing was so great that the Father sent an angel to strengthen Him during these prayers. Yes, we also find ourselves agonizing in prayer at Gethsemane as we wrestle between these two wills, but rest assured, the angel of the Lord will strengthen us during this time of prayer. He will strengthen us until we have come into full submission unto the Father and peace with the cross we must bear. At Gethsemane, we pray our hardest prayers, for there, we learn to choose the will of God over our own will, we learn to choose the will of God over our own comfort, and we learn to choose the will of God over our own crushing. There in Gethsemane, we are pressed over time, and the oil begins to flow in a greater manner as we cry out, not my will, but Thy will be done.

During these times in Gethsemane, we also learn more about ourselves. Sure, we learn that it is not the will of the Father to have the cup pass from us, but we also learn more about the inner man in this Garden of Olives. We learn more about our relationship with God. We learn that we love God above our own will, or we will learn to love God above our own will. We learn that we hold God's will in higher esteem than our own comfort, or we will learn to hold God's will in higher esteem than our own comfort. We learn that we value God's call upon our life to be more important than our crushing, or we will learn to value God's call upon our life to be more important than our crushing. Whether we learn these truths in the Garden or have it manifested that we already had these qualities before we came to Gethsemane, we come to the place where God's will is more important than our will. Gethsemane reveals who we are in so many ways. It reveals to us that we hold God and His ways above our own, or we will learn to hold God and His ways above our own. Either way, at Gethsemane, we say, not my will, but Thy will be done. Yes, this is the most difficult prayer we will ever pray.

Not my will, but Thy will be done is the sound that will be heard coming from our lips in this precious Garden as we agonize in prayer. Here in this Garden, our will comes to the place where it can no longer be seen, for the will of God swallows it up. Yet, we must also remember that God will never send us out of this Garden without sending His angel to minister unto us, and we will not come out of this Garden until we are at peace with the will of the Father. We will be strengthened there in Gethsemane for the crushing we must endure that the will of the Father may be fulfilled in our lives.

In Gethsemane, Jesus prayed His hardest prayer, as He wanted to know if it was possible to remove the cup from Him and the will of the Father still be accomplished. It wasn't possible, and through these agonizing prayers, Jesus' will became the will of the Father. Jesus came to this place through prayer at Gethsemane, and once Jesus' will became the Father's will, then Jesus was at peace with it and ready to embrace the cross. These agonizing prayers of Jesus were to cause Jesus' will to become the Father's will. Jesus came to this place through prayer in the Garden of Gethsemane. This was the hardest prayer Jesus ever prayed, and it will also be our hardest prayer. It is hard for our will to become the Father's will in these times, but this seeming impossibility becomes a reality in the Garden of Gethsemane.

After Jesus' will became the will of the Father, such a peace fell upon Him, although the cross lay directly in his path, and the same will be true with the Saints, no matter what we face. If submitting unto the Father's will over His own will was the hardest prayer Jesus ever prayed, then never doubt that it will also be the hardest prayer we ever pray, for in the oil press of Gethsemane, we too will cry out with Jesus, not My will, but Thy will be done.

It is important for us to come to Gethsemane and have our will swallowed up by God's will so that we may embrace the crushing that is soon to come, which is so important to our calling. We must be steadfast in the Father's will, or we will vacillate during the crushing. We won't be as strong or have the peace we could have during this crucifixion of the flesh if we haven't come to the place where our will has become God's will. We will call out for the twelve legions of angels to deliver us if they are offered. We will take an off-ramp if we see one. We will choose to escape the crushing if we can. We will have the cup removed if possible.

There are times in which we are unwilling to be crushed, yet we have no choice. There are times in which we are drug, kicking and screaming into the fires of tribulation because it is necessary for our growth, calling, and God's glory, yet we still try to escape it. Yes, we are forced into it. Yet, in the Garden of Olives, we say, not my will, but Thy will be done. Gethsemane causes us to embrace the will of God over our own crushing, which gives us strength, resolve, and peace in the crushing at hand.

At Gethsemane, our will becomes the Father's will as we submit completely unto Him. Therefore, great peace comes upon us as we embrace it. We are strengthened to perform the will of God, and the oil now flows in a greater manner, for our will has now bowed down unto the will of the Father. We are now willing and desirous that our flesh be thoroughly crushed that the will of God would be performed in our lives, for the oil has been pressed out of us at Gethsemane, and we cry out, not my will, but Thy will be done! We are now ready and willing to embrace the cross and have the flesh nailed unto it, for we not only hold God's will above our own, but now we are ready to have it performed in our lives, although it requires a crucifixion of our flesh.

God has called us to a greater work, which requires a greater killing of our flesh, and therefore, Gethsemane is necessary, for it brings us to the place where God's will swallows up our will, as we embrace the cross, even before we are nailed to it. At Gethsemane, we not only want God's will above our will, but in this Garden of Olives, we become willing to have the flesh crucified.

Gethsemane teaches us what the will of the Father is. The will of the Father was for Jesus to be crucified. In the Garden of Gethsemane, we learn this. The cross of Christ is displayed as the Father's will in this Garden of Olives. The finished work of Christ is the Father's will. The finished work of Christ is the crucifixion of Christ, the burial of Christ, and the resurrection of Christ. The Bible teaches that we must believe in the entire work of Christ if we are to be saved, for we can't be saved without trusting in the cross of Christ, and we can't be saved without trusting in the resurrection of Christ either (Romans 10:9; 1 Corinthians 15:13-17). Paul described the gospel as Christ's death, burial, and resurrection (1 Corinthians 15:1-4).

The cross is the centerpiece of Christ's finished work because there would have been no burial or resurrection if there were no cross. Yet, we also know that we must have a risen Christ, or our justification wouldn't be complete, for the scriptures say Christ was delivered up (crucified) for our offenses (sins) and raised again (resurrected) for our justification (Romans 4:25). We must also have a buried Christ, for He had to taste death as a judgment for our sins. The law demanded death for our sins (Romans 6:23), and Christ tasted death for every man (Hebrews 2:9). Without a crucifixion, we wouldn't have the shed blood of Jesus for our sins; without a death and burial, we wouldn't have the penalty of death determined by the law for our sins paid for; and without a resurrection, Christ wouldn't be our eternal High Priest after the order of Melchizedek. Therefore, all three are necessary for salvation. At Gethsemane, we see that the Father's will is the finished work of Christ, and if Saints are going to walk in the will of God, they must trust in the finished work of Christ. There is no salvation outside of faith in the finished work of Christ. There is no peace in eternal salvation outside of faith in the finished work of Christ. There are no answered prayers outside of faith in the finished work of Christ. There is no sanctification outside of faith in the finished work of Christ. There is no blessing outside of faith in the finished work of Christ. The entire gospel is given unto us through faith in the finished work of Christ. At Gethsemane, we see the Father's will is the finished work of Christ, and if we are going to live in the Father's will, it will only be done through faith in the finished work of Christ. Let's look at the words of Jesus concerning the Father's will.

John 6:39-40. *"And this is the Father's will which hath sent me, that of all which he hath given me I should lose nothing, but should raise it up again at the last day. And this is the will of him that sent me, that everyone which seeth the Son, and believeth on him, may have everlasting life: and I will raise him up at the last day."*

Matthew 7:21. *"Not everyone that saith unto me, Lord, Lord, shall enter into the kingdom of heaven; but he that doeth the will of my Father which is in heaven."*

In these verses, we see the Father's will, which is for us to believe in the One He sent. This is the only way of salvation and sanctification. The Father's will is for the Saints to place their faith in the finished work of Christ. We know from scripture that no person can enter the Kingdom of Heaven, but by faith in the finished work of Christ, and we see that it's not those who say, Lord, Lord, that enter the Kingdom of Heaven, but those who do the will of the Father. We know that everlasting life only comes through faith in the finished work of Christ, and we see that the Father's will is to give everlasting life unto all who place faith in the finished work of Christ. The will of the Father is the finished work of Christ, and if Saints are going to walk in the will of the Father, they must do it through faith in Christ's finished work. There is no salvation outside of faith in the finished work of Christ, there is no sanctification in the lives of Saints outside of faith in the finished work of Christ, there are no answered prayers outside of faith in the finished work of Christ, and there is no peace outside of faith in the finished work of Christ.

At Gethsemane, we agonize in prayer as our will collides with the Father's will. We learn that it is not our will but the Father's will that must be embraced. Through this agonizing pressure, we learn that our abilities aren't sufficient for the godly task we are called to. We see ourselves as being weak, as our pride is crushed under the pressure of the olive press. There, we learn to submit unto the will of the Father as we forsake our fleshly abilities and trust Christ's finished work for godly living. When we have come to this place, the oil will flow, for the Holy Spirit will move in a greater manner in our lives, seeing we have forsaken all confidence in the flesh and have placed faith in the finished work of Christ for our sanctification.

The Holy Spirit will move in our lives when our faith is in the finished work of Christ, for this is God's prescribed order for sanctification. The Holy Spirit works through faith in Christ's finished work, and God's promises are manifest in our lives through faith in the finished work of Christ. Here, in this Garden of Olives, we see that the Father's will is the finished work of Christ, and the only way we can fulfill the Father's will is through faith in the finished work of Christ. It wasn't the Father's will to remove the cup from Jesus, and it's not the Father's will that we should try and live for Him in any other fashion other than faith in the finished work of Christ. Gethsemane presses our will into pulp so that we may trust in the finished work of Christ for eternal salvation, sanctification, and blessing, which causes the Holy Spirit to flow more abundantly in our lives. So often, our will is to walk in the flesh, trying to live for God by our own abilities. However, at Gethsemane, we forsake the flesh and embrace the finished work of Christ for eternal salvation, sanctification, blessing, the fulfillment of our calling, etc., as we pray unto the Father, saying, not my will, but Thy will be done.

Gethsemane is an agonizing place, but it is also a very beautiful place, for there we are prepared to willingly embrace the Father's will and have our flesh crushed. This Garden of Olives is designed to cause us to submit to the will of the Father. In the Garden of Gethsemane, we wrestle with these two wills: God's will and our own will. There, these two wills collide. There, we must stay until our will is crushed, and the only will left standing in our lives is the will of God.

Let's notice why Jesus prayed in such agony at Gethsemane. Jesus was praying about the cross. Jesus wanted the cup to pass from Him, but not at the expense of God's will. There, at Gethsemane, Jesus prayed until He came to a place where He was at peace. There, He embraced the cross, and having the cup pass from Him were no longer thoughts or issues.

Now, let's ask ourselves what the will of God is for our life. I'm not talking about a specific calling but how we are to fulfill this calling. At Gethsemane, Jesus saw that it was impossible for the cup to be removed from Him (His will) and the will of the Father (the cross) to be done. One of these two wills must be forsaken to accomplish the other. Jesus chose to embrace the will of God and forsake His own will, although Jesus came into the Garden having already placed the will of the Father above His own will. At Gethsemane, we pray such agonizing prayers as our will collides with the will of God. God's will is the cross. Not a literal crucifixion of ourselves, but a spiritual crucifixion of ourselves. God's will is the cross of Christ, for He desires us to be crucified with Jesus. God's will for our lives is for us to trust in the cross of Christ for eternal salvation, sanctification, blessing, etc. So often, our will is for us to achieve God's purpose through the means of the flesh. It is impossible for both these wills to come to pass, for one must be forsaken to accomplish the other. These two wills collide in the Garden of Olives. There, we pray in agony as we seek to hold onto the flesh (our will), but God's will is for it to be crucified with Christ.

Crucifixion is a very humbling thing, for it is a place of humiliation and pain. Remember, Jesus humbled Himself unto the cross, for He endured the cross and despised the shame (Hebrews 12:2). It is a place where the flesh is laid bare in front of us and even others, for it is very likely Jesus was crucified naked in front of everyone on a mountain. On the cross, pride is broken. The cross is not only humbling but also a very despised place. It isn't respected in this world. Yet, Christ didn't make Himself of any reputation (Philippians 2:7). The cross is where our strength and life are drained from us. These things, and more, must decrease in our lives so that God may increase in us. We must not seek to make ourselves of any reputation, as our pride is crushed in the olive press, for he who glories, let him glory in the Lord (2 Corinthians 10:17).

The cross is where we must lose ourselves in the will of God. It is a place where we are conformed to the image of Christ. We are afraid of this, for at the cross, we must say, make me nothing or kill me that Christ may be glorified. Sure, that's what we want. Sure, we want the will of God, but the process is very hard for us to embrace. This is what we want, as we say unto the Father, not my will, but Thy will be done, but we are so afraid of the process and even wonder if we will have the ability to operate in our calling afterward. We wonder, will anyone want to listen unto a crucified preacher after his flesh has been laid bare, in full view of the entire community, or will I be able to recover from the crucifixion to minister afterward? Yet, we must remember that although Christ was crucified in weakness, He was raised in power (2 Corinthians 13:4), and though He was shamed at Calvary, the Father has honored Him with a throne above all thrones (Hebrews 7:26; Philippians 2:7-

11). Yes, it is a fearful thing to be crucified and have the flesh killed, but it is the will of the Father.

We have come unto the Garden of Gethsemane, and our will collides with God's will. There, we agonize in prayer, and there, we must stay until we have come unto the place where we say, not my will, but Thy will be done. We must forsake all confidence in the flesh, as our will is crushed into oblivion, and the only will that remains standing in our lives is the will of God. After we have submitted ourselves unto the will of God and are willing to be crucified spiritually, we rise, embracing His will, as we solely trust in the finished work of Christ for everything. Christ has become our life, strength, respect, exaltation, clothing, etc. Christ has become everything unto us, and Christ has become our means to live for God. We have forsaken all the things of the flesh that Christ may live greater in our lives. We have come to the place where we can truly embrace our calling in the power and wisdom of the Spirit. We have now come unto the place where the oil will flow. We have come unto the place where we are willing to have our flesh crucified.

Now, we have forsaken the flesh after this agonizing process and trust only in the finished work of Christ, which causes the oil to flow. We know it is impossible for God's will and our will to occur simultaneously. We know it is impossible to walk in newness of life without a crucifixion. Yes, we wrestle with these two wills in agony until God's will is the only will left alive, for the olive press has crushed our will. After all prayer is ceased (the angel of the Lord having strengthened us in this submissive prayer), we find peace in submitting to the will of God and willingly embrace the crucifixion of the flesh. If there are twelve legions of angels on the ready to deliver us at our word, we will not pray unto the Father to send them, for our will has become God's will. Now, we are completely submissive and have made the finished work of Christ our only object of faith. Now, the oil flows greater in our lives. There, in this Garden, we are pressed out of measure and above our strength (2 Corinthians 1:8) that we may trust in the finished work of Christ to resurrect us by the power of the Holy Spirit so that we may walk in newness of life. We, with Paul, are no longer praying for the messenger of Satan who is sent forth to buffet us to be removed, but are glad for it, for this is the means through which the power of Christ may rest upon us. These prayers were agonizing because the will of the Father was the horrors of the cross, and Jesus was asking if He could escape them and still perform the will of God.

In this Garden of Olives, where the oil press is erected, we learn to willingly embrace the cross, although we know it may be or will be a painful, shameful, and torturous death. Though we came into this Garden desiring to have the cup removed from us, something special has happened here; for now, we no longer want the cup removed but desire to drink it. At Gethsemane, we pray as Jesus prayed, saying, *"O my Father, if this cup may not pass away from me, except I drink it, thy will be done."*

Gethsemane is the place where we are prepared for the cross. This is the place where we learn to embrace the cross willingly. At Gethsemane, our will and God's will collide. There, we agonize in prayer until God's will swallows up our will. Our will is to preserve the flesh, and God's will is to see it crucified with Christ. There, we agonize in prayer until we say, *"Not my will, but thine, be done."* At Gethsemane, our will is crushed so that we may embrace the will of the Father, which is to submit unto the cross of Christ, and through the crucifixion of the flesh, the oil flows.

Remember, the Holy Spirit wasn't given until Christ was crucified (John 7:38-39). At Gethsemane, Christ was pressed immensely until His will became the will of the Father. At Gethsemane, we are pressed until we do the same, for then we have fully submitted ourselves unto the cross of Christ, and we are crucified with Him, which causes the oil to flow. There, we learn to embrace the will of God over our own will, learning to forsake all confidence in the flesh and trust solely in the finished work of Christ. When we do this, we are crucified with Christ, as the flesh hangs on the cross, and our faith is entirely in His finished work. At Gethsemane, our will is crushed in the olive press that the oil may flow, for the Holy Spirit will greatly move in our lives when our faith is in the finished work of Christ.

Gethsemane crushes the flesh in this respect. We are allowed to feel some of the horrors of the cross beforehand. This is very terrifying to us. We see it coming but don't want it to happen. Yet, the pressure increases when a foretaste of the coming cross lies heavily upon us. We can hardly hold up under such pressure as we cast ourselves upon the ground, praying, let this cup pass from me. However, as the pressure increases, more oil flows, strengthening us and bringing us closer to embracing the Father's will. We are clutching tightly to the flesh because the cross terrifies us. Yet, we are experiencing a foretaste of the cross, and the pressure continues to increase.

Little by little, we turn loose of the flesh—little by little, more oil flows. Little by little, we embrace the will of the Father. The pressure continues to the point that we can't bear it, but the Father sends an angel to minister unto us. Though there is no physical crushing of the flesh at Gethsemane, we learn to embrace the crushing of the flesh there. We are taught how to embrace the cross there. At Gethsemane, we feel the emotional parts of the cross before the cross comes. We feel the inner sufferings of the cross ahead of time. We feel the anxiety, fear, and shame of the cross at Gethsemane before the crucifixion of the flesh takes place. This pressure is enormous, for we have been placed into Gethsemane's oil press. The pressures of the cross are real, and we don't want to see the flesh crucified, but at Gethsemane, we eventually turn loose of the flesh and submit it to the will of God. We are placed under this immense pressure until we turn entirely loose of the flesh and say, Thy will be done. Therefore, our will to preserve the flesh is crushed into pulp at Gethsemane. We are now willing to be crucified with Christ, trusting that the Glory of the Father will raise us to walk in the newness of life. This causes the oil to flow mightily, giving us the heavenly strength to endure the cross. Though we despise the shame of the cross, we are now ready to endure it, for the fear of the cross has been experienced and overcome at Gethsemane beforehand. The pressures of the cross have been placed upon us at Gethsemane so that when the cross comes, we won't have to deal with them and the cross at the same time. In short, some, many, most, or all of the inner agonies of the cross are placed upon us at

Gethsemane before the cross comes so that we don't have to bear them and the cross at the same time. Gethsemane prepares us for the cross, and the cross prepares us for our calling. The cross is meant to prepare us for our calling. However, it may be too much for us to bear. Therefore, God sends us to Gethsemane first to prepare us for the coming cross. The oil needed to embrace the cross flows at Gethsemane. Now, we have the heavenly strength to embrace the cross when it comes.

There at Gethsemane, our will is crushed so that we may embrace the Father's will, which is the crucifixion of Christ. At Gethsemane, our will is crushed so that we may fully submit unto the Father's will, which is the cross of Christ, as our old man is crucified with Him so that we may walk in the newness of life (Romans 6:4-6). There, in this Garden of Olives, we learn to embrace the will of God, which is to trust in the finished work of Christ as our flesh is placed upon the cross.

Now, we can say with Brother Paul, *"I am crucified with Christ: nevertheless I live; yet not I, but Christ liveth in me: and the life which I now live in the flesh I live by the faith of the Son of God, who loved me, and gave himself for me"* (Galatians 2:20). There, in Gethsemane, we are brought unto the place where we embrace the cross of Christ as the only means of eternal salvation, sanctification, and blessing. We embrace it as the means by which we fulfill our callings and receive all the promises of God, etc., as we say unto the Father, *"Nevertheless not as I will, but as thou wilt."*

# CHAPTER 15
# HAST THOU CONSIDERED MY SERVANT JOB

Job 1:8. *"And the LORD said unto Satan, Hast thou considered my servant Job."*

As God blesses us to continue to look at Job and the affliction brought on him by Satan, let's pray for spiritual understanding in this matter. We know that Satan brought all this upon Job, but we also know that God allowed it.

Job was an exceedingly godly man who went through some extremely trying times. God willing, we want to look at these circumstances and try to understand why it was necessary for Job to go through the things that he did. What was its purpose, and why did God allow it?

The scriptures teach us that Job was very wealthy and influential before this fiery trial came upon him. We know that God said Job was perfect and upright, feared God, and eschewed evil, and there was none like him on Earth before this fiery trial came upon him. We also know that Job lost his health, wealth, children, and household when he was afflicted. We can also see that Job lost his influence and respect during this hard time, for Job said he had become the song of fools who abhorred him and spat in his face (Job 30:8-10). Job also said, *"But now they that are younger than I have me in* derision, *whose fathers I would have disdained to have set with the dogs of my flock"* (Job 30:1).

We can also see that Job's friends didn't understand his situation, as they accused him of having secret sins, which, they said, caused his calamity.

Job was also confused during these times, but he knew this wasn't brought on him because he was a hypocrite. Job couldn't understand why this was happening to him. However, he knew he would come out of this tribulation as if he were tried gold. God didn't show him why this was happening unto him, although he prayed unto the Lord about it, for Job prayed unto God but received no answer from Him during this time.

Yet, towards the end of the Book of Job, we see that God appeared and spoke unto Job out of the whirlwind, and we also know that God caused Job's wealth to double from what it was before he went through this tribulation.

It should also be noted that God mentions Job to Satan, not vice versa. So, what brought this on? Why did God mention Job to Satan? Why did the Lord bring Job's name up in this conversation? Satan had previously boasted that he had the ability to do anything he desired on Earth. Then God asks him if he has considered His servant Job. In other words, God is saying you can't do all you say you can do. You say you have been walking to and fro in the earth, up and down in it, and having your way wherever you go, but I haven't seen you walking in the land of Job, the biggest spread in the East. God is saying unto Satan, you don't have total dominion in the earth, for the land of Job is unoccupied by you. Satan says he can't walk in the area belonging to Job because God has placed a hedge about him, but if the Lord would allow him to walk there, Job would curse the Lord to His face. We know God allowed it, and we know Job didn't curse the Lord to his face as Satan said he would, but the question is, why did God permit Satan to do all these things to Job? Why would God mention Job to Satan in the first place?

We have already stated that God brought Job's name up in this conversation to rebuke Satan's false report of being the victor of the earth, but there is more to it than that. There would be something worked in the life of Job, and God willing, that's what we want to look at as we continue.

The Bible mentions other instances in which God allowed Satan or his messengers to afflict His children. Satan was granted permission to sift Peter as wheat, and a messenger of Satan was allowed to buffet Paul. In both these accounts, we are told why. Satan was allowed to sift Peter as wheat so that Peter would be a strengthener of the brethren, and the messenger of Satan was allowed to buffet Paul so that the power of Christ would rest upon him.

Sometimes, God allows Saints to be tempted or tested so they may be increased. Job was increased in possessions, but more importantly in revelation through this fiery trial. These tribulations are a means to bring us closer to God. Through this, we see that Job increased in wealth, but we also see that Job increased in revelation. Job spoke to God in the whirlwind at the end of this trial. At that time, Job saw a greater revelation of God, and he also saw a greater revelation of himself. Job saw he wasn't as holy as he thought he was. Job also saw that

God was more glorious than he had ever imagined. Through this revelation, Job would grow spiritually.

God doesn't give Satan free rein to do whatever he wants, nor does God allow such things to come upon His children for no reason, but God does allow such testing of His Saints that they may grow closer to Him.

Through this greater revelation of God, Job grew closer to the Lord, and through such tribulations, we also grow closer to the Lord, getting a greater view of God and of ourselves as well. Through the revelation of God in the whirlwind, it is evident that Job had ungodly things in his life that he didn't even know about. During this amazing experience, Job says unto the Lord, *"I have heard of thee by the hearing of the ear: but now mine eye seeth thee. Wherefore I abhor myself, and repent in dust and ashes."* (Job 42:5-6). This doesn't mean Job was a terrible person, nor does it mean he intentionally walked sinfully, for he was perfect, upright, feared God, and eschewed evil. However, it does mean that Job saw more of himself than he had ever seen before he was brought into the light of God's glory.

Though we may not see God in the whirlwind as Job did, God still allows us to see more of His glory and more of ourselves as well. God may do this in several different ways. Sometimes, it is through trials, tribulations, and chastisements. Other times, it may be through us beholding His glorious creation (Romans 1:18-20).

Yet, another common way for this to happen is by the washing of the water of the word (Ephesians 5:26-27). We learn more about God and of ourselves through reading and hearing God's precious word. The more about God and His ways we understand, the more the Lord's glory is revealed to us; therefore, we see vile things in our lives that we didn't even know were there. These revelations we receive from the word of God cause us to get a greater view of the Lord, which causes us to revere and worship Him in a greater way. These revelations that come to us by reading or hearing the word of God cause us to see more of ourselves in relation to this greater view of the Lord we received. This grants us the ability to see the vile things in our lives we previously didn't see before, for the light of God's glory has shone upon them and revealed them to us. The more we see of God's glory, the better we can observe them. The more God's glory is revealed unto us through the word, the greater our ability to see. The more God's glory is revealed unto us, the greater the light will be in our lives. Through a greater revelation of God's glory, His glory shines brighter before our eyes and brighter upon our lives. Therefore, God becomes more glorious in our sight, and His glory allows us to see more of ourselves as well. Before this greater revelation of God's glory, we couldn't see certain ungodly things in our lives, but afterward, we can. Therefore, we seek to repent from things previously unknown to us, for we are being washed by the water of the word. By the washing of the water of the word, we learn how to order our lives better. We learn more about ourselves and more about God. This causes us to have greater reverence and worship of God. This also causes us to repent from the sinful things in our lives that we previously didn't see, for the water of the word is washing us.

When God spoke to Job out of the whirlwind, Job saw that there was room for repentance, which he had never seen before, and therefore, this granted him the ability to move closer to God. Through this, Job humbled himself more than before, which also caused him to come closer to God. Through this, Job saw a greater revelation of God's glory, which caused him to magnify God greater than before.

In all of this, we see that God allowed this to come upon Job so that he would have a greater revelation of Him, which would cause him to have a greater relationship with Him. Through this greater revelation and relationship with God, Job was increased in the earth. Therefore, God says to Satan, *"Hast thou considered My servant Job?"*

The same is true with all Saints. There are times when God allows us to go through tribulations so that we may grow closer to Him. A greater revelation of God needs to come into our lives, and certain things need to fall out of our lives. When this happens, we are increased in the earth as our calling becomes more powerful. Sure, it is uncomfortable when God allows us to be buffeted by a messenger of Satan, and we cry bitter tears when Satan is allowed to sift us like wheat, but the fruits of it are glorious and worthwhile, as the power of Christ rests upon us.

Job was miserable during this fiery trial, but he came forth as tried gold, and God knew this would be the case before He ever mentioned His name to Satan. Therefore, God says to Satan, *"Hast thou considered My servant Job?"*

Notice that Job is increased in the earth, for his possessions double after the tribulation ceased. Why is this important? It is important because this was the reason God allowed Satan to afflict Job. This was the main purpose of God mentioning Job's name to Satan. Yet, we may ask, does God care so much about possessions that He would allow an already extremely wealthy man to be afflicted in such a fashion as Job was for the purpose of giving him more wealth? Was Job so focused or desirous of more wealth that he would have been willing to go through all of this to simply become richer, although he was already the wealthiest man in the East? The answer to both questions is no. So why was it so important to increase Job in the earth? Why was it so important that the Lord felt it was worth allowing Job and all that he had to be touched by Satan?

Again, let's notice what Satan said when the Lord asked him where he had been. Satan said, *"From going to and fro in the earth, and from walking up and down in it"* (Job 1:7). Satan is bragging about the power, dominion, and authority he has in the earth as the god of this world. God then asks Satan, *"Hast thou considered My servant Job, that there is none like him in the earth, a perfect and upright man, one that feareth God, and escheweth evil"* (Job 1:8)? This question is a layered response to Satan's boasting.

One of the things we can get out of God's question is that Satan doesn't have complete power, dominion, and authority on Earth. Satan's pride would have been wounded when God said, *"Hast thou considered My servant Job."* In other words, God is letting Satan know that he doesn't have complete and total power, dominion, or authority on the earth because the land of Job hasn't been conquered. God is asking Satan if he has considered Job in this equation. Did you consider My servant Job when you claimed to have free rein throughout the earth?

The mention of Job was a rebuke of Satan's previous statement. The mention of Job would have not only stopped Satan's boasting but would have placed a burr in his saddle as well. Satan wouldn't have liked this at all, for he just shot off his mouth, boasting of his greatness in the earth, and the mere mention of Job exposed his statement to be a lie and himself as a liar. Therefore, God says unto Satan, *"Hast thou considered My servant Job?"*

Why was it important for God to increase Job's wealth? Why was it important for God to double everything Job had? Why was it so important for Job's possessions to be doubled? Why was it so important that God would see fit to allow Satan to afflict Job as he did? It was very important, but before we mine in that vein, let's look at why it was necessary for Job to go through this affliction before his wealth was doubled.

Job's wealth and influence on Earth would be doubled, but Job had to be prepared spiritually so that he would have the ability to handle the responsibility that came along with this increase. With this 100% increase came greater responsibility, but Job wasn't prepared for such an increase in the earth before Satan touched him and all that he had. Therefore, this tribulation was necessary before Job was increased on Earth. We must often wander in the wilderness before entering the Promise Land. Why? We must learn how to live in the Promise Land before we possess it. Job had to be prepared for the increase God would give him before the Lord would increase him. Therefore, God says unto Satan, *"Hast thou considered my servant Job?"*

Now, let's get back to the previous question. Why was it important for God to increase Job's wealth? Why was it important for God to double everything Job had? Why was it so important for Job's possessions to be doubled? Why was it so important that God saw fit to allow Satan to afflict Job as he did?

Let's look again at what Satan said when the Lord asked him where he had come from. Satan replied, *"From going to and fro in the earth, and from walking up and down in it"* (Job 1:7). Again, Satan is bragging about the power, dominion, and authority he has on the earth as the god of this world. Satan proclaims that he has this power, dominion, and authority in every place of the Earth. God points out that Satan doesn't have total and complete power, dominion, and authority on Earth when He mentions Job's name, saying, *"Hast thou considered My servant Job?"*

Although Satan hadn't completely conquered the earth, much of what Satan said was true. Satan did have great power, dominion, and authority on Earth. This, too, is a reason for God mentioning Job, for God will countervail Satan's evil power and influence upon the earth by increasing righteous Job. The more Job increases on Earth, the more Satan decreases. The most righteous man on the earth at this time seems to have been Job, for God said there was none like him on the Earth. Therefore, the more power, dominion, and authority Job has on Earth, the less power, dominion, and authority Satan has therein. The more Job is increased, the more righteousness will be increased in the earth, and the more Satan is decreased, the more wickedness will be decreased in the earth. Satan has gone forth, conquering throughout all the earth, but one place he hasn't conquered belongs to Job. Job's power, dominion, and authority on earth were strongholds of righteousness. Satan can't defeat it, although he has conquered all over the earth. The more Job increases in the earth, the more Satan decreases therein. Therefore, God says unto Satan, *"Hast thou considered My servant Job?"*

Notice the first thing Satan does when the Lord allows him to touch all that Job has. Satan takes his wealth by killing or stealing his animals, his posterity, by killing his children, and his household by killing all but four of his servants, for he only left one servant from each horrific event to survive so that they may report these calamities unto Job. The more Job has, the less Satan has, and the less Job has, the more Satan has. This is the reason God was going to increase Job in the earth. Satan bragged about his power, dominion, and authority in the earth, and it was enormous. Therefore, God was going to increase Job, which would weaken Satan.

Yet, before Job can be increased, he must be decreased (John 3:30). Something must be done in Job's life. Something that will cause him to decrease so that he may increase. Sure, Job decreased in wealth and posterity, but there was something more needful for Job to decrease in before he could be increased on Earth. Job's flesh had to decrease. Although Job was a perfect and upright man who feared the Lord and eschewed evil, the flesh remained. Before Job will be increased in the earth, his flesh must be decreased, which will cause him to increase spiritually. Before Job was increased in the earth, his flesh must be decreased. Therefore, God says unto Satan, *"Hast thou considered My servant Job?"*

So often, this is the case with the Saints of God. Too much of the flesh is in our lives, which hinders us from increasing. In many cases, God will not allow us to increase in the earth while there is too much of the flesh in our lives, no more than He would allow Adam and Eve to eat of the tree of life after falling headlong into the flesh in Eden. So often, God increases us according to how much we have decreased in the flesh. Yet, many times, Saints can't see that they need to decrease in the flesh. Therefore, God allows Satan to afflict us so that the flesh would be broken and marred to the point that we could increase spiritually according to His call upon our lives.

God's call on Job's life determined that he needed to increase in the earth. Therefore, God's call demanded his flesh be decreased. It was the call of God upon the life of Job, which made it necessary for him to be afflicted by Satan. The fleshly part of Job that was alive and well had to be broken and marred. The fleshly part of Job, which was in direct conflict with the call of God on his life, had to be crushed. Job couldn't be increased in the earth all the while this fleshly part lived. Remember, dear Saints, we live by dying and are increased by decreasing. God was not going to increase Job in the earth all the while these fleshly parts of him were alive and well. Therefore, God says unto Satan, *"Hast thou considered My servant Job?"*

If Saints are increased before they are properly prepared, then there is a great likelihood that they will fail. There is too much of the flesh working in them to handle this godly responsibility, and there is too much at stake for God to allow this.

Job was the most powerful force for righteousness on earth, but God wanted him to become more powerful. Yet, God wasn't going to increase Job's power and influence while he was unprepared for it; no more than we will give a 5-year-old the keys to our car. Why? If we can understand the dangers of giving a 5-year-old the keys to our car, then we should also be able to understand this.

Many Hamans, Herods, and Hitlers litter our history books. They are examples of people who had great power but used it for evil. It is a great responsibility for a person to wield such power, for the founding fathers of America taught that power can even corrupt good men.

John Dalberg was an English Catholic historian, politician, and writer. Dalberg said, "Power tends to corrupt, and absolute power corrupts absolutely. Great men are almost always bad men, even when they exercise influence and not authority. There is no worse heresy than that the office sanctifies the holder of it."

It is a great responsibility to wield such power, and before God increases Job in the earth, He will first see that he is decreased in the flesh. Therefore, God says to Satan, *"Hast thou considered My servant Job?"*

Now, I'm not saying that Job was a bad person before this tribulation came upon him by any stretch of the imagination, for he was quite the opposite, but there were fleshly things in Job that would have hindered him after being increased. Job didn't know this, but God did, and therefore, God said unto Satan, *"Hast thou considered My servant Job?"*

Job must repent of some things he doesn't even know are in his life. He must repent of some things he didn't know needed to be repented of. Job needs to become humbler, and he needs to hold God in even higher esteem than he does at the time of this conversation between God and Satan. To do this, Job will need a greater revelation of God and a greater revelation of himself than he already has. Therefore, God mentions Job unto Satan, for God will use the tribulation of Satan in the life of Job to reveal this unto him.

God isn't fully revealed unto us at any time in this life, for no man can look upon the face of God and live. God is only revealed unto us according to how much we are decreased in the flesh. The more we are decreased in the flesh, the more God will be increased in our lives.

Other than Jesus, Moses got the greatest recorded look at God of anyone in history, but we must also consider what the Bible says about Moses. The Bible says that Moses was the meekest man on the face of the earth (Numbers 12:3), which is why Moses was blessed to see the back side of God. This is a determining factor in the measure of the revelation of God that Saints have. According to how much we are decreased in the flesh will be how much God is increased in our lives. This means Job must decrease so that God may increase in his life. Before God increases Job, Job must be prepared. Job must be prepared for the power, dominion, and authority God is going to give him. Therefore, God says unto Satan, *"Hast thou considered My servant Job?"*

This truth is also seen in other areas of the Bible. David was anointed king years before he set on the throne of Israel. Yet, many of those years were spent being pursued by Saul. David suffered much during that time, and although David may not have learned everything about being the king of Israel during these hard times, he learned much, for David was prepared to be king through the tribulations that came upon him when Saul sought his life. Therefore, God says unto Satan, *"Hast thou considered My servant Job?"*

Joseph was a great dreamer. God gave Joseph dreams, which let him know he would one day be exalted to a position of great authority and people would bow down to him. Yet, harsh tribulations came before the authority was manifested in his life. He was betrayed by his brothers, sold as a slave, falsely accused of attempted rape by Potiphar's wife, and cast into prison. However, the deep, dark, damp prison couldn't destroy the prophetic dreams, for they would come to pass and surpass what Joseph could have probably even imagined.

Joseph was prepared to be the governor of Egypt through betrayal, slavery, and being in prison. These harsh tribulations worked a work in Joseph, which prepared him for the governor's chair. Therefore, God says unto Satan, *"Hast thou considered My servant Job?"*

It is no coincidence that both David and Joseph suffered before coming to great power, dominion, and authority, and it is no coincidence that Job did as well. The anointing was there, but the flesh was also there. Many times, before and after God grants authority unto a person, God must prepare them for it. Many times, it is necessary for that person to be placed in the sieve of Satan for this preparation. Often, they must be placed in the furnace of affliction to be prepared for the calling of God upon their lives. In the sieve, Satan sifts us that the chaff may be broken in our lives and taken away, and the furnace mars us so that the flesh can be revealed unto us to be what it truly is. Therefore, God says unto Satan, *"Hast thou considered My servant Job?"*

It is incredible to see how much confidence we place in the flesh. Therefore, we must be sifted in Satan's sieve and afflicted in the furnace. In these times of tribulation, we see who we really are. We see a part of ourselves that we hide from everyone, even ourselves. We even see parts of ourselves that we haven't ever seen before, though they have always been there. We even see actions and thoughts that we feel are godly but are revealed to be sinful. Yes, in the sieve of Satan, pride is broken, and in the furnace of affliction, the flesh is marred. We see who we truly are and are appalled and frightened by the sight we behold. We learn that we aren't everything we thought we were in ourselves. We learn we aren't as strong as we thought we were in ourselves. We learn we aren't as righteous as we thought we were ourselves. We are pressed like the olives at Gethsemane, and our flesh becomes the pulp. Yes, we are placed under some of the most severe pressures because it is essential that we be crushed. The point is that the flesh must be broken so that we would no longer have confidence in it. Sometimes, it is one part of the flesh, and sometimes another, but the flesh must be broken. The flesh must be marred in the furnace so we can see this horrible sight and learn not to trust in it. We must stay in this painful place until we learn to trust God. Yes, in this pressure cooker, our hard hearts are tenderized so that they may be soft enough to receive a greater revelation of God. In this pressured-filled place, we learn about

God, for Solomon says He dwells in the thick darkness (1 Kings 8:12).

We learn about God in the sieve of Satan and the furnace of affliction. Why there? Can't we learn of God in more comfortable places? Sure, we can, but in the sieve of Satan and the furnace of affliction, we learn some of the greatest things about God and more about ourselves.

Why? The sieve of Satan and the furnace of affliction teach us all that we are not. We learn we are not paragons of righteousness, all-powerful, or all-knowing. The sieve of Satan and the furnace of affliction cause the flesh to be laid bare so that we may truly see it for what it is. There, in the sieve of Satan and the furnace of affliction, the true colors of the flesh are revealed. For the most part, it seems, we have a hard time seeing the flesh for what it is anywhere else. Yet, in the sieve of Satan and the furnace of affliction, we see a truer reflection of the flesh than we often do in any other place. We see how weak and wicked it is. We see how abhorring it is. We also see how foolish and sinful it is to trust in it.

There, in the sieve of Satan and the furnace of affliction, the flesh becomes more apparent to us. The sight we behold turns our stomachs as we cry out with brother Paul, saying, *"O wretched man that I am! who shall deliver me from the body of this death"* (Romans 7:24)?

Sure, we know from the scriptures that the flesh is sinful, but, so often, we don't realize or refuse to realize how much we walk in it. So often, we don't realize how we adorn the flesh and trust in it. So often, we don't realize how much we rely on the flesh. We are often ignorant of how much we like and rejoice in the flesh.

It is sinful to cling to the flesh, but we often hold tightly to it. Yes, we often refuse to forsake it after seeing its sinfulness. Oh, how miserable this is! Therefore, it is expedient that we find ourselves in the sieve of Satan and the furnace of affliction so that we may see the flesh for what it truly is, so that we may forsake the flesh we cling so tightly unto, and that we may despise the flesh we love so dearly.

There, in the sieve of Satan, our pride becomes loathsome in our eyes, and in the furnace of affliction, the flesh is marred and no longer appealing unto us. Yes, many times, the sieve of Satan and the furnace of affliction reveal the flesh unto us in a truer manner than we can behold it anywhere else.

It is profitable for us to find ourselves in the sieve of Satan and the furnace of affliction because they cause the flesh to become undesirable unto us. The flesh we love so dearly and cling so tightly unto becomes undesirable and loathsome in the sieve of Satan and in the furnace of affliction.

Once we see the flesh for what it is, we become desirous to forsake it. We are often unwilling to forsake the flesh, but in the sieve of Satan and the furnace of affliction, the lipstick is burnt off of the pig as we see the flesh for what it truly is. There, we get a clearer view of the flesh, as we have such a problem getting this view anywhere else. The flesh no longer looks so desirable after we are placed in the sieve of Satan and the furnace of affliction, and there, we are willing to forsake it. Therefore, God says unto Satan, *"Hast thou considered My servant Job?"*

There are times that Saints may be placed in an unsolvable maze so that we may learn not to trust in our own knowledge and wisdom, or an immoveable obstacle may be placed in front of us so that we may learn not to trust in our own strength, or our character may be destroyed so that we may learn not to trust in our own righteousness, &, etc. There, in the sieve of Satan and the furnace of affliction, we see the flesh for what it truly is: Insufficient!

Yes, the Gethsemane's of life are designed to crush our will so that we may embrace the cross of Christ, which causes the oil to come out. So often, the Holy Spirit doesn't flow from our lives as He would because we are trusting in the flesh. The Holy Spirit will not honor our pride, for He is the Spirit of Life in Christ Jesus (Romans 8:2), not the Spirit of Life in the flesh. The Holy Spirit works in our lives through faith in Christ, but all the while, our faith is in ourselves (the flesh); the Holy Spirit doesn't move in our lives as He would if our faith was in Christ's finished work, for the Holy Spirit will not honor our prideful way when we are trusting in the flesh. When we trust in the flesh for eternal salvation, sanctification, and blessing, our ways are perverse, and the Holy Spirit will not honor that. If the Holy Spirit honored us while we were trusting in our own abilities for eternal salvation, sanctification, and blessing, then we would boast in ourselves as the hand of pride patted us on the back. No, this isn't the honorable and right way, for it is perverse. The Holy Spirit will not honor it, for he who glories, let him glory in the Lord (1 Corinthians 1:31). It is idolatry, for we are worshipping the works of our own hands when we trust in the flesh and, in essence, look unto it as our power source and savior (Isaiah 2:8; Acts 7:41).

Therefore, we find ourselves in the sieve of Satan or the furnace of affliction so that we may see the flesh for what it truly is, which will cause our love for it to turn into hate, causing us to no longer place confidence in it. We see the flesh to be like Pharaoh in many ways, for it is as a reed, and if a man leans upon it, it will pierce his hand (Isaiah 36:6), and so it is unto all who place confidence in the flesh.

When Saints lean on the flesh, weakness, harm, and trouble will eventually follow if we don't judge ourselves and forsake it. Weakness is coming, and God's power will not be as manifest as greatly as it could, would, or was in our lives. Confidence in the flesh greatly hinders all Saints and the call of God that rests upon their lives. Therefore, God says to Satan, *"Hast thou considered My servant Job?"*

It is very important for Saints to see the flesh for what it truly is, for it is abominable and a hindrance, but often, we see it as lovely and complimentary. Oh, how confused even the Saints of God can become. Such confusion is repeatedly seen in the Epistles of the Bible.

After being taught the great doctrines of the Bible by the very Apostles of Christ, the early church often fell into legalism, as they embraced a perversion of the gospel (Galatians 1:7). Although they were Christians, they began to walk in the flesh, trusting in it, instead of trusting in the finished work of Christ completely. They began to trust in their own abilities to secure their salvation, sanctify them, please the Lord, have God's power displayed in their lives, and earn God's blessings.

Oh, what a miserable mistake this is. Consider the gravity of this error. Yet, they couldn't plead ignorance because Paul testified that they had received the message of Christ with such magnificence and clarity that it was as if they were present at the foot of the cross during Jesus' crucifixion (Galatians 3:1).

They had embraced the wrong teachings, which moved them away from the doctrine of grace and placed them in the camp of legalism. This wouldn't work out for their good. They became sick and weak through this, for this legalistic teaching was like a virus in the church body.

Saints who walk in the flesh are walking down a destructive path, whether confused as Eve was or intentionally embracing it as Adam did. This is not the way of God, nor is it the way of peace for the Saints. This path leads to destruction, and God desires us to walk on the straight, narrow path that leads to life.

Sometimes, we are confused into thinking that we are walking godly when, in all reality, we are walking in the flesh. God sends us words of grace during these times, but most of the time, we don't understand how far out in left field we really are. Though we hear and read the words of grace during these times, we are so confused that we don't understand how to apply them in our lives. We are confused, and what is it that confuses us? It is the flesh! We see it as beautiful and a proper sacrifice to send up to God. We are so confused that we feel God is pleased with it. Oh, how backward the Saints of God can become. We are trying to add to Christ's finished work, although we may not understand it in those terms. We are so confused that we feel Christ's finished work isn't enough for eternal salvation, sanctification, and blessing. Therefore, we look to our own abilities to fulfill what Christ left undone, although He completed all.

Saints of God walking in the flesh may say, that's ridiculous; this is not our goal. Yet, when we trust in our own abilities, we are walking in the flesh and not trusting Christ for that part of our life. What can the filthy rags of the flesh add to the finished work of Christ? Absolutely nothing! Nothing at all! The flesh only takes away the advantages of grace in our lives. Not that the grace of God is ever diminished in His Saints, but the workings of grace in our lives are diminished when we trust in our own abilities.

Remember this: people make two great mistakes concerning the cross of Christ. Either they don't come all the way unto the cross and stop short of salvation, or they try to go beyond the cross after salvation. To find salvation, one must come all the way to the cross, trusting completely in the finished work of Christ, but after one is saved, one needs to be careful not to try to go beyond it. Trying to go beyond the cross is one of the greatest mistakes the Saints of God make.

Understand this: to try to go beyond the cross is to backslide. Although not coming all the way unto the cross for salvation is self-explanatory, going beyond the cross is a phrase that may not be understood. Trying to go beyond the cross is to try and add something to the finished work of Christ, which is what Saints do when they trust in their own abilities. When Saints trust in their own abilities, then, in all reality, we are saying that the finished work of Christ isn't enough. Although we may not say it in those exact words or understand it in those terms, our actions and thought processes proclaim it. Again, to go beyond the cross is to backslide, for we are leaving Calvary and returning to Sinai.

Think of this just for a moment. If Saints believe that they must do something to secure their salvation (remain saved), produce sanctification (godly living), or do something (some deed) to have their prayers answered (earn blessings), etc., then we are proclaiming that faith alone in the finished work of Christ isn't enough. This is how confused Saints can become. When this happens, we must see clearly if we are going to return to the straight path. In these times, we need to see exactly what we are trusting in when we lean on our own performance. To see clearly, often, it is necessary for us to find ourselves in the sieve of Satan and the furnace of affliction, for there, we see the flesh for what it truly is. We see how weak, frail, and marred it is so that we would turn from trusting in it, seeing that it is incompetent and completely inadequate for the godly task at hand. We see that our performance cannot meet God's standards, and our abilities aren't great enough to please God. Yes, in the sieve of Satan and the furnace of affliction, we see the flesh for what it truly is, and we must stay there until that part of our flesh dies. Therefore, God says to Satan, *"Hast thou considered My servant Job?"*

Oh, we are so confused sometimes, for we are so prone to try and resuscitate the flesh after it has been slain in the sieve of Satan and the furnace of affliction. We feel that we need it in our lives; we think we would be less without it. Yet, all the while we try to resuscitate the flesh, the sieve of Satan continues to sift it, and the furnace of affliction continues to mar it, and we must stay in this troublesome place until we willfully let it die. We must stay there until we are willing to forsake the flesh. Yes, we must stay there until we say, not my will, but Thy will, dear Father. We must continue to be sifted in Satan's sieve and marred in the furnace of affliction until we willingly give up all efforts of CPR on the flesh. Therefore, God says unto Satan, *"Hast thou considered My servant Job?"*

Speaking of Saints becoming confused, let's look at an extremely godly king named Hezekiah. What a great blessing he was to the Jews during his reign. When he first ascended to the throne, Judah was in a mess. Their economy and military were in shambles, for the kings before him had forsaken the Lord, sealed up the temple, and went headlong into idolatry. This caused Judah to be brought very low. Yet, when Hezekiah ascended the throne, the first thing he did was open the doors of the temple, cleanse it, set the priests in their ordained places, make a sin offering for the inhabitants of Judah, and make a covenant with God that they would walk in His ways. God, in return, blessed Hezekiah and Judah immensely.

Yet, when God blessed Hezekiah, he became prideful, as is often the case with the Saints of God. It is God Who blesses us, but sometimes we become prideful when we are blessed by Him. These blessings are the work of God in our lives, but mankind is very frail when it comes to combating pride. So often, we step into its snare and are greatly hindered by it.

Unfortunately, Hezekiah stepped into the snare of pride, and the Bible says something very interesting about him. The Bible says, *"God left him, to try him, that he might know all that was in his heart."* (2 Chronicles 32:31). What does this mean? When we are to walk down into The Valley of Humiliation, it is as hard to walk down into this valley as it is to walk up a mountain (to paraphrase Bunyan in The Pilgrim's Progress). I will add this to it. I feel that it is easier to walk up

Prideful Mountain than to walk down into The Valley of Humiliation because we are so often affected by the feelings of our flesh. It seems to be harder for us to have our flesh killed than to have it fed. It is more destructive spiritually, but we seem to desire the feeding of the flesh and loathe the killing of it. Therefore, I feel that walking up Prideful Mountain is more pleasing to us than going down into The Valley of Humiliation.

Yet, I would also like to add that we must walk alone when we walk down into The Valley of Humiliation. Notice, *"God left him"*. God left Hezekiah. Why alone? We must go down into The Valley of Humiliation with our own power, strength, and wisdom only, and not in God's power, strength, and wisdom. We go down into this valley with our own abilities, not with the abilities of God. There, in The Valley of Humiliation, we will see how mighty we truly are as Satan tracks us down and wages war with us. As we face the Dark Prince in this valley, we will see how mighty our flesh truly is.

Satan, or certain members of his kingdom, are always encamped in The Valley of Humiliation, with their fiery weapons of war always ready. They encamp there, hoping and always looking for a Saint to stumble down into this valley. When they see a Saint come into this valley, they immediately blow their trumpets of war, gathering the entire host within earshot of the trumpet, sending messengers to gather far-off reinforcements, and then attacking with all the force they can muster. They intend to rip us to shreds and trample us in the mire while we have no strength but our own. They see their opportunity and seek to take full advantage of it. They desire to kill us, but I firmly believe that the Lord has already stipulated that they can't, and therefore, they will inflict all the punishment they can upon us while we are in this humbling valley.

Notice that God left Hezekiah so that he may be tried. The purpose of this trial was for Hezekiah to see what was in his own heart. Not that God would know what was in Hezekiah's heart, but that Hezekiah would know what was in his own heart, for God could clearly see it.

Often, Saints don't truly know what lurks within their own hearts. There are times that Saints can be exalted so greatly in pride that they don't even notice what is in their hearts, for pride is like a sniper accustomed to many different camouflages.

Mr. Pride may come to us promoting legalism while wearing the camouflage, called an angel of light, or promoting self-righteousness while wearing the camouflage, called please God. His wardrobe is massive, for he has many garments, but he always chooses the camouflage that best blends into his surroundings. He can blend into almost any environment. However, there are a few settings he can't blend into, such as the glory and presence of God, the word of God, or the Holy Spirit and His power. Yet, he tries to mimic them to the best of his ability through self-righteousness, legalism, and impure religious zeal. Oh, he is a master chameleon and is almost undetectable; although the word of God identifies him, the Spirit of God unmasks him, and the glory of God causes his camouflage to melt away. It is no wonder he has been so successful in the hindrance of Saints, for he is often undetectable by us, frequently disguising himself under the guise of walking in the Spirit while promoting the flesh.

Mr. Pride often walks in our hearts, and we don't even see him. Mr. Pride tries to remain unnoticeable while walking the length and breadth of our hearts. Mr. Pride camouflages himself, hoping that Saints won't see him, and he has been very successful throughout the ages. Mr. Pride, clothed in his ghillie suit, blends seamlessly into his surroundings, often unnoticed by the Saints. Yet he is a sniper, wielding a powerful rifle.

Mr. Pride camouflages himself, takes up a position in our hearts, and continually looks through his scope, scoping out the godly works we seek to do. When he sees us endeavor to do godly things through the means of the flesh, he pulls the trigger, and the rifle fires. Yes, he shoots down these works in their infancy, for they aren't founded upon Christ in many respects but rest upon our pride. He wounds these works, and they don't prosper or fulfill their task, although we spend much time and energy performing CPR on them. Why? The power of God isn't in them, for their origin is pride, not faith in the finished work of Christ.

This often confuses the Saints, causing us to wonder why these works aren't prospering. We wonder, if I'm trying to walk in godliness, why are these works failing? We go to great lengths, trying to resuscitate these works to no avail, for there is no life in them, seeing they are dead (Hebrews 6: 1; 9:14). Why? They are wrought by our own power and forged through our own strength. They are our own creations. They are our own offspring. They are fashioned in our own image and likeness, not possessing the DNA of the Holy Spirit. This is why these works fail, and this is why we find ourselves repeatedly having to try and prop them up, seeing that they can't stand on their own, for we are attempting to live for God by our own abilities. It is pride that causes these works to fail. Though we can't see him, nor do we recognize who is doing the shooting, it is Mr. Pride, the great camouflaged sniper, who has taken up a position in our hearts.

Mr. Pride has many kills attributed unto him, for he has shot down many of the works Saints have endeavored to perform. He has a trophy room filled with the dead works of the Saints. Saul's kingdom is one of his most prominent trophies, although many others hold an esteemed place in his trophy room. He is an extremely decorated sniper, one of the greatest enemies Saints will ever encounter. Yet, this great enemy is often unnoticeable unto the Saints, for they can't see him, although he dwells within them. His presence glares in the sight of the Lord, the spiritual realm, and often unto other Saints, but we can't see him, although he has taken up a position in our hearts. We are unable to see him, and are ignorant of his presence in our hearts, although his appearance is glaringly obvious. He is like a deer hunter wearing a bright orange vest, which is very apparent to other hunters but unrecognizable to the deer, for the deer can't see the bright orange, although it glows in the brown brush. God sees Mr. Pride easily, the spiritual realm sees him easily, and many other Saints see him easily, but we can't, although he has taken up a position in our hearts.

We try to walk in godliness, but our works don't have the power to flourish because we are unaware that we are trying to perform them through pride. We are trying to live for God by our own power and abilities, which is pride. Therefore, these works won't prosper, although they are godly, for we have sought to do them in an ungodly way.

How? We aren't trusting in the finished work of Christ to perform them, for we are trusting in our own abilities. This is pride, and although we can't see him, it is Mr. Pride camouflaged in our hearts, and we have made him the foundation of working godliness in our lives. This will never prosper, although we are trying to walk in godliness.

Pride is the wrong foundation to support godliness in our lives. Though pride can be extremely strong, it doesn't possess the power to do the works of God. Its strength is our own strength; its wisdom is our own wisdom, and its abilities are our own abilities, which is insufficient for godliness, for we are trying to live for God by the means of the flesh.

Our faith can't be in ourselves if we are to walk in godliness because this will make the flesh our power source, which is never sufficient. Our faith must be in Christ's finished work, which will cause the Holy Spirit to be the power source in our lives, Who is always sufficient for any and all tasks.

Notice that God left Hezekiah so that he may be tried. Hezekiah must face this trial with his own power, strength, wisdom, and righteousness, the very things he takes pride in. The trial begins, and Hezekiah's pride will be his wisdom, weapons, and armor, but he will soon find that they aren't sufficient, for Satan is stronger than the fleshly abilities of Hezekiah. Hezekiah tries to wage war but fails at every turn. He makes critical errors because he is being led by his pride. He is now defeated in the battles he once fought so courageously, successfully, and victoriously. In times past, Hezekiah was victorious because the Lord was with him, but now all he has is his own fleshly abilities, and he is defeated decisively. The war rages on, and Hezekiah loses one battle after another. He is defeated repeatedly, which will eventually cause him to see what lies within his heart. Now, while wallowing in continual defeat, Mr. Pride becomes apparent, for the trial has stripped him of his camouflage. Though Hezekiah sees what is in his heart, he is still in The Valley of Humiliation and must remain there until he despises the pride within him.

What a gloomy sight it is to behold our own hearts! It is a frightful sight to see! To look deep into our hearts can be horrifying! To see the wickedness that lies within us can be terrifying! We are often surprised and even shocked to see the evil that lurks within us. Our hearts are so wicked that we can never truly grasp how evil they are, for the scriptures say, *"The heart is deceitful above all things, and desperately wicked; Who can know it?"* (Jeremiah 17:9).

It isn't a pretty sight when we are forced to walk down the corridors of our own hearts, for it is scarier than any haunted house or horror movie we will ever experience. It is horrific and extremely disturbing when our hearts are laid bare before us, and we see what they look like without the influences of God's grace upon them. Yet, we must behold this unsettling sight, for we are forced to behold our hearts in this manner so that we can see how wicked they truly are. The sight turns our stomachs and causes us to cry out with Paul, saying, *"O wretched man that I am! who shall deliver me from the body of this death"* (Romans 7:24)? There, finally, we see what God wanted us to see, as we have explored the bowels of our own hearts and have truly despised the sight we saw. Our pride has been broken in The Valley of Humiliation. Now, we not only behold the pride of our hearts but also despise it.

The sieve has not only broken our pride, but the furnace of affliction has marred it in our eyes. It is one thing to see our pride, but entirely another to despise it. Therefore, we remain in The Valley of Humiliation until both are wrought in our lives. At that moment, repentance comes knocking, and we joyfully answer the door as God leads us out of The Valley of Humiliation and shows us that we are seated in heavenly places in Christ (Ephesians 2:6).

There, in the Valley of Humiliation, our pride is broken and despised as we learn to trust completely in the finished work of Christ, not in ourselves. We learn that salvation, sanctification, and blessing don't lie in our own hands but in the nail-scarred hands of Christ alone. Then, we lean solely on the cross of Christ, not on ourselves, and the Great Shepherd of our souls leads us out of The Valley of Humiliation. Therefore, God says unto Satan, *"Hast thou considered My servant Job?"*

We have already stated that God allowed Satan to afflict Job, for Satan couldn't have afflicted him unless God permitted him. So why does God permit Satan to afflict the Saints? Sometimes, it's to chasten us; other times, it's to try us. For the sake of the point we're endeavoring to speak about and to go along with the context of Job, let's look at it from the standpoint of being tried, for Job wasn't being chastised for something he had done wrong but was going through tribulation so he could be increased in the earth.

All Christians have been given the Holy Spirit, Who is given for profit withal (1 Corinthians 12:7). In other words, the Holy Spirit is meant to work godliness in our lives. When

Saints trust in anything other than the finished work of Christ for eternal salvation, sanctification, or blessing, then the Holy Spirit will not move in those areas of our lives as He would if our faith was in Christ and His finished work. Yet, the thing most Christians are prone to trust in other than the finished work of Christ is the flesh. We trust in our own fleshly abilities to secure our salvation, our fleshly abilities to live a sanctified life before God, and our fleshly abilities to secure blessings from God. This is not God's way. This is not God's prescribed order of victory. God's prescribed order for these things to be supplied and displayed in our lives is through faith alone in the finished work of Christ for all of God's grace and workings. The godly workings of a Christian are works of grace, and the promises of God are accessed by faith, for the scriptures teach us that grace only comes through faith (Ephesians 2:8). Yes, faith, not in ourselves for righteousness or godly living, but faith in the finished work of Christ for all. Again, Saints often trust in themselves for these works of grace, and because of this, the Holy Spirit doesn't move in our lives as He would if our faith was in the finished work of Christ. Therefore, Satan is allowed to touch us and our possessions, and we are thrown into his sieve and cast into the furnace of affliction. This causes the flesh to be broken and marred before our eyes. We then see that the flesh is insufficient, and we are only left with one option: trust in Christ's finished work. Remember, the Gethsemanes of this life are meant to crush our will that we would be crucified with Christ, so the oil (Holy Spirit) will flow from our lives. In the Gethsemanes of this life, our will is crushed, and the flesh becomes pulp so that the Holy Spirit will flow greater in our lives. Yes, this is often wrought in our lives through Satan afflicting us. Therefore, God says unto the old serpent, *"Hast thou considered My servant Job?"*

The Lord desires to increase Job on Earth, but God will prepare him first. Job needs a greater revelation of himself and also of God. Saints see a greater revelation of themselves through seeing a greater revelation of God. This is similar to Isaiah's experience when he saw the Lord high and lifted up, and His royal robes filled the temple (Isaiah 6:1-4). Isaiah saw a greater glimpse of God's royalty, majesty, splendor, glory, power, righteousness, etc. In the light of this greater revelation of God, Isaiah said, *"Woe is me, for I am a man of unclean lips, and dwell in the midst of a people of unclean lips."* (Isaiah 6:5). Then, the Lord sent a Seraphim to touch Isaiah's lips with a fiery coal from the altar (Isaiah 6:6). Isaiah was then told his iniquity was taken away and his sin was purged (Isaiah 6:7).

Think about this. Isaiah, during that time, may have been the holiest man on Earth, but in the light of God's glory, he sees something he has never seen before. Isaiah saw that he had unclean lips and dwelled among people with unclean lips. Again, let's ponder this. Isaiah, the great prophet of God, whose lips speak the words of the Lord, sees himself in a different light: not in the light of the world, nor in the light of others, but in the light of God's glory. Isaiah sees that his lips are unclean in God's glorious light.

(Sometimes, our strongest points of holiness and the most essential pieces of our calling must be shown to us in the light of God's glory and refined further for the task at hand. For example, at times, the wise may be allowed to see their folly so that they may become wiser. Though we may not see the

Lord like Isaiah did, God will allow us to see more of Him in other ways. We may see more of His royalty, glory, splendor, power, majesty, righteousness, love, etc., through the scriptures, creation, the witness of the Holy Spirit, etc. There are many ways for God to show us more of His glory. God grants us the ability to see more of Him through every revelation He gives us. We may not be able to see His hand with our eyes, as Isaiah, but we do see what His hand moves. We may not be able to see the Lord naturally, but we see His glorious creation. We may not be able to hear God speak to us as Isaiah experienced, but we can hear His voice through reading the Bible. We also hear His voice when the Holy Spirit speaks to our hearts and teaches us what Jesus said [John 14:26]. Furthermore, we may hear His voice by beholding God's creation, for the Bible teaches that creation preaches to everyone upon the earth [Psalms 19:1-6]. There are so many ways God makes Himself known to us.)

After the Seraphim touched the lips of Isaiah with the burning coal from the altar and told him his iniquity had been taken away and his sin had been purged, something amazing happened. Isaiah heard the voice of the Lord, saying, *"Whom shall I send, and who will go for us?"*. Then Isaiah said, *"Here am I, send me"*. (Isaiah 6:8).

After Isaiah was brought into this greater revelation of God, he was commissioned to proclaim a great prophecy concerning Christ. When Isaiah first saw this greater revelation of God, he saw himself as having sinful lips. Therefore, he would have felt disqualified to speak the righteous words of the Lord. However, after the Seraphim touched his lips with a live coal from the altar and proclaimed that his iniquity had been taken away and his sin purged, Isaiah eagerly volunteered to speak the word of God.

Our calling is greater than we are, and it is important for us to see this. Therefore, we must be shown a greater revelation of God. When we see this greater revelation of God, we, with Isaiah and Job, see things we never saw before. We see how unworthy we are, but in those times, God shows us that He has made us worthy, proclaiming our iniquity to be forgiven and our sins purged. Then, when we see ourselves as totally reliant on God's grace for everything, including our calling, we will be able to do more in our calling than ever before. Job would receive double, and Isaiah would utter one of the greatest prophecies of all time, speaking of The First Coming of Christ and Israel's partial rejection of Him, speaking of the great tribulation period and the end of Israel's partial blindness.

Israel's partial blindness means it can't or won't recognize Jesus as the Messiah nationally. In other words, part of Israel can't recognize or refuse to recognize Jesus as the Messiah. Isaiah was commissioned by God to make Israel's heart fat and their ears heavy and to shut their eyes lest they see with their eyes, hear with their ears, understand with their hearts, and convert, and be healed (Isaiah 6:10).

This great prophecy still resonates to this day. It speaks of the partial blindness of Israel, which will last until the end of the great tribulation period. Though this is a prophecy of Israel's partial blindness, it is also a prophecy of Israel's complete conversion, as every single Israelite on the planet, nearing the end of the great tribulation period, will receive Christ as their Messiah. This was a great prophecy spoken by

God through the lips of Isaiah, which has continued to speak throughout the centuries, even to this day.

The Lord had called the great prophet to speak this amazing prophecy. However, before God charged Isaiah to speak it, God first brought Isaiah unto a greater revelation of the Lord and himself (Isaiah). There, God showed Isaiah his unworthiness but also showed Isaiah His grace. There, Isaiah saw the uncleanness of his lips and the impossibility of him having the ability to perform his calling. Yet, God also showed Isaiah that He would equip him to speak His great words by taking away his iniquity and purging his sins. After Isaiah saw and heard this, he was ready and confident to go forward in his calling, saying, *"Here am I, send me."*

Now, we may ask this question: Why was Isaiah shown a greater revelation of God without going through what Job did? The answer is twofold. First, I don't know, but second, God knows. God knows the hearts of all His servants; therefore, God understands how such revelations should be revealed to them.

Let's look at it from this point of view: The disciples were with Jesus when He fed five thousand men (not counting women and children) with five loaves of bread and two fish. Something interesting happened after feeding them and taking up 12 baskets full of leftovers.

Immediately after feeding the five thousand, Jesus constrains (makes or forces) His disciples to get into the boat and sail across the sea without Him. Then, Jesus sends the multitudes away and goes up the mountain to pray. The disciples are upon the sea, and a great storm comes upon them, and they think they will sink and drown. Jesus sees them on the violent lake, toiling, as they rowed against the storm and done everything in their power and knowledge to fight against it. Yet, Jesus waits until almost daylight to come unto them. The Bible says Jesus came unto them at the fourth watch of the night, walking upon the water. The fourth watch of the night is the last three hours of the night. It would have been from 3 A.M. to 6 A.M.

When Jesus arrives walking upon the water, they see Him and frightfully cry out; it is a spirit. Then Jesus says, *"Be of good cheer, it is I, be not afraid."* Then Peter says, *"Lord, if it be Thou, bid me come unto Thee on the water."* Jesus says, *"Come"*. (Matthew 14:27-29). Then, Peter exits the boat and walks on the water with Jesus.

This is one of the greatest miracles of the Bible. Peter took part in it all the while he trusted in Christ and His word completely. However, Peter eventually takes his eyes off the Lord, sinks, and cries, *"Lord, save me."* The Lord immediately reached down His hand and caught him (Matthew 14:30-31). Then, they both come into the boat, and the storm ceases. At that moment, the disciples begin to worship Jesus, saying, *"of a truth Thou art the Son of God"* (Matthew 14:33). Then, the Bible says something very interesting.

After the disciples worshipped Jesus, saying, *"of a truth Thou art the Son of God,"* the scriptures say, *"for they considered not the miracle of the loaves: for their heart was hardened"* (Mark 6:52). This seems to be very odd. Their hearts were hardened because they didn't consider the miracle of the loaves. What do loaves have to do with this? What do loaves have to do with Jesus coming to them in the storm and causing it to cease? These words don't seem to have any place in the context of this event, yet they have everything to do with it. This tells us why the disciples were forced to get into the boat and sail across the sea into an oncoming storm.

Let's think about this for a moment. Did Jesus know the storm was coming when He forced them to get into the boat and sail across the sea? Jesus would have known a storm was coming. However, He forced His disciples to get into the boat and sail across the sea without Him. Jesus knew a storm was coming, yet He forced His disciples to sail into it.

Now, let's ask why? Let's get the full context of this passage of scripture. Jesus has just fed five thousand men (not counting the women and children that were also fed) with five loaves and two fish, then He forces the disciples into the boat and sends them out into an oncoming storm without Him. Afterward, Jesus comes to them, walking on the water, steps into the boat, and the storm ceases. Then, they worship Him, saying, truly you are the Son of God, for their hearts were hardened because they considered not the miracle of the loaves.

What loaves? The five loaves of bread Jesus miraculously fed the five thousand with. Jesus had shown them a greater revelation of Himself when He fed the five thousand with five loaves and two fish, but they didn't get it. They looked at it, but they didn't see it. They witnessed it but didn't receive it, for it didn't sink in because their hearts were too hard. If they had seen it as the Lord wanted them to, they would have fallen before Him, worshipping Him, saying, truly you are the Son of

God, after He fed the five thousand. So, they didn't get this revelation as they should have, and therefore, they were forced to sail into the storm because their hearts were hard. Their hearts were too hard to get this revelation of Jesus when He fed the five thousand. Therefore, Jesus sent them into the storm to soften their hearts. When their hearts were softened to the point that they could get this greater revelation of Jesus, Christ came walking unto them on the water.

Jesus had given them a greater revelation of Himself on the sunny bank, but they didn't get it, and therefore, they were sent into the storm to soften their hearts to the point that they could get the revelation. This revelation was important to them and their calling. It was essential that they get this, but they didn't get it on the sunny bank because their hearts were too hard to receive it. Yet, it was so important unto them and their calling that Christ wouldn't let them go without it. Therefore, Jesus forced them into the boat and made them sail into the storm. Jesus first showed them a greater revelation of Himself on the sunny bank, but they didn't get it because their hearts were hard. Therefore, sending them into the storm was necessary.

It was one thing when five thousand people were hungry, but entirely another when they thought they were going to die in the storm. They couldn't see their weakness on the sunny bank or their need for a greater revelation of Christ there, for their hearts were too hard to get this greater revelation of Jesus, but they saw their weakness in the storm. In the storm, they saw that their abilities weren't enough to handle what they were up against. In the storm, they saw they needed a power greater than themselves, a power that could only come from God, and therefore, their hearts had been softened enough to receive the revelation of Christ that would be shown unto them. In the storm, they saw their weakness and need, and there, in the midst of the storm, they got a greater revelation of Jesus and of themselves. Therefore, God says unto Satan, *"Hast thou considered My servant Job?"*

The storm is like a mallet that tenderizes the meat. It bangs and beats upon us until our pride is broken. Pride and unbelief cause our hearts to be hard. The storm breaks our pride, and we are more than willing to believe while in the storm; as the old saying goes, there are no atheists in a foxhole. When we see that we don't have the ability to deliver ourselves, we stop trusting in ourselves and look for another with the power to deliver. Our hearts become softer, and we will see Jesus coming unto us, walking on the water. Our hearts are now prepared to receive Christ as our Savior or His greater revelation of Himself.

I'm not sure what caused the disciples' hearts to be hardened. The point is. The storm tenderizes the heart. The storm is bigger than we are. The storm breaks us. The storm humbles us. The storm causes us to look up towards God and not unto ourselves. Therefore, our hearts are softened by the storm. This is why we receive many revelations in the storm. Spurgeon said it something like this: Tribulation is the greatest book in my library besides the Bible. Spurgeon wasn't talking about a literal book called Tribulation. He was speaking of the revelations he received through experiencing tribulations.

Revelations may be all around us, but we can't see them because our hearts are too hard. This is the purpose of the storm, for the storm softens our hearts so that the revelations can sink into it. Tribulations produce revelations in our lives because tribulations soften our hearts. Therefore, God says unto Satan, *"Hast thou considered my servant Job?"*

I feel that this same truth is true for all believers. Sometimes, the Lord wants us to get a greater revelation of Himself. Many or most times, He may show it unto us on the sunny bank, but if our hearts are too hard to receive it, then He will force us into the boat and cause us to sail into the oncoming storm.

God knows what it will take for us to get a greater revelation of Him. God knows if we will get it on the sunny bank or if it will take the storm to tenderize our hearts that we may get it, but we must get it, for God has a great plan for our lives. It is important for our fellowship with God and our calling; for this cause, God shows it unto us.

I believe God mostly shows us a greater revelation of Himself on the sunny bank, but if our hearts are too hard to get it there, He will send us into the storm. Now, I'm not saying that everyone who goes through the storm to receive a greater revelation of God was first shown it on the sunny bank and couldn't get it because of the hardness of their hearts. However, it may very well be so. I believe God shows it unto us on the sunny bank more often than not. Yet, if we don't get it on the sunny bank, we must go into the storm. Whether or not this is the blueprint for all, I cannot say, but I can say that the Lord knows what it takes for the Saints to get a greater revelation of Himself and deals with them accordingly, although all, or some, see it first on the sunny bank.

God showed Isaiah a greater revelation of Himself without mentioning that he went through a storm to see it. God showed Job a greater revelation of Himself without mentioning that He had already been shown it on the sunny bank beforehand. God knows what it takes for us to get a greater revelation of Himself, and our lives and callings are too precious not to have it. Therefore, God sees that we get it, one way or the other.

Although it isn't mentioned that Isaiah went into a storm to see this greater revelation, it is possible that his heart was already prepared beforehand through different experiences. Still, we don't know that for certain.

As we look at Jesus's disciples, we must understand that they had a great calling upon their lives. They would be given great authority in the gospel, so they needed great revelation from God. They were to occupy until Jesus came, as the church is also called to do (Luke 19:13).

The Greek word translated occupy means to be busy. So, the church is to be about the Lord's business until He comes. In this business, the Lord has given us great power and authority (Matthew 13:4; Luke 10:19). Therefore, we have the heavenly power and authority to do the work the Lord has called us to do on the earth. To spread the glorious gospel, which repels the darkness of Satan. To bring the Light of Christ to the dark places of this earth. We are to further the Kingdom until He comes. The Light of Christ, which we are called to spread throughout the earth, has authority and power over the darkness of Satan. The church's calling grants us this authority on Earth, which countervails the power of Satan. The church is the power that hinders Satan on this earth until Christ comes.

In fact, the antichrist can't come to full power until the church has been raptured (2 Thessalonians 2:7).

Seeing that the church has enormous authority, we need great revelation from God. The church must learn to decrease so that God would increase in our lives. Therefore, Christians and congregations are sometimes placed in the sieve of Satan and the furnace of afflictions. We are broken in the sieve and marred in the furnace to weaken the flesh to the point that we stop relying on it as much. Yes, many times, the Lord may allow Satan to sift us, which causes parts of our flesh to die so that our glorious God would increase in our lives. There is much territory to occupy, and Satan doesn't allow these areas to go uncontested. Therefore, we are pressed at Gethsemane that our will would become the will of God, and we would be crucified with Christ so that the oil will come out. God increases our authority on Earth through a greater revelation of Himself, but many times, we must be sifted by Satan and endure the fiery furnace of affliction. Yes, the flesh must be broken and marred so that we would decrease and God would increase in our lives. The more the church occupies, the less Satan occupies. It is imperative that we occupy all the areas God has called us to occupy because if we leave a void, Satan will fill it. Satan wants the Promise Land to be inhabited by the Philistines, Amorites, Hittites, Jebusites, &, etc. God has given us these lands, but so often, we must spend forty years in the wilderness before we come to the proper revelation of God and of ourselves, to the extent that we have the faith to occupy the Promise Land. Therefore, God says unto Satan, *"Hast thou considered My servant Job?"*

The English word occupy can be used as a military term, meaning holding ground that doesn't necessarily belong to you. The land you have taken from the enemy in battle and use as a base camp or stronghold to wage war from. An area that has been taken by the military, which is no longer in the hands of the enemy, an area you have influence over and can decide how things are conducted there, and an area you can cause to be governed in the manner you desire.

The earth is the Lord's and the fullness thereof. It is God's earth, and there is an evil imposter in it. Satan tries to lay claim to God's Earth, and God sends us forth as good soldiers of Jesus Christ to occupy until Jesus comes. We are to recover all the areas God has called us to and not allow Goliath to bellow out from a valley in the land of Judah any longer. Yet, we must be equipped for the mission.

David fought a lion and a bear to prepare him to meet Goliath, for the faith he received in the battle and victory over these two ferocious animals was what he needed to face Goliath. When David defeated the lion and the bear, he saw more of God, for he knew God empowered him to defeat them. David knew God before the lion and the bear. Yet, he got a greater view of God when the Lord blessed him to slay them. Through this, David learned to trust God in a greater manner, and this faith would be required to face Goliath.

So, our flesh must die more and more, and our faith in Christ must rise to greater heights as we are blessed to occupy more and more. If not, then we won't be equipped to occupy that which God has given us. Therefore, God says unto Satan, *"Hast thou considered My servant Job?"*

Israel learned more about how to live in the Promise Land while they were in the wilderness than while they were in the Promise Land. They received the law in the wilderness and had their flesh killed to the point that they learned they didn't live by bread alone but by every word that proceeded from the mouth of God (Deuteronomy 8:3).

We will not conduct ourselves properly in the areas God has called us to occupy if the part of our flesh that should die before we occupy lives. We will occupy the areas but won't be equipped to handle the authority given to us. We will act like tyrants instead of occupiers, we will act like the Philistines instead of the children of God, and we will act like heathens instead of those who have a covenant with the Lord.

Authority in the hands of one who isn't equipped to handle it is dangerous. The Earth has been plagued with it throughout the ages. Many kings and rulers of states, countries, and empires have abused their authority. They have led the nations they had authority over into the abyss and have mistreated the people under their control. Many babies (incompetent people, Isaiah 3:4) have been set on the throne of power and committed great atrocities. Oh, how much better it would have been if they had never ascended to the throne in the first place or were properly prepared for it before they set upon it?

God is not interested in having babies occupy. Therefore, we are equipped for the job before we are placed in that position. Many times, this equipping must be done at Gethsemane, Calvary, in the sieve of Satan, or the furnace of affliction, but occupy we must, for it is the call of God upon our lives, and the Lord will see that we are equipped for the job. Therefore, God says unto Satan, *"Hast thou considered My servant Job?"*

Gethsemane causes us to know and submit to God's will, preparing us beforehand for the cross, as we, with Christ, say unto the Father, not my will, but Your will be done. We must stay there in agony until we are fully submitted to God's will, for God has no interest in us occupying if we are going to rule according to our own will. Therefore, God says unto Satan, *"Hast thou considered My servant Job?"*

Calvary kills the flesh and causes us to decrease so that Christ may increase in our lives. It causes us to be less carnal and more spiritual. It causes us to walk in the Spirit and not in the flesh. Yes, we must hang on the cross so that the flesh may die, for God has no interest in us occupying an area if we are going to rule it according to the flesh. Therefore, God says unto Satan, *"Hast thou considered My servant Job?"*

The sieve of Satan breaks our pride, for we believe we are already equipped for the job at hand before we are. We, with Peter, say, I will never deny you, Lord. Prison or death can't cause me to deny You. Sure, we may feel we are ready to die with the Lord. We may even be ready to die with the Lord if it is a sword fight, but when it comes to the shame and pain of the cross, we will deny the Lord. This is the purpose of God allowing Satan to sift us. After a Saint has been placed in the sieve of Satan, they will no longer care what others think of them or even regard their own lives when it comes to the cause of Christ. They will have the strength the people they are called to need them to have, for they will no longer look unto their own strength, but to the strength of Christ, for God is not interested in you occupying in your own prideful strength, for it is insufficient. Therefore, God says unto Satan, *"Hast thou considered My servant Job?"*

The furnace of affliction mars the flesh, stripping it of its glory in our eyes, showing us that there is nothing in it worthy of trusting in. Yes, in this furnace, we see the flesh for what it truly is: despicable and insufficient. We see it marred by the fire until it becomes so detestable in our sight that we no longer desire it. We see it marred in the fire until we understand it is insufficient for godly tasks. Then we throw it into the Kidron Valley where it belongs because we have come to the place where we see how wicked, counterproductive, and useless it is, for God doesn't have any desire for us to occupy an area if we are going to rule it by glorifying the flesh. Therefore, God says unto Satan, *"Hast thou considered My servant Job?"*

Job was a very blessed and holy man, yet the call of God upon his life was greater than he had yet experienced. God would increase Job on Earth and, by doing so, decrease Satan therein. This was God's call upon Job's life, and the time had come for him to step into it, but Job wasn't prepared. Therefore, God allowed Satan to touch him and all that he had.

Job needed more of the flesh stripped out of his life. Job also needed a greater revelation of God before he would be prepared to be increased on Earth. This preparation called for the fire, and therefore, God allowed Satan to touch Job and all that he had.

The fire seemed to do the opposite of what God's calling upon Job was. It seemed Job was decreased in the earth and Satan increased therein, but God knows what He's doing. God knows what will come out of the fire before one is placed in it. Therefore, God says unto Satan, *"Hast thou considered My servant Job?"*

So, what was God's purpose in allowing Job to be thrown into the fire? What would the fire reveal? Job would get a greater revelation, not only a greater revelation of God but also a greater revelation of himself. Job received both. Job received a greater revelation of God and a greater revelation of himself in the fire. Therefore, God said unto Satan, *"Hast thou considered My servant Job?"*

# CHAPTER 16

# THE LORD APPEARS TO JOB

Job 38:1: *"Then the LORD answered Job out of the whirlwind."*

The time had come for Job's trial to cease. His heart had become malleable enough to receive a greater revelation of God (Job 23:16). Then, suddenly, God appeared to him in a whirlwind.

Though Job didn't sin against God throughout this fiery tribulation, and though he did say he wasn't worthy to plead before God, he said, I wish I could order my cause before the Lord and reason before Him, for I know he would accept it (Job 23:1-17).

Job had prayed many times throughout this trial, but God didn't answer him, which sometimes is also true for us. Remember, those who go down into The Valley of Humiliation must go alone. It's not that the Lord isn't there, but you can't feel Him or see Him.

Job greatly desired to speak to God about his situation, but God didn't answer him. Job desired to order his cause before God personally, genuinely believing the Lord would accept it. Job knew he had done nothing wrong to cause all of this to come upon him. He was confused (as we would have been) about why this happened, and he wanted to order his cause before God.

Now, I must speculate a little here, and I hope I don't misunderstand this as Job's friends did, for this would show me worse than they because I am looking back on it after the fact while they were looking at it during the present.

What was Job saying? It's evident that he knew he was on good terms with God, and he trusted that God would strengthen him. He knew that God would eventually bring him out of this, and he would be as tried gold, but what he wanted to speak personally to God about, I can't say. So, I won't speculate on what Job's thoughts might have been because I probably would do worse than his friends.

Yet, let's try to speculate on how we may have thought if we were in Job's shoes. What would our thoughts have been during such a troublesome time as this? What would we have wanted to say to God during such a fiery trial as this? Would we want to reason with God concerning this trial or hope that we could persuade God to remove this from us? Would we hope to convince God that this is unnecessary, or would we desire to say that our lifestyle doesn't deserve all of this?

I'm unsure what Job desired, but I know Job was righteous and didn't sin throughout this harsh time. I must say that I feel Job would have wanted to speak to God wisely and righteously, possibly trying to understand why this had come upon him and God's purpose for it.

So, God appears to Job in the whirlwind. WOW! What a sight this must have been! A sight that very few have ever had the privilege of seeing! Only a select few have had the privilege of seeing God in such a revealed manner as this. Very few have ever spoken to the God of glory in such a manner as

Job did on this day. God had graced Job with His glorious presence, then said unto him, *"Gird up now thy loins like a man; for I will demand of thee, and answer thou me."* (Job 38:3).

Why did God say this unto Job? Again, I'm not certain, but this may have something to do with it. Usually, girding up your loins involves tying up a robe around one's waist. During Bible times, a person's garment was a robe, not today's modern clothing like blue jeans, tee shirts, or shorts. The robe was gird up so that it wouldn't be flapping around. A person girds up their loins when they walk, run, work, or fight in battle, etc. God tells Job, *"Gird up now thy loins like a man."* Like a man could refer to courage and strength, possibly in a military setting. Gird up your loins like a soldier or a hero. Although this may be the meaning, I'm more inclined to think God meant something else concerning this phrase.

1 Peter 1:13 says, *"Wherefore, gird up the loins of your mind, be sober, and hope to the end for the grace that is to be brought unto you at the revelation of Jesus."* So, here we see that Peter uses the phrase *"gird up the loins"* to refer to the mind that they may be sober, hoping to the end for grace at the revelation of Jesus. 1 Peter mainly speaks of the fiery trials of the Saints. So, this may be the meaning of God telling Job to gird up his loins like a man. Job should think as a man, not a child. Job should hope in God and the revelation to be revealed, keeping himself from allowing the trial to cause him to think like a drunk man. In other words, God may be saying, Job, you must think spiritually, not carnally. God may be saying, let's have a grown-up conversation. God may be saying, Job, put your spiritual thinking cap on and gird yourself with wisdom.

God may be saying, Job, I want you to put your best foot forward, for I will demand of you, and you answer me. Remember, Job wanted to order his cause before the Lord personally. This wasn't sinful at all, but it seems that Job's thoughts may not have been as mature as he thought they were, or Job may have felt that the tribulation wasn't necessary or shouldn't be so harsh. I'm not sure, but it is clear that God wanted Job to understand that He was wiser than him and that Job wasn't as wise as he thought.

So, it was a matter concerning God's wisdom and Job's wisdom. Job's wisdom may not have seen the necessity of such a harsh trial, but God's wisdom did. Job understood that he was being tried and would come forth as tried gold, but maybe he didn't understand that he needed this much trying. Remember, Job was perfect and upright, feared God, and eschewed evil. It may have been hard for him to have understood that such an incredible fire was required, seeing that he lived his life very piously. He may have thought like we do sometimes, feeling that there wasn't enough dross in his life to require so much fire. Have we not thought the same or even said the same unto God? Have we not felt that the fire is too hot? Have we not felt like the dross would have been burned out of our lives with less fire?

So, God has personally graced Job with His presence, and now, Job is granted the privilege of speaking personally to Him concerning his situation. God appears to Job, possibly saying, put your best foot forward. I will ask you some questions and I want you to answer them. God wasn't doing this spitefully but to show Job a true reflection of himself. God wanted Job's wisdom to be fully displayed before him (Job). God wanted

Job to see his own wisdom compared to the small portion of God's wisdom, which the Lord would reveal to him. This would not only show Job God's wisdom but also show Job his lack of wisdom.

Job knew God's wisdom was infinite, but did he truly understand how much wiser God was than him? Job knew God was wiser than him, but did Job really understand how much wisdom he (Job) lacked?

It is one thing to know God's wisdom is infinite, but another to hear it. It is one thing to know that God's wisdom is infinite, but another to have it displayed before us. This would cause Job to see his need for more wisdom, which would cause him to desire more wisdom. If Job must view his wisdom in the light of God's wisdom, then Job will see his lack of wisdom, even his own folly.

We may see a space shuttle and know that it took someone with an amazing mind to be able to design and build it. Yet, so often, we don't truly understand how smart a person must be to figure out everything involved with putting a person into space. Often, we may think or say, how could they do that? We are completely flabbergasted at the mental ability and craftsmanship it must have taken to accomplish something so amazing. Though we know they must be very smart, we often don't understand how smart they actually are. However, if a rocket scientist were to sit down and explain everything involved in a space program, it would boggle our minds. They would bring up things that we never even thought about. Things we never even considered. Seemingly impossible things that had to be calculated and designed. Therefore, their knowledge would be on greater display before us, and we would have a greater appreciation and understanding of how smart they really are.

This is what God is going to do with Job. He will have a short conversation with him, showing him a small amount of His wisdom and almighty power by mentioning some things He has done. God will speak to Job briefly about creation and things He has done and can do. Job has observed these things to a certain degree, but God will reveal more of them to him. Sure, Job may have observed parts of the space shuttle, but there are many things he doesn't know about it. God will ever so slightly reveal more of His wisdom and almighty power to Job by asking him a series of questions, which will cause Job to place his hand over his mouth, understanding that he can't answer any of them, knowing that it would be foolish even to try. These questions will reveal more of God's wisdom and almighty power to Job. This would also reveal to Job how much wisdom he lacked in comparison to God's wisdom.

It is important for Job to see this because he needs a greater revelation of God. Not only seeing the amazing God in the whirlwind but also hearing a small declaration of the Lord's wisdom, power, and sovereignty. Things God has done and understands that Job hasn't considered or even imagined. God lists many things He understands and has done in question form in chapters 38-41 (I'd like to encourage you to read these chapters), and Job is told to gird himself up like a man and answer them if he can. Though God asks him many questions, Job couldn't answer one of them, nor could he match God in wisdom or power.

Sometimes, we think we understand. Sometimes, we feel we should be allowed to speak to God about our situation personally. Sometimes, we think that if God allowed us to order our cause before Him, He would see our point and change His direction. Sometimes, we feel we know enough that God would hear our counsel. Oh, how prideful we are. Sure, we should come to God with our requests and trust Him to answer them, but we must understand that the counsel of the Lord is perfect. God is Omniscient and Omnipotent. We must learn to accept His counsel and trust Him in our lives. If we pray and the Lord doesn't answer, we must believe our understanding isn't complete. We must continue to trust in Him, for Job said this amid his fiery trial, *"Though he slay me, yet will I trust in him"* (Job 13:15). Jesus did the same, for the wrath of God was poured out upon Him on the cross, but He still trusted God to resurrect Him (Psalms 40:1-2).

Job may have felt at odds with his situation, possibly thinking this isn't completely necessary, and now God says unto him, gird up your loins like a man, and I will ask you some questions and see if you can answer them. I will demand wisdom and strength from you in certain matters and let you give what is adequate.

Oh, that we would slightly understand this when we misunderstand God and His purposes. Oh, that we, in our limited knowledge of God, would try and gird up our loins like a man before Him, seeking to put our best foot forward in His presence and hypothetically match wits and strength with Him.

God demands of Job, and Job quickly sees there is no point in trying to put his best foot forward, for it is inadequate because he stands before the Almighty God.

God speaks to Job, asking him some questions. Through these questions, God is letting him know He is all-wise, all-powerful, and all-sovereign. God lets Job know He has the right and wisdom to allow this.

Job quickly discovers that there is much about God that he doesn't know. Job hasn't spoken wrongly about God, as his friends did, but it is apparent that there is much about God that he hasn't considered, and therefore, God says unto Job; gird up your loins like a man.

One may wonder, did Job think he knew more about God than he did? I will not speculate on that, for Job had a wisdom and understanding of God that few in history have obtained. Yet, the fact remains that he doesn't know as much about the Almighty as he needs to know for the call of God upon his life. There is much about God that Job didn't know. Much more than Job probably even imagined.

Something amazing happens when Job stands in God's revealed presence and hears Him speak to him out of the whirlwind. Job sees himself as vile and places his hand over his mouth. Job will not be so foolish as to speak on his own behalf, Job will not be so foolish as to contend with God, and Job won't be so foolish as to counsel God. This is the same thing the princes did when Job spoke in the gate (Job 29:9). Job was so wise that no one would speak after he spoke because they would have been viewed as foolish, but now Job stands before God and does the same. Job can see God's wisdom, power, and sovereignty in a greater manner than he has ever seen before.

In a greater way, Job understands that he doesn't deserve anything from God, for the things of God are His and at His divine disposal. All the things Job had beforehand were objects of God's free grace. Job didn't earn them, nor did Job deserve them, although he was perfect, upright, feared God, and eschewed evil. God simply chose to give them unto him. These things are God's, and through His divine wisdom, He chooses how He distributes them.

Though Job's three friends didn't understand God well enough to cause Job to place his hand over his mouth and declare himself vile, in God's presence, Job does.

May we all understand this about ourselves. None of us laid the foundations of the Earth or set the bounds of the sea, nor did we have the wisdom or power to do so. Therefore, none of us are the all-sovereign, all-powerful, and all-wise God.

Sure, in comparison unto those upon Earth, Job was head and shoulders above them all, for God said there was none like him on Earth, but now Job stands in the presence of God. There, he sees a truer reflection of himself, for he isn't being viewed in the mirror of man's righteousness, wisdom, and power but in the mirror of God's righteousness, wisdom, and power. There, Job sees himself for who he really is and says, *"I have heard of thee by the hearing of the ear: but now mine eye seeth thee. Wherefore I abhor myself, and repent in dust and ashes"* (Job 42:5-6).

Job had heard about God but never heard directly from Him. Job had heard about God but never seen Him. There, in the presence of God, Job sees his own reflection in comparison with God's and understands that he is vile.

There were fleshly things in Job's life that he had never seen before. He couldn't see them because he didn't have the right mirror to show him a true reflection of himself. Job could only view them through his limited knowledge of God. Job could only view them compared to those around him, but now he stands in the Lord's presence. There, he sees how vile he truly is. There, he sees the flesh in his life that he couldn't see before. There, he sees that he lacks many things he didn't even know he lacked. Then, in the light of this, Job says, I repent in dust and ashes.

Repenting in dust and ashes was an outward sign of humility and repentance towards God. Job would not only repent but also do it in a way that made it obvious. Job would make it known to all around him that he was repenting. Job will no longer hold himself to be righteous, for he has seen that he is vile and will declare it openly before everyone in dust and ashes. Job will not only admit to his vileness but also declare God to be righteous by doing so. Job will do as David when he said, *"For I acknowledge my transgressions: and my sin is ever before me. Against thee, thee only, have I sinned, and done this evil in thy sight: that thou mightest be justified when thou speakest, and be clear when thou judgest"* (Psalms 51:3-4).

It is important for Job to repent in such a manner as this. Job wouldn't try to save face in repentance, but he acknowledged his vileness, which would cause God to be justified in the eyes of all who saw him repent in dust and ashes. God allowed this in Job's life, but not without a valid reason. This is made perfectly clear to Job, and he desires this to be made perfectly clear to those who hear about his situation.

It's important not only to repent but also for God to be justified in the eyes of others. God didn't allow this to come upon Job for no reason, and people shouldn't see Job's situation as such. Job declared himself to be vile with his own words, and others should also see this. God wasn't out of line by allowing this to come upon Job; God was just in doing so, which will be declared through Job repenting in dust and ashes.

Job's three friends tried to get him to repent, but they couldn't show him his need for repentance. Yet, now Job stands in the presence of God and sees how vile he is, as the prophet Isaiah had also done (Isaiah 6:1-5). Now, Job not only repents but does it in sackcloth and ashes.

I'm not saying that repentance is to be done before men, but before God, nor am I saying that Saints must go and tell others every time they sin, for this is a matter between God and the Saints. Yet, this situation that came upon Job was a little different, somewhat unique, as sometimes, ours can be. What happened to Job would have been common knowledge to many, and Job also proclaimed that he hadn't sinned to cause this to come upon him. Therefore, many may have felt that God allowed this to come upon Job for no reason or that God shouldn't have allowed this to come upon Job. By repenting in dust and ashes, Job declared that he was vile and that God was just in all that was done.

It is important in such situations that we don't try to hold to our own righteousness while allowing others to view God in a lesser light. Job was declaring God to be just in allowing this in his life and declaring himself to be vile. Job is declaring himself to be vile, and his vileness is the reason God allowed this to come into his life. May God bless us not to show ourselves undeserving of what God has allowed in our lives, which may cause others to view God in a lesser light, if we are ever in a similar situation. We should never seek to hold on to our own righteousness at the expense of God's righteousness in the sight of others. We are vile, and because of our vileness, this has come upon us. Let it be declared. May we never seek to hold on to our own righteousness in such matters. Let us be covered in dust and ashes as we repent and declare God as just before all. Remember the words of David after he committed adultery and murder, which say, *"For I acknowledge my transgressions: and my sin is ever before me. Against thee, thee only, have I sinned, and done this evil in thy sight: that thou mightest be justified when thou speakest, and be clear when thou judgest"* (Psalms 51:3-4).

No, I don't believe we are called to air out our dirty laundry before everyone, but in Job's case, it was necessary for him to repent publicly. Why? God had to be seen as just, and Job needed to be seen as vile in the eyes of others. No, I don't think we have to speak about every sin publicly, and for the most part, that conversation probably should be kept between you and God, but in Job's case, it was necessary because it proclaimed the justness of God unto others. Job's tribulation was done openly, and therefore, Job repented openly.

When the children of Israel came into the Promised Land, God blessed them to win some amazing battles. One of the battles was Jericho. There, God had them march around the city for seven days; then, He miraculously made the wall collapse when they blew their trumpets and shouted (Joshua 6:1-27).

God had given specific instructions concerning Jericho. The people were to give all the spoils of that battle to the Lord (Joshua 6:17-19). Though God had given them specific instructions, Achan took a Babylonian garment, two hundred shekels of silver, and a wedge of gold, hiding it under his tent (Joshua 7:1; 20-21).

Afterward, Israel set their eyes on the land of Ai, which was also inside the borders of the Promised Land. They sent out a scouting party to view the military might of the people. They returned, saying, don't send the whole army to fight with them, for we can take them easily; therefore, send only a portion of the army against them. So, Joshua did what they recommended and only sent out three thousand men. Yet, when they went to battle with them, they were defeated, and 36 men lost their lives. Joshua fell on his face before God, trying to understand what happened—trying to understand why Israel was chased by their enemies (Joshua 7:2-9).

The Lord told Joshua that there was sin in the camp. God told Joshua to have all of Israel gather themselves together. Joshua did so and told them there was an accursed thing in the camp; therefore, they couldn't stand before their enemies. Joshua cast lots before them, and Achan was found to have been the one who had sinned (Joshua 7:10-18).

After the lot determined Achan to be the sinner, the Bible says this, *"And Joshua said unto Achan, My son, give, I pray thee, glory to the Lord God of Israel, and make confession unto him; and tell me now what thou hast done; hide it not from me."* (Joshua 7:19). Then, Achan confessed, telling him that he coveted a Babylonian garment, two hundred shekels of silver, and a wedge of gold, and took it and hid it under his tent (Joshua 7:20-21). Joshua sent some men to get it, and they found it where Achan had said it would be. So, they brought the items back, showing them to Joshua and the children of Israel, and laid them before the Lord (Joshua 7:22-23). Then, the Israelites stoned and burned Achan and all that he had in The Valley of Achor (Joshua 7:24-26).

When the lot fell upon Achan, Joshua told him, *"Give...glory to the Lord God of Israel, and make confession unto Him."* Notice that confession gives glory to the Lord. Achan's confession was to the Lord, yet it wasn't only heard by God but also by the entire army of Israel.

Israel had just lost their first battle in the Promise Land, and thirty-six men died. God had given them this land; therefore, confusion gripped Joshua and must have gripped the others also. They may have wondered why God allowed this after telling them to go and possess the Promise Land. Their faith may have been shaken, wondering if they could trust God to continue to bless them in battle. Yet, God had revealed to Joshua that all of this happened because of sin in the camp (sin among the army of Israel). Therefore, when Achan confessed before the Lord and before them all, God was justified before their eyes.

God is always just, but our view of Him can sometimes become somewhat distorted. Israel's view of God may have done the same during this time. Yet, this confession allowed the Israelites to see what God already saw. Although God's actions were just, this confession justified them in the eyes of Israel. Israel would have already known God's actions were always just, but why God allowed this would have been a mystery unto them. This confession brought to light why God allowed Ai to defeat Israel. This confession brought the just actions of God into view before the eyes of the army. They would no longer have to guess why God allowed them to be defeated in battle. Sure, they knew God was just in all He did, but knowing this is one thing, yet understanding why God allowed this to happen is quite another. Israel could now see what God saw, which would have shown His actions to be just and proper.

Now, Israel would sanctify the army by stoning and burning Achan and all that he had, which would cause them to have their faith increased. They were no longer puzzled as to why God allowed them to be defeated by Ai. They now understood that it was sin in the camp that caused them not to have the ability to stand before their enemies. Now, they could remove this sin from their camp and have confidence in God to bless them on the battlefield again. They could now see why Ai defeated them. Now, they had the ability to fix it by stoning and burning Achan and all he had.

After this sanctifying process, they would have felt cleansed of Achan's sin. This would have strengthened them, as sanctification strengthens us as well. They would now have a greater boldness to face the army of Ai. Therefore, Achan's confession glorified God, showing Him to be just in His actions. It gave Israel the ability to sanctify the army, which strengthened Israel's faith in the battles to come. Therefore, Achan's confession needed to be made public.

Now, as we get back to Job and his repentance, we can see that it wasn't God Who commanded Job to repent publicly, for this was Job's idea. Job wanted to do this because he wanted to proclaim God's justness and his (Job's) vileness in this matter, for Job wanted God's righteousness to be declared openly, even if it meant his (Job's) vileness would have to be declared in the same way. This matter concerning Job's trial was done openly, and therefore, Job desires to repent openly, and by doing so, he openly declares God as righteous concerning all that has come upon him. Job is more concerned with God being glorified than his (Job's) own vileness being displayed before all. This would have openly declared God to be just in allowing the trial to come upon Job, and also declared Job's vileness as the reason for God allowing it.

This worked very similarly to Achan's confession. All Israel could see was that they were defeated in battle by Ai and lost thirty-six men. They knew God's blessing had to be withheld for this to happen. Yet, through Achan's confession, everything was brought into full view. They could now see that Ai was allowed to defeat them because of Achan's sin.

The people who knew and heard of Job would have known that he was the godliest man they had ever known or had even heard of. Then, hearing of his trial must have caused them some confusion. They may have thought that Job doesn't deserve this or something to that effect. They may have had their view of God distorted through this. I'm not sure. Yet, Job's open repentance would have proclaimed the justness of God and the vileness of Job throughout this trial. Therefore, Job's repentance was done openly, in a manner that gave glory unto the Lord.

It required a certain amount of humility for Job to repent in this manner. Yet, we must always understand that we can never show others God's righteousness and glory; all the while, we are trying to show them our own. In anything we do, if we are going to point out God's righteousness and glory, we can't do it by pointing to our own. We never glorify God by holding on to our own righteousness. We never glorify God through pride. The more we are abased and rejoice in God's grace; the more God is glorified in our lives. Job's repentance would have been a debasing act in front of everyone. Yet, if God is to be glorified properly in the eyes of the people, Job must humble himself in this manner. Therefore, Job repents in dust and ashes.

# CHAPTER 17
# WHY DO THE RIGHTEOUS SUFFER

Job 42:10: *"...the Lord gave Job twice as much as he had before."*

I must start this chapter by saying that none of us are righteous in ourselves, for the Trinity of God alone is righteous, but we are made the righteousness of God through Jesus Christ our Lord. We are made the very right-doings of Christ when we are saved through faith in Jesus. So, yes, Saints are righteous, but only because we have been made righteous through faith in Christ Jesus.

So, why do the righteous suffer? This is the question, isn't it? The righteous suffer so that they may get a greater revelation of God and of themselves, that they may increase in the earth. The suffering is important, and God is just in allowing it, for Job needed a greater revelation of God and of himself before he could be increased on Earth.

One may say, why didn't God show it to him without all the suffering? Job's heart wasn't prepared for it. Job needed to be prepared by receiving a greater revelation of God and of himself before the Lord would increase him on Earth. However, Job's heart had to be prepared before he could get the revelation. Job needed to be prepared before increased.

As we have stated earlier in this book, God often shows us a greater revelation of Himself and of ourselves, but often, our hearts are too hard to receive it. Job's heart would have to become softer before the revelation God wanted him to have could be received by him. Therefore, before the increase, his heart would have to be placed in the fire of tribulation until it was softened enough to receive the revelation necessary for the increase. This is the reason tribulations come into our lives. This is the reason we are called to bear the cross. Yes, the cross softens our hearts, for the scriptures prophesied of Christ on the cross in this manner, *"I am poured out like water, and all my bones are out of joint: my heart is like wax; it is melted in the midst of my bowels"* (Psalms 22:14). Also, in the midst of his tribulation, Job said, God makes my heart soft (Job 23:16).

Job needed a greater revelation of himself. Therefore, the furnace of affliction had to mar his flesh so that he could see it for what it truly was. God had called Job to be increased even more than he previously was, but Job had to be prepared first.

What was Job lacking that kept him from being increased? A greater revelation of God and a greater revelation of himself. Through this greater revelation of God and of himself, Job would have become humbler. The Bible teaches us that God resists the proud and gives grace to the humble (James 4:6). Therefore, the suffering came to prepare Job's heart for this revelation, and after his heart was prepared, the revelation came. After the revelation came, God increased Job on the earth. Job now saw God as greater than he had ever seen Him before, and he also saw himself as viler than he had ever imagined. Job repented in dust and ashes, and this greater revelation of God was placed in his heart. Now, Job was prepared to be increased, and God increased him on the earth, which caused Satan to be decreased therein.

So, why do the righteous suffer? The sieve of Satan breaks the flesh so that we would learn not to trust in it. The furnace of affliction mars the flesh, causing us to abhor, despise, and forsake it. Tribulations soften the heart so that more of God can be added to it. We must decrease so that God will increase in our lives. The flesh must decrease so that God will increase in our lives. When God increases in our lives, we are prepared to increase in the earth. After being prepared, God increases us in the earth, which decreases Satan therein.

So, the answer to the question is this: The righteous suffer so that they may increase in the earth—not necessarily monetarily, but in their callings. They become more powerful in their calling and more authoritative on earth. This increases the power of righteousness on the earth and, by doing so, decreases the power of Satan on the earth.

Satan had shot off his mouth in the presence of God and the angels at the celestial gathering. Satan declared himself as the sole power on the earth, but Job was the proof, which proved this hellish statement to be a lie.

However, Satan did have great power in the earth, but God would decrease his power by increasing Job.

Satan declared that Job only served God for His blessings, saying, "let me touch Job and all that he has, and he will curse the Lord to His face." God allowed it, and Satan did it. Satan thought by doing so that he would increase his power in the earth and declare himself to be the victor over righteousness before the world and the celestial gathering, but little did Satan know that he had cast a brick into the air, which would eventually come down and strike him on his own head (to paraphrase Spurgeon).

After the trying of Job, Satan would be weaker than before this trying took place, for Job would be increased in the earth, which caused Satan to be decreased therein.

Earlier in this book, God blessed me to mention a statement made by Napoleon, and I'd like to revisit it for a moment. The story goes like this. After Napoleon was defeated at Waterloo, he was sent into exile. There, in exile, he saw a map, and when he looked at it, Waterloo was marked with a red dot. Napoleon then loudly exclaimed, "Sirs, if it were not for that one red spot, I would have conquered the world!"

Satan knew that he needed to defeat Job to be declared the conqueror of the earth, but though he tried, he failed, for no matter how hard he hit Job, he couldn't knock the grace of God out of him. The little clay pot remained, no matter how hard the dark prince hit it, for the strength of the clay pot wasn't the pottery itself but the grace of God, which was in it. Oh, how Satan must have felt when he was so close, yet so far away, as he looked at this frail clay pot named Job and thought, why can't I break it? This little clay pot is nothing before me! I have hit it hard enough to break kingdom and tear down nations! Yet, it is still upright and the only thing that stands between me and victory in the entire earth!

Centuries later, the Seed of the Woman (Jesus) would arrive upon the earth, and there was none like Him. He was perfect, upright, feared God, and eschewed evil. Satan knew He was coming and was continually looking for Him. Satan knew the

Seed of the Woman was coming to crush his head, for the prophecy God gave against the old serpent in the Garden of Eden after Adam and Eve fell read like this, *"And I will put enmity between thee and the woman, and between thy seed and her seed; it shall bruise thy head, and thou shalt bruise his heel"* (Genesis 3:15).

Satan watched for the Seed of the Woman throughout the ages, and from the time He was born of a virgin, he sought to kill Him. Satan sought to kill Him before the Seed of the Woman could crush his head. Oh, how he sought to kill the Seed of the Woman, or at least destroy His calling, for Herod sought his life as an infant, the Jews sought to kill Him many times after He became an adult, and Satan personally tempted Him in the wilderness. Satan was watching for the Seed of the Woman to be born into this world so that he might destroy Him immediately. Satan had been looking for Him because he desired to kill Him before He could crush his head and fulfill the prophecy.

The last part of Revelation 12:4 says: "*...and the dragon stood before the woman which was ready to be delivered, for to devour her child as soon as it was born."* In this verse, the dragon is Satan, the woman is Israel, and the child is the Seed of the Woman (Jesus). This shows that Jesus was a son of Abraham, of the stock of Israel (the son of David of the tribe of Judah, to be more precise), and Satan was watching for Him to come, with intentions of killing Him as soon as He was born.

As stated earlier in this book, Satan even tempted the Seed of the Woman with the same temptation he used to tempt Eve in the Garden. Satan may have thought; if I could cause Adam and Eve to sin in the Garden of Eden, then surely, I can cause the Seed of the Woman to sin in this harsh wilderness. I tempted Eve with the lust of the flesh, lust of the eyes, and the pride of life, and I will also tempt Him with the same. It worked in Paradise; surely it will work in this fallen, unforgiving wilderness.

Satan is very confident in his abilities, for he thought he could corrupt Job and the Seed of the Woman. Satan knew if he could cause the Seed of the Woman to sin, the purpose of God in His life would be destroyed, and he (Satan) would be declared the conqueror of the earth. Yet, he couldn't succeed in causing the Seed of the Woman to sin, though he tempted Him greatly. Therefore, he would continue to try and kill Him.

Satan tried and tried to kill the Seed of the Woman but failed repeatedly. One attempt upon His life after another was unsuccessful, but eventually, the day came. It was the time of Passover, and Satan would use Judas to betray Him.

Judas did betray Him, and Satan thought he was going to be successful. The temple guard took the Seed of the Woman to the high priest's house, and the Sanhedrin judged Him and condemned Him that night. Then, He was sent to Pilate in the wee hours of the morning. There, Pilate declared there was no fault in Him, but because of the political pressure the Jews placed upon him, Pilate had Him flogged and then commanded Him to be crucified. There, Jesus (the Seed of the Woman) suffered and was nailed to the cross on a mountain called Calvary in the sight of all. Minute after minute, the life of Jesus was being drained, as He was poured out like a drink offering.

Jesus' death was shortly coming, and Satan thought he had accomplished his goal. Satan felt he would be the conqueror of the earth shortly, as the cross slowly drained the life out of Jesus. There, Satan watched, anxiously anticipating his exaltation to becoming the emperor of the earth, which he felt would come to pass as soon as Christ died. Finally, the time came when Jesus gave up the ghost and died. Satan felt that he had flipped the prophecy and crushed the Seed of the Woman's head. Satan thought that he had won.

Oh, how he must have reveled in the moment! It would have been more satisfying than when he touched Job and all he had, when he buffeted Paul, or when he sifted Peter like wheat. Sure, Satan delighted in seeing Job sitting on the ash heap, scraping his boils with broken pieces of pottery, but now he delights even more in seeing Jesus crucified and laid in a tomb.

Satan thinks he has won and will shortly be declared the victor of the earth, but something amazing happened three days later. The tomb's stone was rolled away, and there was no one in it, only some burial clothes and a napkin. The tomb was empty, for keeping Christ in the grave was impossible. He had risen, and it is declared to be true. The evidence is real; there is no escaping it. Satan had only bruised Jesus' heel, but in the process, his head had been crushed.

Job was righteous, but Jesus is the completion of righteousness. Jesus was 100% righteous according to God's standard of righteousness. Not even Job or John the Baptist could have made this claim according to their righteousness. Job was righteous, but Jesus is the righteousness of God. Yet, Christ would suffer more than anyone, for His visage was marred more than any man, and His form more than the sons of men (Isaiah 52:14), meaning that Jesus was beaten so badly that one couldn't even tell that He was a human being.

When Jesus was baptized, God spoke from heaven in the presence of John the Baptist, saying, *"This is my beloved Son, in whom I am well pleased"* (Matthew 3:17). Christ, the most righteous of all, suffered more than anyone and died upon the cross, but it wouldn't be for nothing. His suffering has increased Him in the earth, for Jesus said this about His crucifixion, *"Verily, verily, I say unto you, Except a corn of wheat fall into the ground and die, it abideth alone: but if it die, it bringeth forth much fruit"* (John 12:24).

Jesus' calling has become greater than before the crucifixion, for righteousness is increased in the earth, and therefore, Satan's power is decreased therein. Salvation has now come unto the world's inhabitants by grace through faith in the finished work of Christ. Victory over sin and the sinful nature has now come through faith in the finished work of Christ. Victory over the world, the flesh, and the devil has now come through faith in the gospel of Christ. Grace and truth have now been made available to all. Victory in Jesus is now available to all who will trust in Him. The blood of Jesus has now become the antidote for sin, which defeats every power of darkness. The Saints of God have been empowered from on high with the Holy Spirit. The power of Christ now resides in every single believer. A power that Satan can't resist is in the hearts of Christ's Saints. The very righteousness of God clothes Christians.

Oh, Satan, the cross didn't destroy Jesus; it increased Him in every single believer upon the earth. Christ can be seen in their lives. He has given them the Holy Spirit. His righteousness clothes them. His gospel proceeds from them. His light shines within them, repelling hell's darkness throughout the world. Christ has made them the salt of the earth, like a city set upon a hill that cannot be hidden (Matthew 5:13-14). Christ is not only in Israel, for He can be found in all four corners of the world, for the glorious gospel has girdled the globe and filled the earth. Christ is everywhere a Saint resides, for He lives within them. The crucifixion of Christ increased righteousness in the earth, for Jesus said, *"He that believeth on me, the works that I do shall he do also; and greater works than these shall he do; because I go unto my Father"* (John 14:12). Christ has been increased in the earth through the crucifixion and will one day reign upon the earth, sitting on The Throne of David.

Christ has redeemed the earth from the clutches of Satan. Christ has and will redeem all who trust in Him from the devil's bondage. Yes, the day will come when Satan will be cast into the Lake of Fire, righteousness will reign supreme, saturating the entire earth, filling every molecule of it, and God Himself will dwell with humanity.

Satan is nothing more than a defeated foe. His defeat is decisive! The pit awaits him! He knows his time is short! Yet, a New Heaven and a New Earth await the Saints of God.

All of this and more came solely through the finished work of Christ. Only eternity will be able to partly explain all Jesus provided for us, for every minute that passes throughout the eternal ages will reveal more of the grace of God that has been provided unto the Saints through the sufferings of Christ. Christ endured the cross to make all of this possible. Yes, through the suffering of Jesus, He has been increased in the earth, and Satan's head has been crushed.

Job suffered greatly and was increased in the earth, and Jesus would suffer greater than any and become Lord of the earth. Yes, Satan has once again thrown a brick into the air, never considering that it would fall upon his own head three days later.

Now, the weakened and defeated Satan stares at Calvary's cross, where the blood of Christ was shed, and says, "If it weren't for that tiny red spot, I would have conquered the earth" (to paraphrase Perry Stone). Praise God! Amen.

www.ingramcontent.com/pod-product-compliance
Lightning Source LLC
Chambersburg PA
CBHW071234160426
43196CB00009B/1052